SOUTHERN BIOGRAPHY SERIES

Titles in the
SOUTHERN BIOGRAPHY SERIES

ROBERT TOOMBS

OF GEORGIA

ROBERT TOOMBS
OF GEORGIA

By
WILLIAM Y. THOMPSON

LOUISIANA STATE UNIVERSITY PRESS

BATON ROUGE

1966

To Helen, Sherard, and Richard

Mother and Dad

Acknowledgments

SOME time ago, as a student at Emory University, I became interested in Robert Toombs, the man who *might have been* President of the Confederate States of America—a man who became a legend in his own lifetime. I wanted to discover if the historical Toombs was as fascinating as the legendary one. I hope that these pages have proven this to be so.

Many people through the years have been involved in this study. I wish to acknowledge the kind assistance I received from the staffs of the Southern Historical Collection of the University of North Carolina, the Special Collections Division of the University of Georgia Library, the Emory University Library, the Georgia Department of Archives and History, the Archives Division of the Virginia State Library, the Manuscript Division of the Duke University Library, the Manuscript Division of the Library of Congress, the National Archives, the Schaffer Library of Union College, and the Louisiana Polytechnic Institute Library.

I am grateful to Dr. Henry P. Beers and Mr. Handy B. Fant of Washington, D.C. for their courtesies. Special thanks go to Mr. Carl J. Vipperman for his aid in microfilming manuscript materials at the University of Virginia and to Mrs. Susan B. Tate of the University of Georgia Library for her assistance in securing most of the illustrations in this book. I will always remember the pleasant hours spent in the Toombs mansion in Washington, Georgia, now occupied by his descendants, Miss Kathleen Colley and Mrs. Marion B. Boyd, and in the home of Mr. Bolling DuBose of Athens, Georgia, the senator's great-grandson. I wish to thank Mrs. Mabel Moland, deputy county clerk of Bayfield County, Wisconsin, for her help in locating information on Toombs' land holdings in that state and Judge J. T. Erwin of Arkansas City, Arkansas, for similar labors on Toombs' Arkansas holdings.

Others to whom I am indebted include: Dr. H. J. Sachs and Dr. Dwight A. Lee of Louisiana Polytechnic Institute, who read the manuscript and offered many helpful suggestions; Dr. James Z. Rabun of Emory University, who directed my M.A. thesis on Toombs and maintained his interest in this study; Mrs. Elaine G. King and Mrs. Lyndae J. Gilbert, who cheerfully performed many of the mechanical chores connected with the manuscript; and Dr. T. Harry Williams, editor of the Southern Biography Series, whose valuable criticism improved the quality of the manuscript.

I wish to thank the American Philosophical Society for a research grant and Louisiana Polytechnic Institute for a semester's leave of absence in order to terminate the research on Toombs.

My wife and parents have constantly aided and encouraged me throughout the preparation of this biography. To them I am the most grateful.

WILLIAM Y. THOMPSON
Louisiana Polytechnic Institute

Contents

List of Illustrations

ROBERT TOOMBS
OF GEORGIA

CHAPTER I

The Formative Years

THE old man sat alone in his mansion in Washington, Georgia, gazing through cataract-clouded eyes at the roaring fire on the hearth. He was for the moment contented. His brief speech from the front porch that evening on Grover Cleveland's victory had been well-received, and shouts of "Toombs, Toombs, Toombs" echoed in his ears. His large body was warmed by heat from the fire and by the wine he had shared with his neighbors. Perhaps his musings carried him back through the years to the applause of crowded Senate galleries, to the flash of guns at Burnside's Bridge over the Antietam, to an outlaw existence in the mountains of North Georgia, to moments of tenderness with his wife—but reality closed in upon him again. His family, his old friends, the country for which he had fought were no more. There was very little left for which to live. The old man's cup of bitterness once again began to run over as the fire died down.

Robert Augustus Toombs was born in Georgia on July 2, 1810, about four miles from Washington. His birthplace was not pretentious—a "small farm house in a grove of venerable oaks" [1]—but

---

[1]Augusta *Chronicle*, December 16, 1885. This newspaper appeared at various times as the *Daily Chronicle* and the *Daily Chronicle and Sentinel*. It will be cited herein as Augusta *Chronicle*.

his father, Major Robert Toombs, was a man of substance and standing in the community. Major Toombs had been a soldier in the American Revolution and had come from Virginia with his parents, brothers, and sisters soon after the war with England. The Toombses had been Virginians for over a century. Wills, baptismal records, and court suits place the family at various times in Gloucester and Caroline counties in eastern Virginia and in Charlotte and Lunenburg in the south-central part of the state. William Toombs, the future senator's great-grandfather, registered a will in Charlotte County in 1764. After his wife's death his estate was to be divided equally among his six children; one of these was Gabriel, father of Major Robert Toombs, and by tradition a veteran of the French and Indian War. The Toombses of Virginia will remain largely unknown, however, for their historical record is scant and incomplete. One can assume that they belonged to the colonial era's sturdy yeomanry with means perhaps somewhat above the average.[2]

Wilkes County, Georgia, where Robert and Gabriel settled, had been named for John Wilkes, a member of Parliament who became a popular hero because of his opposition to George III in England before the Revolutionary War. Known as the "mother county" of upper Georgia, it originally embraced a large area which in 1790 contained more than one third of the state's population. The Wilkes boom was induced by state grants of unoccupied land through the headright and bounty systems. Sizeable tracts could

[2]All accounts of Toombs' ancestry appear to follow Pleasant A. Stovall, *Robert Toombs* (New York, 1892), 1–3. Although documentation is meager, it shows, contrary to Stovall's contention, that the first of the clan, William, was the father of Gabriel; Gabriel, the father of William; William, the father of Gabriel (the senator's grandfather); and Gabriel, the father of Robert (the senator's father). See Gloucester County (Va.) Parish Register (MS in Virginia State Library, Archives Division, Richmond), 15, 20, 25, 27, 45; Charlotte County (Va.) Will Book I (Microfilm MS in Virginia State Library), 1; T. E. Campbell, *Colonial Caroline: A History of Caroline County, Virginia* (Richmond, 1954), 365, 461. A thorough search of pertinent documents at the Virginia State Library revealed nothing to substantiate grandfather Gabriel's participation in the French and Indian War, although this does not absolutely preclude his service. The Revolutionary War service of Major Robert Toombs is also clouded by scant documentation. Francis B. Heitman, *Historical Register of Officers of the Continental Army During the War of the Revolution, April, 1775, to December, 1783* (Washington, 1914), 545, gives this information: "Toombs, Robert (Va.) Major Virginia Militia, 1779–1782. (Died 1815)."

be acquired through settlement and military service. According to early biographers, Major Toombs had commanded Virginia troops in Georgia during the Revolution and for this service received three thousand acres from the state. Neither bounty grant records nor tax records bear out this oft-repeated contention.[3]

Major Toombs, twice a widower, took as his third wife Catharine Huling, whose family had originally come from Rockingham County, Virginia.[4] From this marriage five children were born: Sarah Ann, James H., Augustus, Robert Augustus (the future senator), and Gabriel. As the size of his family increased, Major Toombs correspondingly expanded his land and slave holdings in order to benefit from the thriving cotton industry of Wilkes. In 1787 the county tax digest listed him as owning no property. Within a short time, however, he had risen to the status of planter and in 1814, the year before his death, he owned forty-five slaves and 2,200 acres of land in Wilkes, Greene, and Wayne counties. A small portion of his land and a few slaves came through inheritance from his father, who died in 1799.[5]

[3]Stovall, *Toombs*, 2; Ulrich B. Phillips, *The Life of Robert Toombs* (New York, 1913), 4. The original grant and plat records of the Surveyor General's Office in Atlanta show no acquisition of land by Robert Toombs through the bounty system. According to the Wilkes County Tax Digest, 1787, 1793, 1794, 1801, 1805, 1809, 1813, 1814 (MS and Microfilm MS in Georgia Department of Archives and History, Atlanta), Toombs never owned land in quantity approaching three thousand acres.

[4]Toombs' first two wives were a Miss Saunders of Columbia County, Georgia, it is thought, who died without issue, and Sarah (Sally) Catlett of Culpepper County, Virginia, whom he married on September 17, 1798. From this marriage one child was born, Lawrence Catlett Toombs. See Stovall, *Toombs*, 3; *Historical Collections of the Joseph Habersham Chapter, Daughters of the American Revolution* (Atlanta, 1910), III, 169; Grace G. Davidson, "The Ancestry of a Noble Georgian" (Undated Atlanta *Journal* article in Robert Toombs Vertical File, University of Georgia); *William and Mary College Quarterly Historical Magazine*, XI (July, 1903), 71; Catherine L. Knorr (comp.), *Marriages of Culpepper County, Virginia, 1781–1815* (Pine Bluff, 1954), 90; Grace G. Davidson (comp.), *Early Records of Georgia: Wilkes County* (Macon, 1932), 302, hereinafter cited as Davidson (comp.), *Wilkes County*.

[5]Wilkes County Tax Digest, 1787, 1814. Gabriel Toombs' chattel property was appraised at $4,216.31 1/4 after his death. No land is listed; presumably it had been transferred to Major Toombs and his brother, Dawson Gabriel. See Wilkes County Inferior Court Inventories, Appraisements and Sales of Estates, 1794–1806 (Microfilm MS in Georgia Archives), 145–47. Gabriel's will can be found in Wilkes County Wills, 1792–1801 (Microfilm MS in Georgia Archives), 199–201. The will provided that none of his slaves (he owned sixteen) be sold or traded out of the family and that they be used "in a christian like manner. . . ."

Records show very little about Major Robert Toombs. Years later Alexander H. Stephens, Vice President of the Confederacy and a native of the region, said that he often heard some of the old-timers speak of Toombs as a "man of strong and vigorous mind, a good neighbor and citizen, thrifty in business as a planter, and a most excellent, worthy man." His wife, Catharine, Stephens characterized as a "most excellent Christian woman." [6]

Major Toombs died when young Robert was only five years old, but he left his family well provided for. His estate was appraised at $22,510 in chattel goods, nearly $17,000 of which was in slaves; $6,933 in cash; and over $5,000 in promissory notes and bonds—a total of close to $35,000. [7] In his will the father made special provision for his oldest child, Lawrence Catlett, (a son by his second marriage) in the form of land, slaves, and bank stock to be inherited when the boy came of age or married. The rest of the estate was to be equally divided among his wife and the other children, as they came of age or married. "It is my Will and desire," he said, "that all of my children be Well educated & decently maintained. . . ." [8]

Only a few glimpses can be had into the boyhood of Robert Toombs. Pleasant Stovall, his earliest biographer, pictured him as a "slender, active, mischievous lad," small for his age, showing no early signs of precociousness, and living the normal life of a planter's son. He enjoyed unusually good health, in contrast to later years, and was noted for his horsemanship. [9] Estate returns indicate that Robert and his family lived a comfortable life and achieved a high level of education for that day. His half-brother, Lawrence Catlett, attended Franklin College (the University of Georgia) and his sister Sarah Ann went to boarding school in Bethlehem, Georgia, and studied music in Augusta. All of the children probably went to the "old field school" in the neighborhood, usually a one-teacher institution maintained by private sub-

[6]Myrta L. Avary (ed.), *Recollections of Alexander H. Stephens, His Diary Kept When a Prisoner at Fort Warren, Boston Harbour, 1865* . . . (New York, 1910), 425–26, hereinafter cited as Avary (ed.), *Stephens' Recollections.*

[7]Wilkes County Inferior Court Inventories, Appraisements and Sales of Estates, 1812–1816 (Microfilm MS in Georgia Archives), 235–43. No mention is made of real estate in this appraisement.

[8]Wilkes County Wills, 1818–19 (Microfilm MS in Georgia Archives), 108–12.

[9]Stovall, *Toombs*, 4–5.

scription. Family receipts show that in 1819 and 1821 tuition was paid to Christopher Render and Welcome Fanning, schoolmasters. From 1822 through 1824 James, Robert, and Gabriel attended the academy in Washington, Georgia—the same school in which Alexander H. Stephens, Toombs' closest friend, later enrolled.[10] The academy was the backbone of Southern secondary education before the Civil War, serving primarily to prepare students for college.

On July 31, 1824, four weeks after his fourteenth birthday, Robert Toombs was admitted to the University of Georgia.[11] He had successfully stood the required faculty examination in which a candidate for the freshman class had to be able to "construe and parse Cicero, Virgil, the Greek Testament; have a general knowledge of English Grammar and be well acquainted with Arithmetic." [12] With what zeal, if any, he looked forward to his scheduled four years in Athens is not known. One thing seemed certain, however, according to a later writer: although the university had previously admitted some interesting people, there had been "none like the one now permitted to invade its grounds; for here was a fourteen-year-old, plantation-bred upstart who looked askance at all rules, whose hilarious moods knew no bounds, and whose burning tongue and quick repartee seared like brimstone fresh from Hades." [13]

Athens, a town of about one thousand people during Toombs' college days, lay in a plantation belt populated by about as many slaves as whites. Both town and university were on land originally donated to Franklin College by John Milledge.[14] From 1819, when the Reverend Moses Waddel assumed the presidency, to the time of Toombs' entrance, fortunes of the university had considerably improved. It was a school far superior to that entered by Lawrence Catlett some years before.

At the time of Toombs' matriculation, the university was located

[10]Davidson (comp.), *Wilkes County*, 302–303.

[11]Transactions of the Faculty of Franklin College from Aug. 15, 1822 to May 13, 1836 (MS at University of Georgia), 51, hereinafter cited as Faculty Transactions. Although the institution was generally referred to as Franklin College through much of the antebellum period, it will be called the University of Georgia throughout this work.

[12]Washington (Ga.) *News*, October 16, 1824.

[13]Tom S. Gray, Jr., "Bob Toombs," *Georgia Alumni Record*, (May–June, 1928), 194.

[14]E. Merton Coulter, *College Life in the Old South* (New York, 1928), 264–65

on a fenced-in and virtually treeless college yard of approximately thirty-seven acres, containing nine buildings. It had about one hundred students and a small professorial staff operating on an annual budget of about $13,000. [15]

Toombs' freshman year passed quietly. At least, the records of the institution do not reveal any breach of regulations. One may surmise, however, in view of the turbulence of his remaining years that Toombs was learning to "chew tobacco, drink, swear, gamble, and miss prayers; in the mode of the time he was getting collegiate." [16] His sophomore year was doubtless long remembered by the authorities at the university. In early September, 1825, bad blood developed between Toombs and two brothers, Junius and Granby Hillyer. It seems that Toombs applied the school nickname, "Bull," to Junius and "made it the occasion of various shameful and obscene remarks." On the night of September 15 the brothers attacked Toombs and thrashed him. Shortly afterwards the fifteen-year-old invaded their room, threw a bowl at Granby, and aimed a pistol at Junius only to have it wrested away by another student. After a brief respite Toombs attacked a second time with a knife and hatchet, but again he was restrained by a neutral observer. Still under a full head of steam the next morning, he ambushed the brothers with club and pistol as they were on their way to classes. There is no official report on the outcome of the final engagement.

The faculty, undoubtedly shocked by the violence of the incident, resolved on September 20 that the Hillyers be "publicly admonished by the President" and made subject to immediate dismissal for future brawling. Toombs' expulsion was called for. That day President Waddel dismissed him.[17]

The next morning the faculty was greeted by a letter from Toombs acknowledging the "impropriety of his conduct." Accompanying the letter was a petition endorsed by both literary societies, the Demosthenian and Phi Kappa, between whom existed

[15]Augustus L. Hull, *Annals of Athens, Georgia, 1801–1901* (Athens, 1906), 38; Coulter, *College Life*, 17, 177; Minutes of the Board of Trustees of the University of Georgia (Typescript at University of Georgia), II, 122, 297, 320, hereinafter cited as Trustee Minutes, II; Robert Preston Brooks, *The University of Georgia Under Sixteen Administrations 1785–1955* (Athens, 1956), 233.

[16]Gray, "Bob Toombs," 194.

[17]Faculty Transactions, 80–81; Coulter, *College Life*, 99.

a bitter rivalry, calling for a "mitigation" of Toombs' punishment. Impressed, the faculty resolved to remit his sentence and reinstate him on a probationary status. Not wishing to seem irresolute, they made it clear that this act of amnesty must not be considered a precedent by the student body, that a "resort to weapons of a deadly nature" was regarded "with the utmost disapprobation" and would be punished vigorously.[18]

Toombs should have learned his lesson, but he did not. In a sense he never did; contempt for authority would remain a lifelong characteristic. In his senior year, Dr. Waddel had to speak to him now and then about his swearing.[19] On September 18, 1827, the faculty fined Toombs and his roommate, William Rembert, two dollars each for "loud laughing & boisterous conversation in their room" which "upon admonition, waxed worse & worse."[20] On January 2, 1828, Toombs was dismissed by the faculty. No specific reason was given in the faculty minutes for their action, but apparently the long-suffering professors refused to tolerate the incorrigible student any more and ousted him. Toombs had tried to worm his way out of trouble with another letter prior to his expulsion, but this time to no avail. Ironically, his next official connection with the university would be as a member of the Board of Trustees in 1859. [21]

Stories still abound in Georgia about the college escapades of Robert Toombs. Most are fabrications well-embroidered by age, but they reflect his colorful character and indicate the independence and dash which helped make him a political idol later. One such story has it that Toombs and some other students were drinking and gambling when a proctor came upon them. The others ran, but Toombs leaned tipsily against a wall and roared: "The guilty flee when no man pursueth, but the righteous are as bold as a lion!" Another version of the tale says that "Toombs was unable to run." [22] Again, there is the widely held legend that the University of Georgia offered him his diploma after he had won renown in politics and that Toombs refused to accept it.[23] Perhaps

---

[18]Faculty Transactions, 82.
[19]Coulter, *College Life*, 99–100.
[20]Faculty Transactions, 112.
[21]*Ibid.*, 115; Coulter, *College Life*, 100; Milledgeville *Federal Union*, August 16, 1859.
[22]Gray, "Bob Toombs," 195.
[23]*Ibid.*

the most stubbornly persistent myth is that of the "Toombs Oak."
According to this story, Toombs returned to the campus for the
commencement exercises in 1828 (at which time he would have
been graduated but for his dismissal), stood under a majestic oak
near the chapel where the program was underway, and began
such an eloquent address that the chapel benches were soon
emptied. By the middle 1880's, this episode had become a university
tradition. When the old tree was finally cut down, students erected
a marble sundial to mark the historic spot. The tree was once
there; the sundial is still there; Toombs never was.[24]

Shortly after his dismissal from the University of Georgia,
Toombs enrolled in Union College at Schenectady, New York, for
the completion of his college training. There is no clue as to why
he chose to travel so far from home. One could hope that Union's
excellent reputation under the leadership of President Eliphalet
Nott was the magnet, but Toombs' record in Athens would belie
this. There is a good chance that he would have been barred from
matriculation had President Nott had in his possession—undoubtedly he did not—a complete dossier from the University of Georgia.

College records show that he stayed the sessions from January
to April and from April until his graduation in July. His total school
expenses were $49.78: $20.00 each term for "Tuition, Room-Rent,
use of College Library, servant's Hire, Printing, etc. etc."; $1.75
for the use of Blackstone and a copy of the college laws; $8.00
for graduation and commencement exercises; and a three cent fine
for missing one class recitation. Since the custom in this day was
to levy fines for breaches of regulations, it appears that he had
undergone a monumental metamorphosis since he departed his
native Georgia.[25] The only grades available for Toombs show
100 in Blackstone, 60 in Botany, and 80 in Virgil.[26] In July, 1828,
he was awarded his degree.

Toombs belonged to the Delphian Society, a literary group
which had been founded at Union by Southern students in 1819. [27]

<hr>

[24]E. Merton Coulter, "The Toombs Oak," *Georgia Historical Quarterly*,
XLVI (March, 1962), 34–40.
[25]Union College Bill Books (Facsimile of MS at Union College, Schenectady); Fred C. Cole, *Union Worthies, Number Sixteen: Robert Augustus
Toombs, Class of 1828* (Schenectady, n.d.), 5–14.
[26]Charles F. Wilde to author, May 2, 1962. The grades were obtained by
Mr. Wilde from records in the Alumni Office of the college.
[27]*Catalogue of the Members of the Delphian Institute Society, At Union
College, Founded Feb. 22, 1819* (Schenectady, 1830), 8.

There were forty-eight members in 1828, twenty of them Southerners. One of these was William Rembert, whose residence was listed as Petersburgh, Georgia. Apparently this was the same Rembert who was Toombs' roommate and fellow troublemaker at the University of Georgia. What brought him to Union College is not known.

Toombs entered the law school of the University of Virginia on September 18, 1828. He was classified as a junior—a first year student in the two-year law school. Jefferson's university was still a young institution. Although founded in 1819, it had not granted its first degree until the close of the 1827–28 session, just before Toombs' arrival. There were 121 students enrolled during Toombs' stay, 28 in law school. One of these, Robert M. T. Hunter, was to achieve national prominence as a senator from Virginia and would succeed Toombs as Confederate Secretary of State.[28]

Little is known about Toombs' year at Charlottesville. Undoubtedly the most significant event of the year was the typhoid epidemic which closed down the university from early February until the middle of April. Robert probably went home to Washington during the long vacation. In the faculty minutes there are three direct references to Toombs, none of them flattering. On January 1, 1829, mention is made of violations of the school regulation requiring the wearing of uniforms at school parties. Toombs is listed among those students who had several times been guilty of this infraction. On June 25 a faculty member stated that a "disturbing noise was made last night by a number of persons who appeared to be returning from Charlottesville." He said he heard Toombs' name called. At the end of the school year Toombs scored 77 out of a possible 310 on his law examination, tying for low place with another student in a class of 14. [29]

Toombs left the University of Virginia at the close of his first year and went back home to Georgia, his formal education ended.

[28]The Matriculation Book of the Students of the University of Virginia, 1826–1879 (Microfilm of MS in Office of the Registrar, University of Virginia); *A Catalogue of the Officers and Students of the University of Virginia, Session of 1836–37* (Charlottesville, 1837), 16–17; *A Sketch of the History of the University of Virginia* . . . (Washington, D.C., 1859), 6; *A Catalogue of the Officers and Students of the University of Virginia, Fifth Session, 1828–1829* (Charlottesville, 1880), 5–9.

[29]Proceedings of the Faculty of the University of Virginia, from September 5, 1827, to March 12, 1829 (Microfilm of typescript at Alderman Library, University of Virginia), 411; *ibid.,* from March 14, 1829, to February 2, 1831, pp. 432–46, 475, 513.

Certainly there was nothing in his brief sojourn at Virginia to portend the brilliant legal career which awaited him.

Just a little over two years after Robert Toombs was expelled from the University of Georgia, he was admitted to the state bar. The circumstances were somewhat unusual, but this was not out of keeping with the general pattern of his life. On December 19, 1829, the legislature passed a special act permitting Toombs, still a minor, to practice law if found competent and qualified by court examination.[30] He successfully stood his examination and was admitted to practice on March 18, 1830, in the Superior Court of Elbert County. Presiding over the court and signing his license was Judge William H. Crawford, onetime giant in national politics who had been forced from the arena by bad health.[31]

Exactly eight months after Toombs joined the bar, he married Julia Ann DuBose, daughter of Ezekiel DuBose, a wealthy slave-owner from adjoining Lincoln County. She was seventeen; he was twenty.[32] They were not alike in many ways—she was a quiet, pious woman; he was boisterous and profane—but it was a happy marriage that lasted until Julia Toombs' death in 1883. She was the only person outside of Stephens who ever exerted much influence over her strong-willed husband. The couple had three children: Lawrence Catlett, who died in infancy; Mary Louisa, who married William Felix Alexander and died childless in 1855 at the age of twenty-one; and Sallie, who married Dudley M. DuBose and who died in 1866, just before her thirty-first birthday.[33]

Toombs' early efforts in his profession did not meet with immediate success. Stovall states that "he seems to have reached excellence in law by slow degrees of toil." He adds that Toombs' "work in his office was spasmodic, and his style in court too ve-

[30]*Journal of the Senate of the State of Georgia* (1829), 316, 318–19; hereinafter cited as *Georgia Senate Journal*.

[31]Elbert County (Ga.) Superior Court Minutes and Records, 1828–31 (Photocopy of microfilm MS in Georgia Archives).

[32]Davidson (comp.), *Wilkes County*, 357. Toombs and his half-brother, Lawrence Catlett, married sisters. On October 22, 1822, Lawrence married Harriet DuBose. The appraisement of Ezekiel DuBose's estate made in January, 1820, showed ownership of 81 slaves, according to Lincoln County Inventory and Appraisement Book, 1819–28 (Photocopy of microfilm MS in Georgia Archives), 4–46.

[33]Information obtained from grave markers in the Washington, Georgia, cemetery, the Toombs family cemetery about four miles from Washington, and the Alexander family cemetery, also in Washington.

hement and disconnected to make marked impression" in his first years of practice.[34]

The young Georgian rode the northern circuit during the fall and spring terms, attending weekly court sessions in Wilkes, Columbia, Oglethorpe, Elbert, Franklin, and Greene counties. Along with other lawyers, he "put up" at the local tavern while court convened. There he swapped stories and made preparations for his cases and reports, usually dealing with litigation over land and slaves. Toombs developed a reputation for being able to analyze great quantities of material and pick out the salient points with a minimum of effort. Although he did have a quick and penetrating mind, he worked diligently and left nothing to chance. As Stephens expressed it, he was always "a close and hard student" of the law.[35]

Toombs' talent for improvisation in the early days of his law practice was also noteworthy. Some years later a neighbor related how "when Mr. Toombs was riding his circuit, & tore his black pantaloons, the way he mended them was remarkable—he *inked* his drawers, which answered every purpose." [36]

It was in these first years at the bar that Toombs' lifelong friendship was formed with Alexander H. Stephens, a fellow lawyer. "A highly sensitive young man of serious and joyless habits, of consuming ambition, of poverty-fed pride, and of morbid preoccupation with self," [37] Stephens appeared totally incompatible with the robust, wealthy, and convivial Toombs. But this strange comradeship endured with singular accord throughout their lives.

As Toombs matured, he developed into one of the finest lawyers in the state. "As an advocate before juries," said a contemporary lawyer, "he was without a peer." [38] He spoke briefly, building his case around one or two strong points, rather than encompassing side issues. He tried to convince rather than persuade and left the jury feeling that only fools or knaves could find against his client.

[34]Stovall, *Toombs*, 14–15.

[35]Avary (ed.), *Stephens' Recollections*, 426; Stovall, *Toombs*, 15; Richard M. Johnston, *Autobiography of Col. Richard Malcolm Johnston* (Washington, 1900), 114–15.

[36]Clifford Alexander to Edward Porter Alexander, August 4, 1853, in Edward Porter Alexander Papers, Southern Historical Collection, University of North Carolina.

[37]James Z. Rabun (ed.), "Alexander H. Stephens's Diary, 1834–1837," *Georgia Historical Quarterly*, XXXVI (March, 1952), 71.

[38]Johnston, *Autobiography*, 117.

Stephens, no mean lawyer himself, said that he had "never seen his superior before judge or jury." [39]

Toombs was able to convert his legal talents into a sizeable fortune in the years between the Panic of 1837 and his entrance into Congress. The panic had left much potential litigation strewn in its wake—an inviting field for the enterprising lawyer. With the brief annual sessions of the state legislature occupying but a small portion of his time, Toombs plunged headlong into this profitable work and reaped a bountiful harvest.[40]

The code of the Southern gentleman stressed participation in local military affairs; Toombs fulfilled his obligations. In October, 1831, soon after his twenty-first birthday, he was commissioned by the state as a second lieutenant in the Washington Guards of Wilkes County. In 1836, when a Creek Indian uprising called him to active duty, he held the rank of captain.[41]

On December 7, 1835, Governor William Schley in an address to the House of Representatives spoke of the outrages perpetrated on the people of Georgia by migratory Alabama Creeks, particularly in Stewart and Baker counties. He said the citizens were in a "state of uneasiness and even alarm, in consequence of the hostile and predatory attitude of the vagrant savages, who roam through these counties in large bodies, destroying and stealing their property, insulting their feelings threatening their lives and in some instances actually murdering some of the inhabitants." [42] In the spring of 1836 the Indians burned the village of Roanoke in Stewart County and Governor Schley called out state troops. The general attitude of Georgians who had been long involved in the expulsion of the Indians from their state was expressed by the Athens *Southern Banner* when it editorialized: "We hope soon to see a force organized sufficient to exterminate the faithless race, and that no quarter will be extended to the savage miscreants." [43] Toombs commanded a volunteer company of 105 men from Wilkes that

[39]Avary (ed.), *Stephens' Recollections*, 426.
[40]Stovall, *Toombs*, 16–17.
[41][Georgia] Military Records, 1829–1841 (MS in Georgia Archives), 31, 35, 104.
[42]Executive Department Minutes, November 5, 1834–November 6, 1839 (MS in Georgia Archives), 175.
[43]Athens *Southern Banner*, May 19, 1836.

marched to Columbus and with other state troops passed under the command of General Winfield Scott.

An army surgeon was not impressed with the Georgia troops as they arrived in Columbus. He wrote on June 7 that "every ragamuffin of Georgia, deeming himself an invincible warrior, had enlisted under the standard of Mars, which many from their conduct must have mistaken for the standard of Bacchus, as they observed the articles of the latter god with much greater reverence." [44]

Scott's orders were to put down the uprising and compel the Creeks to adhere to treaty stipulations by evacuating their native lands and moving west. He planned to hem the Indians in between the Georgians on the east side of the Chattahoochee River and Alabama forces under General Thomas S. Jesup, second in command of the operation. But Jesup attacked prematurely, "flushed and scattered the main body of Creeks with but small results." [45] Few of the Georgia troops became engaged in actual combat. Most of them were stationed at various points on the Chattahoochee to prevent the Creeks from escaping into Florida. It is doubtful that Toombs saw a hostile Indian. In a letter Scott published originally in the Columbus *Herald*, July 12, 1836, he made specific mention of some Georgia captains and their companies who had made contact with the enemy, and Toombs' name does not appear. He did, however, compliment "the Georgia line" for its "readiness to obey orders, to march against the enemy, and to win honor for itself, for Georgia, and the Union." [46]

[44]James F. Sunderman (ed.), *Journey Into Wilderness: An Army Surgeon's Account of Life in Camp and Field During the Creek and Seminole Wars, 1836–1838* (Gainesville, Ga., 1953), 3.
[45]*Memoirs of Lieut.-General Scott, LL.D.* (New York, 1864), I, 262–63; D. Howden Smith, *Old Fuss and Feathers . . .* (New York, 1937), 200–202.
[46]Milledgeville *Federal Union*, July 19, 1836.

CHAPTER II

In the Georgia Legislature

IN 1836 Robert Toombs was elected to the lower house of the Georgia legislature as a representative from Wilkes County. This was the first of six bimonthly sessions he was to serve in the Milledgeville statehouse, a thick-walled Gothic structure which stood on a slight hill about three-quarters of a mile from the Oconee River. Toombs never aspired to a seat in the state senate; he preferred to season himself in the larger house of representatives.[1]

By the time of Toombs' election, the Georgia political scene had crystallized into some semblance of order after decades of personal politics bearing little relation to the national scene. From the end of the War of 1812 until the nullification controversy in 1832–33, Georgians had rallied under the banner of George M. Troup or John Clark to fight their political battles. There was little that would serve to distinguish between the Troupers and Clarkites— one prominent Georgia historian classified them simply as the "prosperous class of citizens, the other of the less prosperous class," respectively.[2] President Andrew Jackson's strong stand against

---

[1]Nelle Womack Hines (ed.), *A Treasure Album of Milledgeville and Baldwin County, Georgia* (Milledgeville, 1936), 12; *Sesqui-Centennial of Milledgeville and Baldwin County, Georgia, 1803–1953* (Souvenir program in Georgia Archives).

[2]Ulrich B. Phillips, *Georgia and State Rights* . . . (Washington, 1902), 100.

South Carolina's nullification of the tariffs of 1828 and 1832 served to reduce local factionalism and to substitute measures for men to some extent.

Georgia was linked with national politics through two distinct parties. Most of the Troupers, denouncing Jackson's threatened use of force against a sister Southern state, labeled themselves the State Rights party, while the Clarkites, espousing the cause of Old Hickory, adopted the name Union party. These political identifications soon became Whig and Democrat with the rise of the national Whig party, an anti-Jackson aggregation, in the mid-1830's. From 1836 until 1856, Georgians held to the two-party system, voting Whig three times in presidential elections and Democratic twice. The demise of the Whig party in the 1850's left the Democrats preeminent. Frequently Georgians bloc-voted according to economic and social differences. The eastern section of the state, dominated by a planter hegemony, was largely State Rights or Whig, while the mountainous north and pine barrens south voted Union or Democratic. As the cultivation of cotton spread into southwest Georgia, that area swung to the support of the Whigs.

Toombs entered the legislature as a State Righter, although the Milledgeville *Federal Union* identified him as a "Nullifier," a term of opprobrium customarily used by Georgia Democratic newspapers at this time for politicians of opposite persuasion, and misspelled his name as "Tombs." [3] As Toombs took office, one of the most severe depressions in American history began to settle over the country. The roots of the depression went back to the opening of the decade when a speculative fever had pushed forward unprecedented public land sales, the building of canals and railroads, the creation of wildcat banks, and heavy European investment in various American enterprises. A financial crisis in England and Andrew Jackson's erratic fiscal policy helped precipitate a crash in the spring of 1837, and the effects of the ensuing nationwide hard times did not completely evaporate until the mid-1840's.

Georgia lawmakers were under a great deal of pressure in these years to enact legislation for the alleviation of the state's economic distress. Toombs, already on his way to great wealth, emerged from these political battles a staunch and unyielding champion of con-

[3]Milledgeville *Federal Union*, October 10, 1837.

servative financing. Throughout his life he never allowed public calamity, no matter what the degree, to sway him from a tenacious devotion to this principle.

At the heart of the state's financial system was the Central Bank of Georgia, which had been established in 1828 as a sort of state treasury. Its capital consisted of all of the public funds, debts, bonds, judgments and notes held by or owed to the state, plus the shares of stock owned by the state in four state banks. The bank's directors were authorized to issue bank notes which served as currency and could make loans to citizens of Georgia at 6 percent interest.[4] For a while the bank operated smoothly, and with the advent of the depression it was looked to by many as a panacea for the ills that plagued the state.

In the 1837 and 1838 sessions, legislation was passed which allowed the bank to borrow money in order to fulfill promises of citizen loans. Toombs and his friend and fellow Whig, Stephens, unsuccessfully opposed such a move, feeling that the bank should live within its means and that the borrowing would simply accelerate the current inflationary spiral.[5] In 1839 the charter of the bank was extended and its activities, including its lending capacity, broadened considerably.[6] Toombs and a Whig minority entered a strong protest in the *House Journal* denouncing the "principle which asserts that the people should rely on the Government for pecuniary relief. . . ." This principle was "radically wrong," in the opinion of the dissenters, and "an inversion of all proper Government." [7] The Augusta *Chronicle*, a Whig journal, warned of a "fearful spirit of Jacobinism [which] was rapidly and stealthily undermining our institutions." [8]

Toombs, though largely on the minority side of the aisle in his first three sessions, was beginning to make his presence felt in the legislature. An observer of Whig leanings saw him this way at the close of the 1839 session:

This member possesses high genius, a thorough acquaintance with

[4]Robert T. Segrest, "History of Banking in Georgia Before 1865," (M.A. thesis, University of Georgia, 1933), 17, hereinafter cited as Segrest, "Banking."

[5]*Journal of the House of Representatives of the State of Georgia* (1837), 227–30, hereinafter cited as *Georgia House Journal; ibid.* (1838), 290–91; *Acts of the* [Georgia] *General Assembly* (1838), 45.

[6]Milledgeville *Federal Union*, January 21, February 4, 1840.

[7]Augusta *Chronicle*, January 7, 1840.

[8]*Ibid.*, February 18, 1840.

mankind, and is distinguished by his physical and moral courage. Often eloquent, always sensible and convincing, he is a formidable adversary in debate. He is a bold, fluent, sarcastic speaker, ever ready, ever fortunate and clear in illustration—frank and careless in his manner—he appears to be wholly indifferent to rhetorical embellishment. With infinite tact and sagacity, with a commanding talent for the management of men, it is with himself to select his own rank among the rising men of the State. We have heard with regret that he has declined emphatically a place on the Congressional ticket of the State Rights party. Having a handsome fortune, we know no gentleman who could so well sacrifice something to the public; and no one [to] whom we would contribute more cordially to elevate.[9]

In 1840 Georgia gave her vote to the Whig presidential candidate, William Henry Harrison, whose party also captured control of the state legislature. Toombs was busy in the months preceding the election speaking at political rallies in Washington, Milledgeville, Macon, Augusta, and Elberton. The gathering at Elberton on September 4 was fairly typical of the electioneering of the times: free barbecue for the citizens digested against a background of long political speeches, Whig and Democratic, from early morning to evening. Toombs was the fifth speaker of the day, and although the hour was late, "by the brilliancy of his wit, humor, anecdote, and argument, he gained and fastened the attention of the vast crowd of admiring spectators, for between one and two hours. . . ." The young Wilkes County politician attacked the administration of Democratic President Martin Van Buren amid the "most rapturous and deafening bursts of applause," reported a Whig paper.[10]

The Milledgeville *Southern Recorder* labeled Toombs and his Whig colleagues the "Reform Legislature" and looked forward to its "wise and salutary legislation . . . to correct the abuses of the past, and to devise measures of wisdom for the future." [11] The Whigs tried to please. Toombs was made chairman of a committee to look into the affairs of the bank. The report of his committee inspired a number of corrective measures which included curtailment of further issues of the already depreciated Central Bank notes, the redemption of those in circulation, and the requirement that all banks in Georgia resume specie payment upon pain of forfeiture of charter for refusal.[12]

[9]*Ibid.*, January 7, 1840.
[10]*Ibid.*, September 22, 1840.
[11]Milledgeville *Southern Recorder*, November 3, 1840.
[12]*Ibid.*, December 8, 1840; Augusta *Chronicle*, August 17, 1843; *Georgia House Journal* (1840), 334.

Late in the 1840 session the Democratic governor, Charles J. McDonald,[13] called upon the Whig legislature to devise some means of general relief for the citizens of the state. In his message he pointed up the failure of the state's cotton crop that year, the lack of action on the part of the legislature to meet the emergency, and his disinclination to call a necessarily expensive special session of the legislature for that purpose.[14] This was undoubtedly in part a political maneuver designed to embarrass the reform-minded Whigs who were attempting to deflate, not enlarge, the inflationary bubble. On a motion by Toombs, the house tossed the issue back at the governor, asking him to lead the way. McDonald responded with a proposed bond sale, the proceeds of which were to be deposited in the Central Bank for loans to the people. The scheme was referred to a special house committee, chairmaned by Toombs. The committee's majority report, adopted by an 88 to 79 vote, rejected the proposals of the governor, saying in part:

While we are duly sensible of, and deeply regret the pecuniary embarrassments of many of our fellow-citizens, we feel constrained by a sense of public duty, to declare, that we deem it unwise and impolitic, to use the credit, and pledge the property and labor of the whole people, to raise money to supply the *private* wants of a portion only of the people. The use of public credit, is one of the most important and delicate powers which a free people confide in their representatives; it should be jealously guarded, sacredly protected, and cautiously used, even for the attainment of the noblest public ends; and *never*, for the benefit of one class of the community, to the exclusion or injury of the rest, whether the demand for it grows out of their cupidity, or zeal, or real or supposed pecuniary difficulties.[15]

The committee's views may have been financially sound, but in a depression era they were politically disastrous. The Democrats successfully portrayed the opposition as a "cruel [,] haughty and oppressive set" who came into office crying reform "but seated in the chair of power, deal out the heaped and running over measure of TYRANNY."[16] The year 1841 saw the reelection of McDonald and the return of the Democrats to power in the legis-

[13]McDonald had been elected for two years in 1839 before the Whig sweep of 1840.
[14]Augusta *Chronicle*, December 17, 1840.
[15]*Ibid.*, December 22, 1840; *Georgia House Journal* (1840), 427.
[16]Milledgeville *Federal Union*, December 22, 1840.

lature. Toombs did not seek office at this time. Perhaps he sensed defeat and chose to stay out of contention, but it is likely that he could have won, for even in defeat the Whig gubernatorial candidate, William C. Dawson, carried Wilkes County.

In 1842 Toombs returned to the fray, but now as a member of the minority party, for the Democrats still held power. He did not find being outnumbered an uncomfortable position. In fact, his talent for biting sarcasm and slashing invective seemed at times more commensurate with the destruction of opposition than with the construction of leadership. Quotations from the correspondent of the Augusta *Chronicle* in Milledgeville give a glimpse of Toombs in the heat of legislative debate. "Mr. Toombs opened his artillery and kept up an unremitted fire for half an hour." Again, "Mr. Toombs, who *rolled* over them last Saturday evening like a steam car under full pressure." And finally, "Mr. Toombs replied in a very appropriate manner—not very remarkable for its balminess or conciliation. . . ." [17]

The Central Bank was still an issue but less so now than in earlier sessions. Its capital was gradually being drained away by legislative appropriation and its notes had depreciated markedly. Only the manner of its demise remained for debate. A Democratic bill for this purpose temporarily extended the bank's life while its activities were being wound up. The bill passed 116 to 71. Toombs and thirty-five other members took this occasion to trot out old objections to the bank and add some new ones pertinent to this bill. Particularly did they object to using state revenue to pay off bank debts. This was "indirectly levying money from the pockets of the people, not for the legitimate purpose of supporting their Government, but to support a rotten exploded system of Banking." [18] The protests were long and loud but seemingly useless, for as a student of the bank has written, "The career of the first and only state bank of Georgia was ended." [19]

Toombs also opposed the passage of a stay law designed to give relief to Georgia debtors by delaying the enforcement of contracts. Although another Whig member of the legislature officially wrote a minority report opposing the measure, the real author was prob-

[17]Augusta *Chronicle*, December 6, 15, 1842.
[18]*Georgia House Journal* (1842), 446.
[19]Segrest, "Banking," 24.

ably Toombs.[20] The report termed the bill "both unconstitutional and inexpedient," working "moral wrong, by legalizing violation of moral and legal obligations" and working "political injustice, by depressing one portion of our fellow-citizens of their acknowledged rights, for the benefit of another." [21] The bill failed to pass.

The general question of railroad building found Toombs on both sides of the political fence, supporting Governor McDonald on one issue and attacking him on another. In 1836 the state legislature provided state aid under certain conditions to railroad companies in the form of stock subscription on the authority of the governor. In 1842 McDonald, satisfied that the Monroe Railroad and Banking Company had met stipulated requirements, subscribed in the name of the state to $200,000 of the company's stock. Nevertheless, the house refused by a vote of 100 to 72 to appropriate money to honor the state's obligation. The argument advanced by the Democrat-dominated lower house was that the company had not fulfilled its part of the contract and hence was not entitled to the appropriation. It is more likely that the continuing hard times caused the lack of enthusiasm among the legislators. Hard times or no, Toombs and thirty colleagues entered a protest in the *House Journal* saying "they would be false to their principles, and unworthy of the place they occupy, did they not proclaim, and record their entire dissent to what they (with pain) regard as a violation of the plighted faith of the State." [22] Chief Justice John Marshall was no greater champion of the sanctity of contracts than was Robert Toombs.

Within a short time Toombs had bounded across the fence and was taking potshots at the governor for alleged misuse of state funds in connection with the building of the state-owned Western and Atlantic Railroad. Under provisions of an 1841 legislative enactment, all money received by the state from the Federal government was to be applied toward the payment of the state's public debt. McDonald had $80,000 of Federal money drawn from the treasury to pay for iron needed in the construction of the state road. Toombs, a self-appointed watchdog of state finances, charged that the money had been used unlawfully. The 1841 statute obviously referred to public debts then in existence, not those to be contracted in the future, as was the case in the purchase of the iron. Characteristically, the young legislator's criticism was strong.

[20]Phillips, *Toombs*, 21.
[21]*Georgia House Journal* (1842), 138–39.
[22]*Ibid.*, 276–77; Phillips, *Toombs*, 21–22.

"In the language of Mr. Toombs, the 'Governor has robbed' the public treasury," declared the *Chronicle*.[23] No official inquiry was made, however, and the legislative session came to an end without any further action. Toombs' attack on McDonald boiled up into quite a newspaper controversy. The Whig *Chronicle* on December 29 warmed to the defense of Toombs and in doing so intimated that he had charged the governor with appropriating the money for his private use.[24] The Democratic *Federal Union*, although holding no brief for Toombs' "vulgar denunciations," denied that such an inference had been made. "Not a man in the Legislature," it said, "considered him as charging anything more than perhaps some mistake in the construction of the law. . . ."[25] On January 10 Toombs broke into print assailing the action of Governor McDonald and the Democrats but denying that he had attacked the private character of the state's chief executive.[26] The *Federal Union*, wanting the last word, called Toombs' letter a "tedious specimen of the stuff out of which the Whig party manufacture the laurels of their great men. . . . The trash he has raised by his little whirlwind sails harmlessly around, to fall unregarded." [27]

Toombs completed his service in the legislature in the 1843 session. The Whigs were back in power, having elected George W. Crawford governor while capturing control of both houses. It was a busy season for Toombs, although less explosive than some of the previous ones. He worked for the establishment of a state supreme court, but the house bill failed to carry the senate by three votes.[28] Toombs explained to a friend that the Whig majority in the senate was very small and some of the party members unmanageable. "Hence, we are always defeated in that body when any *two* of our friends disagree with us." [29] The court was finally established by the next legislature.

[23] Augusta *Chronicle*, January 4, 1843.
[24] *Ibid.*, January 10, 1843.
[25] Milledgeville *Federal Union*, January 3, 1843.
[26] Augusta *Chronicle*, January 10, 1843.
[27] Milledgeville *Federal Union*, January 17, 1843.
[28] Toombs to Alexander H. Stephens, January 1, 1844, in Ulrich B. Phillips (ed.), *The Correspondence of Robert Toombs, Alexander H. Stephens, and Howell Cobb* in *Annual Report of the American Historical Association for the Year 1911* (Washington, 1913), II, 53, hereinafter cited as Phillips (ed.), *Correspondence.*
[29] Toombs to Adam Leopold Alexander, December 17, 1843, in Alexander-Hillhouse Papers, Southern Historical Collection, University of North Carolina.

Toombs supported the continuation of work on the Western and Atlantic Railroad and introduced a measure designed to put the raising and distribution of money for the poor school fund on a more permanent basis.[30] He opposed and helped defeat a bill providing protection for the rights and interests of married women.[31] Chivalry was not dead—it was just not a part of nineteenth-century politics.

The battles of state politics were not, of course, fought in a vacuum. National issues obtruded into the local scene, and Toombs was as aware as any young Georgia politician of the interdependence of Washington, D.C. and Milledgeville. In 1838 Toombs voted against a Democratic resolution that a national bank, a Whig-endorsed institution, was unconstitutional.[32] In 1840 he took the stump in eastern Georgia for William Henry Harrison and was so bold as to cross the Savannah River into South Carolina to debate George McDuffie, a Democrat of national prominence, in his home territory.[33] Toombs kept in touch with the polished Whig senator, John McPherson Berrien, apprising him of developments on the local front and suggesting procedures for him in Washington. The younger Toombs was not reluctant to give the veteran Berrien advice. In 1842 he urged boldness of action in Congress, saying that the people were "much more apt to support a party which enacts bad measures than one which has no measures at all, or what is the same thing which changes them every moon. . . ." [34]

Toombs fought unsuccessfully a resolution of censure of Senator Berrien by the legislature in 1842 for his stand in favor of a national bank. The Whigs battled back with their own party-adopted resolutions praising Berrien's actions and denying that members of the legislature were the "proper constituents of Senators in Congress." [35] Toombs wrote Berrien afterwards, advising an address to the people on the matter and that the Democratic

[30]Augusta *Chronicle*, December 20, 1843; *Georgia House Journal* (1843), 67, 124, 309, 420.
[31]Augusta *Chronicle*, December 6, 1843.
[32]*Georgia House Journal* (1838), 239. The Democrats were successful by a vote of 90 to 67.
[33]Phillips, *Toombs*, 32; Stovall, *Toombs*, 45–46.
[34]Toombs to Berrien, July 6, 1842, in John MacPherson Berrien Papers, Southern Historical Collection, University of North Carolina.
[35]"Resolutions of the Whig members of the Legislature of Georgia, Milledgeville, Dec. 23, 1842 to Hon. John M. Berrien, Washington," in Berrien Papers.

resolution be handled "with gloves off. . . . You have," Toombs stated,

the hearty & thorough support of the Whig party of the State, and recent events have increased the interest which is felt in your position and nothing could be so disastrous to you or them as to think for a moment of being driven from your position by the clamor or insults of such a body of men as the democratic party of Georgia, who are a combination of the vilest crew of desperate, unprincipled scoundrils [*sic*] that ever deceived and betrayed an honest people.[36]

By 1844 Robert Toombs was ready to join his friend Stephens to do battle with the Democrats in Congress. He was hardly a man of the people with his wealth and imperious manner. But his handsome, imposing appearance, undoubted ability, and boldness of speech appealed to Georgians, who kept him in national office until the Civil War brought him home.

[36]Toombs to Berrien, January 7, 1843, in Berrien Papers.

CHAPTER III

Early Washington Years

THE Whig party, through which Robert Toombs hoped to enter the United States House of Representatives, was one of the most unusual political groups in American history. Often called an "organized incompatibility," it resembled a multicolored patchwork quilt covering the nation with as many shades of opinion as patches. A coalition of Southern planters, Northern merchants and manufacturers, and Western farmers was embraced by the flexible party structure which took form around 1834. The Whig party started as an opposition party and, because of its heterogeneous nature, it remained largely so, achieving the most success at the polls when it presented no specific aims or platforms.

The merger of its component parts began in the late 1820's when Jacksonian Democracy threatened to change the United States from an aristocratic republic to a government of the masses. Alarmed conservatives were driven into a resistance movement against all things Jacksonian. The fact that Andrew Jackson was philosophically a states-rights advocate but a strong nationalist when he believed the Union was in danger opened the Whig ranks to strange bedfellows. The Tennessean's threatened use of force against South Carolina in the nullification crisis alienated Southern states-righters, while his opposition to the National Bank and Federally-assisted internal improvements angered broad construction nationalists in the North and West. Hoping to weld these disparate groups into a successful national party, Henry Clay of Kentucky emerged as the Whigs' greatest leader. Although by no means endorsed by all factions within the party his American System, aiming at national self-sufficiency through a protective tariff, internal improvements, and a national bank to facilitate credit and exchange, became as much of a platform for the Whigs as they ever had.

With the exception of South Carolina, which became solidly Democrat under the leadership of John C. Calhoun,[1] every Southern state developed a two-party system. Though no firm pattern prevailed, in the lower South most planters joined the Whig party, disliking some of Clay's proposals but fearing more the threat to privilege and property interests posed by the Jacksonian equalitarianism. Furthermore, the magnetic Clay was able to persuade the majority of Whig congressmen from the South that a moderate tariff was to the best interest of their section.

In the upper South, the Whigs included not only the planters but also business and commercial groups who needed no persuasion that tariff protection served them well. The crisscrossing of Whig party interests North and South prevented for about two decades the rise of any strong, purely sectional political group. The impact of slavery, however, proved stronger than party ties. In the mid 1850's, it destroyed the Whig party and gave birth to the Republican party, sectionalized in the North. Most Southern Whigs joined the Democratic ranks and faced the secession crisis in solid phalanx with their former political enemies.

Early in 1844 Robert Toombs wrote Senator Berrien: "I doubt not we shall achieve a brilliant victory in November for Mr. Clay." [2] It seemed a foregone conclusion that the nomination of "Harry of the West" would be agreed upon by all Whigs in the coming convention. Under Clay's guidance, John Tyler, who had succeeded to the presidency at the death of Harrison, had been read out of the party for vetoing the fulfillment of the American System. As Tyler led a small group of states-rights Whigs back into the Democratic party, Clay reigned supreme as leader of the remainder.

[1]Calhoun aligned himself temporarily with the anti-Jackson forces after his break with the President, but later, unable to support the nationalistic aims of Clay, swung back into the Democratic party.
[2]Toombs to Berrien, January 28, 1844, in Berrien Papers.

Toombs had been busy about party business. He told Berrien that Whigs in the southwestern part of the state, where Toombs had a plantation, were "full of hope and energy, the spirit of forty [1840] is already rife among them." Since he returned to his home in Washington, he had written several letters to prominent friends over the state calling for concerted action and a "grand rally" for the Whig cause.[3]

In the spring, just before the Whig convention at Baltimore, Henry Clay made a political tour through the South. His presence in Georgia helped shore up Whig strength. In April he wrote a letter from Raleigh, North Carolina, to the editors of the *National Intelligencer*, a Whig newspaper in Washington, in which he opposed the immediate annexation of Texas by the United States. At the same time, the likely nominee of the Democratic party, Martin Van Buren, issued a similar statement. It seemed apparent that both men, perhaps by earlier arrangement, had agreed to eliminate the troublesome question from the approaching campaign. Alexander H. Stephens, who had entered Congress as a Whig in 1843, pronounced Clay's letter as "very full, clear, and satisfactory."[4]

At Baltimore, where Toombs was in attendance, Clay was nominated as expected. The platform followed the traditional Whig position on the tariff and internal improvements but sluffed off any mention of Texas or a national bank. Later in the month, the Democrats, meeting in the same city, unexpectedly rejected Van Buren, rallied behind James K. Polk of Tennessee and boldly proclaimed a platform calling for the annexation of Texas.

Most Southern Whigs stood behind Clay's stand on annexation, but it was necessary in some areas to refine the issue a bit as the Democrats were making capital of it. In Georgia, where annexationist sentiment was strong, the Whig state convention adopted resolutions drawn up by Stephens which voiced no opposition to the

---

[3]*Ibid.*

[4]Quoted in Richard Malcolm Johnston and William Hand Browne, *Life of Alexander H. Stephens* (Philadelphia, 1878), 170. Writing years later Stephens claimed that as Clay passed through Georgia he urged the Kentuckian not "to come out with such a letter," Avary (ed.), *Stephens' Recollections*, 19. As this Raleigh letter appears to have cost Clay the election, Stephens may well have been wishing he had influenced the candidate not to publish it.

future acquisition of Texas.[5] Clay himself crawfished on the matter by writing letters in which he said he would be willing to accept the admission of Texas if it could be done honorably and without war.

While the national campaign that ended in Clay's defeat rolled on, Toombs was waging vigorous efforts to get himself elected to the House as representative from the Eighth Congressional District. His opponent was Edward J. Black, a Democrat who had served in Congress since 1838. It was not easy for a young politician even with Toombs' talent to defend a national bank, a protective tariff, and opposition to Texas in a Southern district in 1844. Popular sentiment was running in opposite directions, but Toombs campaigned with great energy and forcefulness. He labeled the bank constitutional from a broad construction point of view, as constitutional, he said, as a lighthouse for which there was no specific authority to build. He denied that a protective tariff was systemized robbery, pointing out that more American industry meant greater employment and increased consumption of American raw materials, including cotton. This was "practical evidence" of its benefits.[6] Toombs believed, as did Clay, that the annexation of Texas would lead to war. "A people who go to war without just and sufficient cause, with no other motive than pride and love of glory, are enemies to the human race and deserve the execration of all mankind." [7] The Milledgeville *Federal Union* likened Toombs to Pericles of ancient Athens, a great orator but a man who bankrupted his state and lived to see it invaded and ruined. A "noisy orator," he was telling Georgians to disregard their own interests in counseling them to oppose the annexation of Texas.[8]

In the course of the electioneering, Toombs was accused of being "soft" on slavery, a surprising charge in view of his staunch support of the institution at that time and later.[9] He dismissed the whole thing as dirty politics by the Democrats to confuse the issues at stake and to play upon the fears and passions of the people. "I

[5]Avary (ed.), *Stephens' Recollections*, 17; Arthur C. Cole, *The Whig Party in the South* (Reprint ed.; Gloucester, Mass., 1962), 112–13.
[6]Quoted in Stovall, *Toombs*, 49.
[7]*Ibid.*, 53.
[8]Milledgeville *Federal Union*, August 13, 1844.
[9]*Ibid.*, September 24, 1844.

have no language to express my scorn and contempt for the whole crew," he stated.[10]

On July 31, Toombs participated in a Whig rally at Madison, in north-central Georgia, which reflected the excitement and enthusiasm attending antebellum politics. For two days Whigs had poured into the little town from every part of the state, swelling the convention encampment to over fifteen thousand, according to a Whig newspaper, but calculated at only five thousand by a Democratic sheet.[11] At seven in the morning on the thirty-first, the "most inspiring procession ever witnessed in the interior of any Southern State" formed in the public square and marched over a mile to the convention site where speeches were given until noon. Then the customary barbecue dinner was served on combined tables that stretched "just a few feet short of a mile." Afterwards there were more speeches, including a two hour affair by Stephens, until six o'clock. Toombs spoke several times but his remarks were not recorded.[12]

In October Whigs and Democrats met head-on in debate in Augusta, the largest city in Toombs' district. The main contestants were Toombs and George McDuffie, the South Carolina Democrat with whom Toombs had clashed before in 1840. Each spoke for two hours and ranged over the entire political spectrum. Toombs' concluding remarks revealed clearly the moderate political philosophy with which he was to enter Congress: the constitution guaranteed to rational and tolerant men, both North and South, sufficient protection for the rights of all. He said: "We have lived under the present order of things for fifty years, and can continue to live under it for one thousand years to come, if the people of the South are but content to stand upon their rights as guaranteed in the Constitution, and not work confusion by listening to ambitious politicians: by taking as much pains to preserve a good understanding with our Northern brethren, the vast majority of whom are inclined to respect the limitations of the Constitution." [13]

Toombs defeated Black by a vote of 4,665 to 3,309, carrying every county but one in the district. Wilkes County gave him 525 votes to 349 for his opponent.[14] The new congressman-elect had

[10]Quoted in Stovall, *Toombs*, 47.
[11]Milledgeville *Southern Recorder*, August 6, 20, 1844.
[12]*Ibid.*, August 6, 1844.
[13]Quoted in Stovall, *Toombs*, 50.
[14]Milledgeville *Federal Union*, October 22, 1844.

over a year to wait before he could take his seat in the House for the opening of the first session of the Twenty-ninth Congress.[15] The long delay meant little to him, however, for he had his large law practice to look after together with the surveillance of his plantation in Stewart County. Around the first of the year Toombs was struck by a severe attack of rheumatism which incapacitated him for several weeks. Unable to leave his home, he spent some time in correspondence. Very much on his mind was the Texas problem, still unsettled. He feared that more and more it was becoming a sectional issue to the distress of the Whig party and the Union. "I think it of the greatest consequence to the union," he wrote Berrien, "to settle the question & that speedily. The agitation daily embitters the feelings of the two great divisions of the Union & gives strength to the abolition movement & to the Southern Democracy, for clamour is the livelihood & agitation the stock in trade of both of those heartless, unprincipled factions." [16]

The question was finally put to rest a few days before Polk's inauguration when Congress, by joint resolution, decided in favor of the annexation of Texas, the House voting 120 to 98 and the Senate 27 to 25. Whig party lines crumbled as eight Southern Whigs, including Stephens in the House and three in the Senate, voted with the Democrats to carry the measure through.[17] Toombs would doubtless have voted against the joint resolution. He told Stephens after his affirmative vote but before the Senate vote which Toombs assumed would be negative, that he had misgivings about his friend's course of action.[18] For with the Senate's rejection, the fat would be in the fire again. With the issue now closed and only minimum damage done to Whig unity, Toombs probably was content.

In June, Stephens accompanied Toombs on a trip to Florida for his health. They were accused by a Florida newspaper of promoting Whiggery and intermeddling in the politics of the state, but the charges proved to be untrue and were subsequently withdrawn.[19] During the rest of the summer and fall Toombs attended to his

[15]This situation which produced "lame duck" Congresses was eliminated by the Twentieth Amendment, which called for opening sessions in January following the November elections.
[16]Toombs to Berrien, February 13, 1845, in Berrien Papers.
[17]Cole, *Whig Party*, 117–18.
[18]Toombs to Stephens, February 16, 1845, in Phillips (ed.), *Correspondence*, 64–65.
[19]Augusta *Chronicle*, June 7, 13, 1845.

law practice as he looked forward to the challenge of Congressional service at the end of the year.

Toombs had been to the nation's capital before, probably several times, and so when he arrived in November, 1845, he could not have been surprised at what awaited him. Some visitors were. Washington in the 1840's was still very much an overgrown village, despite the presence of nearly 50,000 people in the District of Columbia. It was several decades away from becoming the pride of the nation. The Capitol, burned by the British in the War of 1812, was yet unfinished, and the Washington Monument was still in the planning stage. The straggling streets and walks were largely unpaved and ill-kept. Harriet Martineau, a British traveler, wrote in 1835 that in making calls about the city she "had to cross ditches and stiles, and walk alternately on grass and pavements, and strike across a field to reach a street. . . ." [20] Government office buildings were drab with plain brick facades and private residences were "destitute of architectural pretention." [21]

The shabby physical appearance of the city was offset to some extent by its social life when Congress was in session. In the early years, Washington society tended to center around the presidential coterie and the diplomatic corps. But in the mid-century decades, more and more congressmen were bringing their families to the capital and establishing their own social pattern. This was true of Toombs, who with his wife spread a fine table and entertained lavishly.

At twelve noon, December 1, 1845, Toombs was present in the House of Representatives for the opening of the first session of the Twenty-ninth Congress. The 224 duly elected guardians of the nation[22] were housed in what is now Statuary Hall, a semi-circular chamber about 96 feet in diameter and 57 feet high with a dome-like ceiling. John Randolph of Virginia pronounced it "handsome and fit for anything but the use intended." [23] At the south end of the hall were the Speaker's chair and table mounted

[20]Quoted in *Washington: City and Capital*, American Guide Series (Washington, 1937), 53.

[21]Rufus R. Wilson, *Washington the Capital City and Its Part in the History of the Nation* (Philadelphia, 1901), II, 158.

[22]This is total membership. Only 212 were actually present on December 1.

[23]Quoted in *Washington: City and Capital*, 238.

on a four foot rostrum befitting the great political power which this officer possessed at the time. Tables for reporters and clerks were nearby. Behind the Speaker's chair were crimson curtains to absorb acoustical peculiarities which plagued the room. Stretching out in front of the Speaker on a marble floor with mosaic tiling were the desks and chairs of the representatives arranged in concentric semicircles. Around the outer row was a curtained iron railing. At the north end of the hall just beyond the railing was the lobby for the members and above this lobby the galleries with seats for some five hundred visitors.[24]

Frequently noisy and disorderly, the House lacked the veneer of sedate dignity which prevailed in the smaller Senate chamber. A South Carolinian visiting the House in the summer of 1846 was shocked by what he saw: "The appearance and character of the members . . . fell as far short of my expectations as the Capitol exceeded them. I have rarely seen more rudeness, insolence and vulgarity manifested in a court yard or at a muster field, than I witnessed immediately on going into the House of Representatives." [25] Nonetheless, it was almost always an interesting and exciting place where representatives from all parts of the country debated, argued, and sometimes fought in hammering out legislative policy.

Only three of the eight-man Georgia delegation were Whigs—Toombs, Stephens, and Thomas Butler King. The most prominent Georgian across the aisle was Howell Cobb, portly Athens lawyer and future governor of the state, who was serving his second term in Congress. The Twenty-ninth Congress was an unusually strong one. From Massachusetts there was ex-President John Quincy Adams, the only chief executive so to serve; from Illinois, Stephen A. Douglas, short, thick-set, tobacco-chewing orator of great ability and ambition; William L. Yancey and R. Barnwell Rhett from Alabama and South Carolina, respectively, fiery apostles of Southern rights; from Mississippi, freshman Representative Jefferson Davis; and a future president, Andrew Johnson from Tennessee. Among the Southerners in this Congress were those leaders who were to figure most prominently in the crisis-ridden years just before the Civil War.

[24]*Ibid.,* 239; Wilson, *Washington,* 160–61.
[25]Quoted in Augusta *Chronicle,* August 3, 1846.

Toombs' first major speech was delivered on January 12, 1846. The issue under consideration by the House was the magnificent, sprawling Oregon Territory, which had been under joint occupation by the United States and Britain since 1818. The two nations had not been able to agree on a line of demarcation, although the United States had on several occasions suggested the continuation of the 49th Parallel westward to the Pacific Ocean. In the early 1840's, beset by "Oregon fever," Americans by the hundreds began to make the long trek into the territory until by 1845 around five thousand Yankees called Oregon home. The matter might have been settled amicably by the diplomats, but the Oregon question was thrown into the 1844 presidential election and the arena of partisan politics. The Democrats in their platform aggressively asserted the claim of the United States to the whole territory, thus cleverly offering to the nation potential free states to balance the slave state of Texas whose annexation they also favored. After his election Polk backed down a bit from his campaign posture on Oregon and once more offered to divide the Oregon country at the 49th Parallel. Upon Britain's refusal, the President in his annual message to Congress in December, 1845, asked that notice be given to Britain that joint occupation would end in a year. Polk's militance provoked loose war talk on both sides of the Atlantic. It was at this juncture that Toombs made his thoughts known.

His maiden effort lasted nearly an hour and according to reporter for the Baltimore *American* was delivered "with great force and ability" and "commanded great attention." [26] Toombs derided the idea that the question of war or peace was involved here. It "did not weigh a feather; it had nothing to do with it," he said.[27] There were but two factors involved—our rights to the Oregon Territory and the proper time to claim those rights by terminating joint occupation. He reviewed the history of Oregon and concluded that the President's assertion that the United States had a clear and unquestionable title to the entire territory was unfounded, although the American claim was better than that of the English. Toombs believed that notice should be given for ending

[26]Milledgeville *Southern Recorder*, January 20, 1846; Augusta *Chronicle*, January 17, 1846. For Toombs' speech, see *Congressional Globe*, 29th Cong., 1st Sess., 185–86.

[27]*Congressional Globe*, 29th Cong., 1st Sess., 186.

joint occupation, but that it should be done by the President and not by Congress, and at his discretion rather than immediately. This was the only way the United States might perfect its title to the whole of Oregon, and he felt the President was in a better position than the legislature to decide when the time was propitious for termination. He would not, he said, distrust the President's wisdom or patriotism in the matter.

Toombs' speech was viewed as patriotic and statesmanlike by the Whig press in Georgia. Governor Crawford wrote Stephens that it was the "best speech which I have had time to read" and "showed more coolness than I supposed he could exhibit on a question which is so eminently fitted for Buncombe." [28] The motives prompting it seemed something less than patriotic and statesmanlike when they were revealed in a letter from Toombs to Crawford dated February 6. In Toombs' mind, Polk, the "vilest poltroon that ever disgraced our Government," was engaged in political trickery of the lowest order. He was playing a game of "bluster" designed to enhance the fortunes of his Democratic party and weaken the Whigs. Toombs believed that Polk really expected the Whigs and Calhoun followers to reject the idea of giving the British notification, thus enabling him to keep the issue alive for another presidential campaign or a "second heat," as the Georgian labeled it. Toombs wanted the Whigs to give Polk what he publicly asked for by placing the power of notification in his hands. This would effectively block any opportunity for getting more mileage out of Oregon. But some Whigs were falling for Polk's bait and opposing notification on the grounds that it would lead to war. They were crying peace, peace, and working themselves into a position from which there was no return, just as the President had planned.

Actually, said Toombs the Southerner, "I don't [care] a fig about *any* of Oregon and would gladly get ridd of the controversy by giving it all to anybody else but the British if I could with honor. The country is too large now, and I don't want a foot of Oregon or an acre of any other country, especially without 'niggers.' " [29]

[28]Crawford to Stephens, January 29, 1846 in Alexander H. Stephens Papers, Emory University.
[29]Toombs to Crawford, February 6, 1846, in Phillips (ed.), *Correspondence*, 73–74.

On February 9, before crowded and excited galleries, the House voted 163 to 54 in favor of a resolution that the President give notice forthwith to Britain that joint occupation of the Oregon Territory would be annulled and abrogated within twelve months. An amendment which would have left the time of notification to the President's discretion was rejected. Toombs voted for the amendment, but along with Stephens cast his ballot against the resolution. The other Georgia Whig, Thomas Butler King, did not vote on the final passage of the resolution.[30]

Toombs was attacked by state Democratic newspapers for inconsistency of action, in that he favored notice to Britain and then voted against it. In a letter to the Augusta *Chronicle* dated February 28, 1846, he answered his critics by saying that he had opposed the method of giving notification, not notification itself. Furthermore, the President had withheld some correspondence on the issue from the House and it was inexpedient, he thought, to act on such a grave problem without knowledge of all the facts. Additionally, "The extraordinary and indefensible pretensions assumed by our Government, . . . have caused many able and prudent men, in and out of Congress, who believe with me, that the convention of 1818 [which originally set up joint occupation] ought to be abrogated, to doubt the propriety of doing so until our government shall be in safer and abler hands than the present Cabinet." [31] The *Chronicle* found quite reasonable Stephens' negative vote because he thought such notification would lead to war. It justified King's lack of action on the grounds that he felt he did not have sufficient information to make a decision.[32]

The Senate debated its own resolution on Oregon for nearly two months. Finally, on April 16, it adopted a proposal similar to that of the House. After a week of adjustment by a joint committee, a joint resolution was passed by Congress on April 23, the House voting 142 to 46 and the Senate 42 to 10. The resolution, couched in moderate and conciliatory language, authorized the President *at his discretion* to give notice to Britain for the termination of joint occupation. This was what Toombs had originally proposed, although his motives were highly partisan in doing

[30]*Congressional Globe*, 29th Cong., 1st Sess., 349–50; Athens *Southern Banner*, February 17, 1846; Augusta *Chronicle*, March 10, 1846.
[31]Augusta *Chronicle*, March 10, 1846.
[32]*Ibid.*, February 26, 28, 1846.

so. Stephens and King voted for the joint resolution, while the record shows no vote for Toombs at all.[33]

Despite the bluster of expansionists, the government was reluctant to precipitate a war with Britain over Oregon. Polk's administration was deeply involved in a dispute with Mexico which was soon to explode into war. Consequently when the British proposed to settle the difficulty by the extension of the 49th Parallel, as the United States had suggested several times previously, Polk decided to submit the compromise plan to the Senate, which recommended acceptance. A treaty signed in June, 1846, brought the Oregon controversy to a close.

While the United States was clasping hands with Britain, it was drawing the sword against Mexico. Since the annexation of Texas, which Mexico had never recognized, the two countries had drifted toward war, and the accession of the pugnacious Polk to the presidency did not contribute to its avoidance. Polk and the expansionists were determined to acquire California and New Mexico, through purchase if possible, through force if necessary. Their impatience was quickened by the inability of American citizens to collect claims against the Mexican government, a dispute over Texas' southern boundary, and the refusal of Mexico to negotiate any of the problems. In January, 1846, Polk ordered General Zachary Taylor and his command to move from the Nueces River, the longtime boundary of Texas, to the Rio Grande, the newly-claimed boundary. This was an aggressive move across an area to which the American claim was at best tenuous. When his last attempts at negotiation failed, Polk prepared to send a war message to Congress. He was relieved from what would have been a feeble justification for conflict when in late April Mexican forces crossed the Rio Grande and attacked a portion of Taylor's army. His hastily-revised call for war now was based on the statement that American blood had been shed on American soil. On May 13, Congress declared war on Mexico, the House by a vote of 174 to 14 and the Senate 40 to 2.

Toombs, along with most Whigs, voted for war and the necessary military appropriations. But it was the only time in the conflict that the two parties seemed to be pursuing the same goals. Even as the Whigs were caught up in the initial flush of excitement

[33]*Congressional Globe*, 29th Cong., 1st Sess., 717, 721.

that produced their affirmative votes, it was evident that they were not enthusiastic about what they were to label derisively "Mr. Polk's war." War sentiment diminished rapidly in the North and East where it was viewed by many as another land grab by the slavocracy, while Southern Whigs found little reason to support anything that enhanced a Democratic administration. Even before the war began, the *Chronicle* was deploring Taylor's movement to the Rio Grande. "Mr. Polk desires the glory of having the Mexicans thrashed during his administration," it editorialized. "It would be the glory which a giant would obtain by knocking down a Lilliput!" [34] The tune for the Whig press remained the same after hostilities commenced.

On May 18, five days after war was declared, Toombs spoke in Congress. It was a short, impromptu speech given in some anger, which probably accounted for the fast delivery that Stephens said made accurate reporting impossible.[35] Toombs was upset over what he believed to be the injection of political partisanship into war preparations. An appropriation bill had been prefaced by a statement endorsing Polk's actions prior to hostilities and declaring that the war had been forced by Mexico. Representative John H. Lumpkin, Georgia Democrat, made the support of the preamble a test of patriotism. At this Toombs bridled. He declared that the defense of Texas, since it had become a part of the United States, was a duty which he was ready to perform. He and the Whigs were also prepared to vote all necessary supplies to repel invasion. But he did not agree that the territory between the Nueces and Rio Grande rivers was a part of Texas. In fact, he declared, the movement of American forces to the Rio Grande at Polk's command "was contrary to the laws of this country, a usurpation on the rights of this House, and an aggression on the rights of Mexico." As Toombs flung this statement into the face of his Democratic colleagues, he pugnaciously invited them "to make the most of [it] . . ." [36]

As the Whig potshots at the prosecution of the war continued,

[34]Augusta *Chronicle*, April 30, 1846. Word had not yet been received of the Mexican attack which took place on April 25.

[35]Stephens to Linton Stephens, May 23, 1846, in Alexander H. Stephens Papers, Emory University.

[36]*Congressional Globe*, 29th Cong., 1st Sess., 837; Augusta *Chronicle*, May 22, 1846.

Toombs in July delivered his second major speech in Congress.[37] It was an attempt to head off a Democratic tariff framed by Secretary of the Treasury Robert J. Walker of Mississippi and embodying much of his free-trade theory. Walker had been impressed by the success Britain was experiencing in abandoning protection, and furthermore President Polk had pledged a lowering of the tariff in the 1844 campaign. Toombs, speaking as a moderate protectionist, called the proposed measure a "hybrid bill which asserts and maintains no principles—which neither harmonizes with the principles of free trade nor protection—but which mixes up so unskillfully the principles of each as to neutralize both." [38] He charged that lowering duties would reduce revenue at a time when government expenditures were increasing. Also the bill's abolition of specific duties in favor of the *ad valorem* principle would make difficult an appraisal of anticipated revenue because of changing market values. Britain, "the workshop of the world," could well afford her free trade, Toombs claimed, and compete in the world market because of the excellence of her manufactures and the low wages of her workers. The United States could not.

The bill was not completely indefensible in Toombs' eyes, but he thought further study and revision of the present tariff structure was called for, not this injudicious combination of incompatibilities. He was under no illusions, however, that he could stem the Democrat majority vote. "We no longer sit here," he said, "as a deliberative assembly, but to register, to give vitality, under the forms of our Constitution to edicts originating in party necessity. Every department of your Government is becoming its slaves, and the people its victims." [39] The tariff bill passed, 114 to 95, with Toombs and Stephens voting nay. According to a reporter, when the vote had been completed, the "free-traders sent up a shout at what had been done, which the friends of Protection responded to with a hiss." [40]

Toombs' misgivings about the Walker Tariff were not realized. It was a success as a revenue measure while business and manufacturing continued to flourish. The entire industrial development of the country was benefited by cheaper iron. As the tariff ques-

[37]*Congressional Globe*, 29th Cong., 1st Sess., 1030–35.
[38]*Ibid.*, 1030.
[39]*Ibid.*
[40]Augusta *Chronicle*, July 8, 1846.

tion became involved in the broader slavery issue, Southern Whigs tended to become somewhat disenchanted with the notion that they should support protection in the interest of party and national unity while their Northern colleagues were assailing Southern institutions. This, of course, foretold for the Whig party the demise which finally occurred in the 1850's.

On August 8, shortly before the adjournment of the first session of the Twenty-ninth Congress, a young Democratic congressman from Pennsylvania named David Wilmot arose in the House. To a bill appropriating money for the President's use in prospective negotiations with Mexico, he proposed an amendment stipulating that slavery be excluded from any territory acquired from Mexico. There thus was raised an issue that most politicians hoped had been laid to rest with the Missouri Compromise.[41] The House twice approved the Wilmot Proviso, but each time it failed in the Senate, where the South still had equal representation. Both of the major parties tried to sweep it under the rug and out of sight, but it kept popping out as a disruptive force to national party unity and sectional harmony.

Toombs and Stephens came home together from Washington around the middle of August. No immediate respite was in store for Toombs, as he had recently been unanimously nominated by a Whig convention in his district to run for another term in the House. His selection was accompanied by the strong endorsement that "in him we have a statesman whom we are proud to honor with our confidence and sustain with our suffrage." [42] Toombs kept his campaigning to a minimum, apparently confident of victory and also desiring to attend to his law practice. He refused to canvass the district with his Democratic opponent, R. W. Flournoy, stating that it had not been the practice in that area of the state for candidates to address public meetings unless asked to do so by the voters themselves.[43] The Democrats had little ammunition to use effectively against the popular Toombs. The Eighth District was his private preserve, and in the minds of the majority of the people Bob Toombs could do no wrong throughout his public career. He was reelected to Congress without difficulty.

[41]The Missouri Compromise of 1820 had prohibited slavery in the Louisiana Territory north of 36°30' with the exception of the state of Missouri.
[42]Augusta *Chronicle*, July 13, 1846.
[43]*Ibid.*, September 26, 1846.

In November, Toombs and Stephens were admitted to practice before the recently established state supreme court.[44] The two friends teamed up to plead their initial case before the high tribunal, but lost, something unusual for both men.[45] Toombs' legal adversaries before the court in these early years constituted a roll call of future governors, United States senators, and secession leaders: Herschel V. Johnson, Charles J. Jenkins, Thomas R. R. Cobb, brother of Democratic Congressman Howell Cobb, Augustus Reese, and Benjamin H. Hill. Toombs was outstanding even among these luminaries, and in the opinion of many stood without a peer as a lawyer in the state of Georgia.

Toombs was three weeks late in returning to Washington for the last and short session of the Twenty-ninth Congress. Not until December 28 did he take his seat.[46] This was to become fairly regular procedure for Toombs, who frequently found that the press of affairs at home interfered with his duties as a congressman. During this period he made only one speech, in which the continued Whig opposition to the prosecution of the Mexican War was reflected.[47] The immediate occasion was a proposed bill authorizing ten additional regiments of regular soldiers for the war. Toombs opposed the bill for several reasons. First, he preferred the use of volunteers to regular soldiers. They elected their own officers, whereas the President appointed the officers to command regulars. In Toombs' mind the volunteers had acted in this capacity "with much greater judgment, skill, and patriotism" than Polk. The President throughout the war had played politics in appointments and would doubtless continue to do so. Furthermore, said Toombs, the "battles of the republic ought to be fought by its citizen soldiery" who were faithful to its institutions and interested in good government. He was not implying that the present administration was looking toward a Caesar-type dictatorship but the time might come when "you have a bold man, as well as a bad one, in the White House." This was not to be the last time that Toombs demonstrated a strong antipathy toward the regular army. His

[44]*Report of Cases in Law and Equity Argued and Determined in the Supreme Court of Georgia, at Atlanta*, I, vii–viii, xxiii, hereinafter cited as *Georgia Cases*.
[45]*Georgia Cases* I, 595 (1846).
[46]*Congressional Globe*, 29th Cong., 2nd Sess., 31.
[47]*Ibid.*, 140–42.

opposition became almost neurotic during the Civil War as he saw in West Point-trained officers a major cause of the downfall of the Confederacy's military efforts.

After his remarks on the "ten regiment bill," Toombs launched into a review of the war itself. He again charged the President with deliberately provoking hostilities and with attempting to discourage freedom of debate in the House by charges of disloyalty toward those who questioned war policy. In muscular language, he labeled some Democratic members "common sewers to pass those denunciations and aspersions through this House to the country." He censured Polk for inadequate support of General Zachary Taylor, who had already won several outstanding victories in northern Mexico and whose growing popularity and Whig support made him anathema to the Democratic administration. Toombs desired peace, but he wanted no dismemberment of Mexico to accompany it. We have territory enough, he said, and should improve what we have. Here he was following the Southern Whig line, which for the sake of party and national unity sought to repress the issue of territorial extension, intertwined as it was with the disruptive question of the slavery expansion.[48] Although as a unionist he deplored the agitation engendered by the principle of the Wilmot Proviso, he warned that as a Southerner he would not stand idly by and see his section shut out of any acquired territory. He stood firmly for the right of his people "wherever the American flag waved over American soil to go with their flocks and their herds, their maid servants and their men servants." Southerners "would be degraded, and unworthy of the name of American freemen, could they consent to remain, for a day or an hour, in a Union where they must stand on ground of inferiority, and be denied the rights and privileges which were extended to all others." Almost fourteen years later Toombs was to say virtually the same thing in the Senate and then help lead his state out of the Union.

His speech made a favorable impression on his colleague and fellow Georgian, Stephens. Writing his half-brother Linton on January 13, he said:

It was decidedly one of the best speeches I ever heard Toombs make, and I have heard him make some fine displays. It was even superior to his Oregon speech. He had fully prepared himself, was calm and

[48]Cole, *Whig Party*, 119–23.

slow, much more systematic than usual, and in many points was truly eloquent. The House was full, and the galleries crowded, and all ears were open and all eyes upon him. He commanded their entire and close attention from the beginning to the end, and the effort has added full fifteen cubits to his stature as a statesman and a man of talents in the opinion of the House and the great men of the nation. I was better pleased with it than any speech I have heard this session. . . . He is destined to take a very high position here.[49]

Toombs returned to Georgia for the long congressional recess from March to December and reentered his roles of lawyer, planter, and businessman. He never quite forgot politics in the off-season, however, using those months to rebuild his fences at home and keeping his finger on the public pulse through innumerable personal contacts wherever he journeyed. Toombs rarely engaged in lengthy correspondence with anyone, preferring the handshake and private encounter as a means of staying abreast of developments and winning support. He was an excellent raconteur, and the man who was to become a legend in his own lifetime had already begun to spin his web of charm, bombast, and colorful earthiness that so intrigued Georgians and rendered impregnable his political stature.

The first session of the Thirtieth Congress which opened on December 6, 1847, saw Toombs and his Whig colleagues holding a slight majority in the House. They consequently were able to elect Robert C. Winthrop of Massachusetts as Speaker of the House on the third roll call.[50] Some doubt existed among several Southern Whigs as to whether they should rally behind Winthrop because of his alleged abolitionist connections. But in the interest of national unity, the glue which held the party together, they fell into line.[51] Furthermore, said Stephens, Winthrop "was a scholar and a gentleman." [52]

The year 1848 saw the close of hostilities with Mexico and the election of a war hero, Zachary Taylor, to the presidency. Toombs had not by the end of the war changed in his opposition to the acquisition of territory, causing him to offer this resolution in the opening weeks of Congress: "That neither the honor nor the interest of this Republic demands the dismemberment of Mexico, or the annexation of any portion of her territory to the United States

[49]Quoted in Johnston and Browne, *Stephens*, 218–19.
[50]*Congressional Globe*, 30th Cong., 1st Sess., 2.
[51]Cole, *Whig Party*, 123–24.
[52]Johnston and Browne, *Stephens*, 220.

as an indispensable condition to the restoration of peace." [53] Whigs and Democrats for the first few months of the session continued to debate the prolongation of the war, but the bitter dispute was cut short by the signing of a peace treaty in February and its ratification by the Senate, 38 to 14, in March. A majority of both Whigs and Democrats voted affirmatively for the acquisition of a huge land mass, over 500,000 square miles, embracing California and most of the present day Southwest. "Mr. Polk's war" was over.

The close of the war brought to Congress with fresh emphasis the problem of territorial organization, made more troublesome now by increasing opposition to the extension of slavery. Diametrically opposed opinions seemed a stumbling block impossible to remove. Most Southerners insisted that neither Congress nor territorial inhabitants had the constitutional authority to exclude slavery from a territory, while Northern sentiment swung behind the idea that slavery could be so prohibited. Southern Whigs like Toombs worked to stem the flow of sectional partisanship on the matter, but such efforts were becoming increasingly unavailing. In July the question of governments for Oregon, California, and New Mexico was referred to a select committee equally divided between Whigs and Democrats, Northerners and Southerners, and headed by Senator John M. Clayton of Delaware. Shortly thereafter, Clayton presented a proposal, the Clayton Compromise, which provided for territorial governments in all three areas, with slavery excluded in Oregon and determined in California and New Mexico ultimately by decision of the United States Supreme Court.

The Clayton bill passed the Senate but failed in the House, where Toombs voted for it and Stephens against it.[54] Toombs supported the plan as a hope for conciliation between North and South, while Stephens feared that a court decision, in a sense the final decree, would make irrevocable the exclusion of slavery from a territory.[55] And so the debate continued. Finally in August, just before Congress adjourned, the Oregon Territory was organized without

[53]*Congressional Globe*, 30th Cong., 1st Sess., 61.
[54]*Ibid.*, 1007.
[55]Phillips, *Toombs*, 57. According to Phillips, Toombs was not hidebound in support of the Clayton Compromise. Within a month, he appeared to have considerable doubt concerning the measure and was talking in strong terms of preserving Southern rights within the territories. A surrender of such rights, he said, "would degrade and demoralize our section and disable us from effective resistance to future aggression." Phillips says that Toombs was in a quandary, but one concerned with the "tactical advantage" of the Clayton bill rather than with the fundamental rights of the South.

slavery, but no decision was reached on the territories to be carved out of the Mexican cession.

In this, his second term in the House, Toombs emerged as a staunch advocate of frugality in Federal expenditures, just as he had been on state spending at Milledgeville. He opposed unsuccessfully an increase in salary for the principal examiner of the Patent Office and the printing of ninety-thousand extra copies of a Patent Office report.[56] Toombs also entered with great warmth into the debate over increasing the size of the peacetime standing army. The Georgian wanted to keep the army small. He reiterated his belief that the citizen-soldier, not the professional, was the defensive backbone of the republic. He considered a large standing army too expensive and a "source of corruption and great danger to the Republic." A strong navy he was willing to support, but an army was "wholly unnecessary." [57]

In the spring of 1848 a fine description of Georgia's outstanding Whigs, Toombs and Stephens, was given by Varina Howell Davis, the Mississippi senator's wife, who shared a common "mess" with the couple from Washington.[58] Of the former she wrote:

. . . One could scarcely imagine a wittier and more agreeable companion than he was. He was a university man, and had kept up his classics. He had the personal habits of a gentleman, and talked such grammar determinately, not ignorantly, as the negroes of this day eschew—unless he became excited, and then his diction was good, his wit keen, and his audacity made him equal to anything in the heat of debate. . . . Mr. Toombs was over six feet tall, with broad shoulders; his fine head set well on his shoulders, and was covered with long, glossy black hair, which, when speaking, he managed to toss about so as to recall the memory of Danton.

His coloring was good, and his teeth brilliantly white, but his mouth was somewhat pendulous and subtracted from the rest of his strong face. His eyes were magnificent, dark and flashing, and they had a certain lawless way of ranging about that was indicative of his character. His hands were beautiful, and kept like those of a fashionable woman. His voice was like a trumpet but without sweetness, and his enunciation was thick.

Mrs. Davis said that Toombs was an avid reader of books of imagination and travel—in fact, of anything which would help him

[56]*Congressional Globe*, 30th Cong., 1st Sess., 400, 403, 481, 483.
[57]*Ibid.*, 1035, 1063.
[58]Varina Howell Davis, *Jefferson Davis, Ex-President of the Confederate States of America: A Memoir by His Wife* (New York, 1890), I, 409–12.

lace his speeches with colorful phrases. At the height of the political excitement in 1850, when Toombs was repeatedly on his feet, he arose at daylight to take French lessons with his two daughters. There he sat with one hand full of a reporter's notes on his speeches to be corrected and in the other a French play over which he roared with laughter. He told Mrs. Davis that "these plays take all the soreness out of me." Mrs. Toombs was described as a "pleasant, kindly woman, and cheerful like her husband."

Stephens, whom Mrs. Davis said Toombs loved "with a tenderness that was almost pathetic, and was as much beloved by him" was

not small, but he looked so, from the shortness of his body. The shape of his head was unpolished and immature. His arms were disproportionately long, and his beardless, wrinkled face gave him the look of one born out of season. His eyes were clear hazel, and had a fine, critical, deliberate expression that commanded attention. His voice was thin, and piercing like a woman's, but there the resemblance ended. His was a virile mind sustained by an inflexible will; and, in all matters of importance, Mr. Toombs came up, in the end, on Mr. Stephens's side.

Mrs. Davis noted that her husband, the future Confederate President, and Toombs, the Confederacy's first Secretary of State, were "never congenial," differing in manners and habits. "But we all went on amicably enough," she concluded. During the Civil War this rapport was to wear extremely thin, to the distress of the South.

The campaign to make General Taylor, Mexican War hero, the Whig nominee and the President of the United States began long before 1848. As early as December, 1846, Alexander H. Stephens was instrumental in organizing a Taylor Club in the House of Representatives. Its original seven members, known as the Young Indians, were Stephens and Toombs of Georgia, Truman Smith of Connecticut, Abraham Lincoln of Illinois, William B. Preston, Thomas S. Flournoy, and John S. Pendleton of Virginia. This group with later additions cooperated closely with John J. Crittenden, influential Kentuckian in the Senate, and as Stephens phrased it, "put the ball in motion." [59]

[59] Avary (ed.), *Stephens' Recollections*, 21–22; George R. Poage, *Henry Clay and the Whig Party* (Chapel Hill, 1936), 157–58, hereinafter cited as Poage, *Whig Party*.

After the battle of Buena Vista in February, 1847, the Taylor boom became widespread. There was some question as to the general's party affiliation, but by the summer the "Democratic press had practically conceded him to the Whigs." [60] Stephens succeeded in getting a Georgia Whig convention on July 1 to nominate him, and all that remained was his acceptance by the national party and then the nation. Southern Whigs were particularly interested in Taylor, who as a Southerner and slave-holder could be expected, more than the titular party leader, the nationalistic Henry Clay, to protect their interests. Moreover, the glamor of a conquering general with simple tastes had helped gain the Whigs their only triumph in 1840, while Clay had the millstone of three presidential defeats around his neck.

In 1871 Stephens recounted an incident during the 1848 campaign in which unusual efforts were made to establish a Taylor beachhead in New York City. Earlier attempts had been disrupted by Whig "roughs" who supported Clay. Fighting fire with fire, Stephens, acting as entrepreneur, arranged for Isaiah Rhynders, "captain among roughs and shoulder hitters in New York" and in sympathy with the Taylor cause, to insure an uninterrupted hearing for Toombs in a hall in the city. The price was $200.00. At Rhynders' suggestion, Toombs met with some of his boys the night before the speech at a favorite saloon in order to establish some degree of camaraderie. Toombs, "who was able to make himself perfectly at home in such a crowd" as Stephens put it, was most successful. The next evening, as he began to speak, he was interrupted by shouts of "slaveholder" and "hurrah for Clay." This was repeated several times and then amidst "the greatest row you ever saw," the hall was cleared of some forty troublemakers in about two minutes. It appears that Rhynders' men had circulated among the crowd during the initial heckling and had chalked the backs of the enemy. Then on the order "Put them out," they were bodily ejected. Toombs went on to deliver "one of his masterly popular harangues" extolling the merits of Old Zach, and the victory was won. [61]

On April 16, 1848, Toombs revealed his views on the Clay-Taylor

[60]Poage, *Whig Party*, 157.
[61]Avary (ed.), *Stephens' Recollections*, 22–24.

contest for the Whig nomination in a letter to James Thomas, prominent Sparta, Georgia, lawyer, whose daughter married Stephens' half-brother, Linton, in 1852:

Clay has behaved very badly this winter. His ambition is as fierce as at any time of his life, and he is determined to rule or ruin the party. He has only power enough to ruin it. Rule it he never can again. . . . The truth is he has sold himself body and soul to the Northern Anti-Slavery Whigs, and as little as they now think it, his friends in Georgia will find themselves embarrassed before the campaign is half over. I find myself a good deal denounced in my district for avowing my determination not to vote for him. It gives me not the least concern. I shall never be traitor enough to the true interests of my constituents to gratify them in this respect. . . . I am a Taylor man without a second choice.[62]

Two weeks later Toombs told Thomas that if Clay got the nomination he would resign his congressional post and return to private life.[63]

Meanwhile Stephens, Toombs, and Crittenden were making determined efforts that Clay should not be the nominee. They jointly authored a letter and sent it to Taylor in Baton Rouge, hoping that he would be persuaded to adopt it as his own Whig manifesto. By coincidence, Taylor, with the aid of some New Orleans supporters who were aware of Crittenden's thinking, had already formulated a clarification of his political beliefs which duly appeared in the New Orleans *Picayune* on April 23 as a letter to his brother-in-law in Louisville, Captain John S. Allison. So similar were the letters that Stephens always contended the original draft had been written in Washington.[64]

In the Allison letter the general stated that he was a Whig but not an ultra Whig and if elected he would not be a mere party president. He would use the veto only in clear-cut cases of constitutional violation or ill-considered action by Congress. On the subjects of currency, tariff, and internal improvements, he would allow Congress to carry out the will of the people. He deplored war and rejoiced at the prospect of peace. This letter helped secure

[62]Phillips (ed.), *Correspondence*, 103–104.
[63]*Ibid.*, 105.
[64]Albert D. Kirwan, *John J. Crittenden: The Struggle for the Union* (Lexington, Ky., 1962), 218–20; Holman Hamilton, *Zachary Taylor: Soldier in the White House* (Indianapolis and New York, 1951), 77–79.

for Taylor the Whig nomination and served as the party's platform, as much as the platitudinous Whigs cared to make use of
one, in the campaign.[65]

The Democratic convention was held in Baltimore in late May.
Torn badly by factionalism, the party chose a colorless party
wheel horse, Lewis Cass of Michigan, as its candidate, "not a man
to inspire enthusiasm anywhere." [66] Although Cass was a champion
of "squatter sovereignty," allowing the people of a territory to
determine the status of slavery, the platform of the Democrats
ignored the issue altogether. The Whig convention, nearly three
hundred strong, met in Philadelphia and nominated Taylor on the
fourth ballot. Clay had considerable support, but the switch of
Webster delegates from the Massachusetts senator to Taylor killed
Clay's chances.[67]

Dissatisfied elements from both major parties joined with the
abolitionists to form a third party, the Free Soil party, with Martin
Van Buren as presidential candidate. Its principles were "free soil,
free speech, free labor and free men." Although without much
prestige, the Free Soilers garnered nearly 300,000 popular votes
and elected several congressmen.

In July, Toombs made a long, partisan speech in Congress, upholding Taylor and the principles set forth in the Allison letter
and assailing Cass and the Democratic party.[68] Toombs eulogized
the Whig candidate's "wisdom and firmness, his lofty character and
unsullied purity" and labeled his platform one "constructed out of
constitutional materials, . . . broad enough and strong enough to
hold every man who does not prefer party to his country." As to
various resolutions adopted by the Democrats at their convention,
Toombs said they could be divided into three classes: "the first
affirms what nobody denies; the second denies what nobody affirms; and the third asserts what nobody believes." In particular
he singled out for ridicule Cass' doctrine of squatter sovereignty,
which Toombs called giving to "Mexicans, Indians, negroes, and
mixed races whom we have conquered" the right to exclude
slavery from territories. Actually, said Toombs, this right existed
nowhere. Congress had no such right. These conquests were the

[65]Hamilton, *Zachary Taylor*, 79–81.
[66]Allan Nevins, *Ordeal of the Union* (New York, 1947), I, 193.
[67]*Ibid.*, 201.
[68]*Congressional Globe*, 30th Cong., 1st Sess., 841–46.

common property of all the people and all were "entitled to an effectual legal equality in the enjoyment of this common property." Toombs was sure that in General Taylor the country had a leader whose prudent and conciliatory counsel would enable the country to work out its destiny in peace and safety.

Toombs and Stephens returned to Georgia as soon as Congress adjourned to spread the Taylor gospel and, incidentally, to get themselves reelected to Congress. The burden of both tasks fell largely on Toombs, for his friend was almost killed in an altercation with Judge Francis H. Cone in Atlanta in early September. Cone had taken serious objection to Stephens' stand on the Clayton Compromise, and when they met face to face further words led to a fracas between the ninety-pound congressman and the two-hundred-pound lawyer. Stephens was cut repeatedly and for some time his life was in danger.[69]

Toombs was equal to the task, as was usually the case. When the speeches, barbecues, and parades were finished, Taylor had won Georgia, Toombs had carried all but one county in the Eighth District, and Stephens was safely reelected.[70]

Political affairs seemed well in hand in Georgia. Not so for the nation. As the Georgia congressmen prepared to return to Washington for the short session of the Thirtieth Congress, the formidable issue of governments for California and New Mexico still remained to be settled. For a moment, sectional tensions had been abated by the exciting news of the discovery of gold in California. But the presence of a wild and lusty population of over 100,000 in an area which previously had embraced a few sleepy Mexicans and some mud huts gave an entirely new dimension to an already troublesome matter—statehood for California.

[69]Stovall, Toombs, 62; Augusta Chronicle, September 5, 1848.
[70]Toombs' total was 4,232, that of his Democratic opponent, 2,551. Taylor carried Wilkes County by 452 to 293, Augusta Chronicle, October 26, 1848; Milledgeville Federal Union, October 17, 1848.

CHAPTER IV

The Compromise of 1850

O N February 8, 1849, Howell Cobb wrote his wife from the nation's capital: "Washington as is always the case is the scene of much excitement and the most agitating question of the day is still the subject of slavery." [1] Robert Toombs had ardently hoped that this short session would see the burial of the slavery issue in order that the incoming Taylor administration might be free from its shackling effects. But such was not the case.

John C. Calhoun, fearful of the Northern majority and scornful of compromise, had come to Washington determined to organize a Southern party which, under his leadership, would hold the line against Northern aggressions. His opportunity came in December when a House resolution was passed instructing the committee on the District of Columbia to report a bill prohibiting slavery therein. Around eighty incensed Southerners responded with a closed door, Senate chamber caucus, and Calhoun went to work.[2] An executive committee of fifteen, one from each slave state, was appointed, and in addition a subcommittee of five to present an address on Southern rights and slavery. It was soon apparent, however, that most of the Southern Whigs viewed Calhoun's efforts with great

[1]Cobb to his wife, in Howell Cobb Papers, University of Georgia.
[2]Brief accounts of the caucus are given in Cole, *Whig Party*, 138–40, and Richard H. Shryock, *Georgia and the Union in 1850* (Durham, 1926), 181–85.

distrust. Shortly after the adjournment of the first meeting, Toombs branded the movement as a "bold strike to disorganize the Southern Whigs and either to destroy Genl. Taylor in advance or compel him to throw himself in the hands of a large section of the democracy [the Democratic party] at the South." [3] He explained to Crittenden that the Southern Whigs had decided "after mature consideration . . . to go into the meeting in order to control and crush it; it has been a delicate business but so far we have succeeded well and I think will be able to overthrow it completely on the 15th Inst." [4]

The second meeting saw Toombs play a major role in blocking the immediate acceptance of the subcommittee's address, authored chiefly by Calhoun. The Democratic leader's "Southern Address" was an able paper, cataloguing the transgressions of the North against the institution of slavery, calling on the South to defend itself, and warning that if not arrested the antislavery movement would lead to abolition, the ultimate of Southern horrors. [5] The Charleston *Courier* spoke of the "vehement opposition" shown by the Georgian as he led the successful fight to recommit the address to the reporting committee. [6] Toombs told those present, as he later recounted to Crittenden, that

the Union of the South was neither possible nor desirable until we were ready to dissolve the Union; that we certainly did not intend to advise the people now to look anywhere else than to their own government for the *prevention* of apprehended evils; that we did not expect an administration which we had brought into power would do any act or permit any act to be done which it would become necessary for our safety to rebel at; and that we thought that the Southern opposition could not be sustained by their own friends in acting on such an hypothesis; and that we intended to stand by the government until it committed an overt act of aggression upon our rights, which neither we nor the country ever expected. [7]

[3]Toombs to John J. Crittenden, January 3, 1849, in Phillips (ed.), *Correspondence*, 139.
  [4]*Ibid.*
  [5]Nevins, *Ordeal of the Union*, I, 224–25; Shryock, *Georgia and the Union*, 183.
  [6]Quoted in Augusta *Chronicle*, January 22, 1849. See also article from the Baltimore *American* in Augusta *Chronicle*, January 20, 1849.
  [7]Toombs to Crittenden, January 22, 1849, Phillips (ed.), *Correspondence*, 141–42.

This was the statement of a Southern moderate colored slightly by party expediency. It remained Toombs' creed through the difficult times ahead.

The final Southern caucus, which many Whigs boycotted, was held on January 22. Senator Berrien of Georgia presented a mild paper addressed to the whole country rather than to the South. The distinguished old Whig appealed for a compromise on slavery while there was still time, but his address was rejected 34 to 27. Toombs and Stephens, opposed to any address whatsoever, abstained from voting on Berrien's paper. Calhoun's paper was then adopted 42 to 17 by party vote, with all of the Whigs, except a representative from Alabama, and four Democrats voting in the negative.[8]

Calhoun had thus failed in his objective—a Southern Rights party transcending Democratic and Whig lines. One of the Democrats who failed to sustain Calhoun was Howell Cobb. He had no sympathy with the schismatic notions of the South Carolinian, the "old reprobate," which were a threat to the "honor of the South & . . . the permanence of the Union. If it could please our Heavenly Father to take Calhoun . . . *home* I should look upon it as a national blessing," he wrote his wife.[9] Toombs, Stephens, and Cobb had thus found common cause. This trio, with the love of union as its bond, would help keep Georgia within the national framework in the 1850 crisis.

Having foiled Calhoun's Southern Rights movement, the Southern Whigs in the House rallied around a plan by which they hoped the slavery controversy would be put to rest. Introduced by William B. Preston of Virginia, it called for the admission of all the territory acquired from Mexico as a single state as soon as was constitutionally possible. The new member of the Union would undoubtedly be free. But only one state would be added to Northern strength, and furthermore it was highly unlikely that slavery could ever flourish in the arid Southwest anyway. Additionally, the prickly Wilmot Proviso would be bypassed by this legislation, as the state could determine its own institutions. Toombs

[8]Augusta *Chronicle*, February 2, 1849; Milledgeville *Federal Union*, February 13, 1849; Cole, *Whig Party*, 140; Shryock, *Georgia and the Union*, 182–83.

[9]Cobb to his wife, February 8, 1849, in Howell Cobb Papers, University of Georgia.

wrote Crittenden that the bill would easily pass the House.[10] But unfortunately for Whig hopes the House tacked an antislavery amendment, a political trouble maker, to the bill and it failed to carry a single affirmative vote.[11] Toombs was disconsolate, saying that "all chance of pacification was at an end." [12]

The Thirtieth Congress, marked by stormy, all-night sessions in its closing days, ended in March without any solution being reached on governments for California and New Mexico. Perhaps there was still a chance that the Taylor administration and a new Congress in December could show the way. Toombs hoped so.

Zachary Taylor was singularly ill-equipped for the office of the President of the United States. Although competent as a professional soldier, he was practically devoid of any knowledge of politics. He had never voted nor held public office; for that matter, he did not appear to be sure of his own political affiliation until shortly before he was elected to the presidency. Championed by the Southern Whigs, he proved to be a source of embarrassment to them. The old soldier had been nationalized by long army service and held no particular affection for the South and its peculiar institution.

In the months following his inauguration in March, it seemed clear that the Northern, antislavery wing of the party was gaining ascendancy over Taylor. Particularly was William H. Seward, New York senator and Wilmot Proviso enthusiast, emerging as a permanent fixture at the President's elbow. Toombs and many other Southerners watching from home were worried over the events on the Potomac. The Georgian acknowledged his concern in a letter to the daughter of his friend, John J. Crittenden, fellow architect of Taylor's triumph and now governor of Kentucky. But, said the still optimistic Toombs,

Genl. Taylor is in a new position, his duties and responsibilities are vast and complicated, and besides, he is among strangers whose aims and objects are not known to him. Therefore that he should commit mistakes, even grave errors, must be expected; but I have an abiding confidence that he is honest and sincere and will repair them when seen.

[10] Toombs to Crittenden, February 9, 1849, in Phillips (ed.), *Correspondence*, 147.
[11] Cole, *Whig Party*, 143; Phillips, *Toombs*, 63.
[12] Quoted in Phillips, *Toombs*, 64.

If I am mistaken in this, no man in the nation will more bitterly repent the events of the last eighteen months than I will, and I think in that event I shall have made my last Presidential campaign.[13]

While Toombs pondered the unfortunate influences on the President, Iverson L. Harris, prominent Georgia lawyer and Whig leader, was just as uneasy about the growing political stature of Toombs, Stephens, and Cobb, the "Georgia triumvirate." He told Berrien, who was falling out of step with his younger congressional colleagues, that "there must be an end to the unhealthy and selfish domination of these gentlemen. . . ." He warned his friend that he would be "unceremoniously" put out of their way when the time was propitious and prophetically spoke of Toombs' desire for his seat in the Senate. There was as yet no open breach in Georgia's Whig delegation, but Berrien for some time had tended to gravitate toward the Calhoun doctrine of Southern solidarity, rather than the preservation of a national Whig party.[14] Harris concluded that Berrien's antagonists were sensible men who realized "that if they do not destroy you—you will destroy them." [15]

In the wake of the anti-Taylor feeling sweeping the South, the influence of Calhoun's Southern Address, and the demand of California for admission as a free state, elections both state and congressional went badly for the Whigs. In Georgia, the Democrats elected G. W. Towns governor for his second term, and wrested control of the legislature from their faltering opponents. Open and aggressive manifestations of sectional resistance became widespread. In Mississippi, where Calhoun's idea of a united Southern front had fallen on fertile ground, a state convention in October issued a call for a convention of all the slave states to meet in Nashville in June of 1850. The success or failure of such a convention would depend on how well the incoming Congress met the sectional crisis.

A worried Toombs arrived in Washington several days before the opening of the Thirty-first Congress. According to his own account he found his party planning to support the Wilmot Proviso, thereby hoping to build up strength at the expense of the

[13]Toombs to Mrs. Chapman Coleman, June 22, 1849, in Phillips (ed.), *Correspondence*, 165.
[14]Horace Montgomery, *Cracker Parties* (Baton Rouge, 1950), 6.
[15]Harris to Berrien, August 17, 1849, in Berrien Papers.

Northern Democrats who were straddling the issue. Understanding that Taylor would not veto the Proviso, Toombs went to see the President and discussed the matter fully with him. Toombs was informed that no pledges had been made either way, but that if the Proviso were made law by Congress he would sign it. "My course became instantly fixed," the Georgian stated. Throwing aside his posture as party preserver, he "determined to put the test to the Whig party and abandon its organization upon its refusal [to disapprove the Proviso]." [16]

The Whigs caucused on the night of December 1, 1849. Toombs presented a resolution, apparently drawn up jointly in Stephens' quarters by several Whig discontents,[17] which read: "Resolved, that Congress ought not to pass any law prohibiting slavery in the territories of California or New Mexico, nor any law abolishing slavery in the District of Columbia." [18] Intense excitement followed, in which some Southerners, though agreeing with the sentiment of the resolution, suggested that the time was not ripe for such action and asked Toombs to withdraw it. He refused, saying that what he had done had come after mature reflection, and that he hoped the issue would be met "fairly and manfully." [19] When the caucus voted to postpone consideration of the resolution, Toombs, Stephens, and Allen F. Owen of Georgia with three other Southerners walked out. Those remaining nominated Robert C. Winthrop of Massachusetts, Speaker of the House in the Thirtieth Congress, to succeed himself in the Thirty-first.[20]

Toombs' course was condemned by several Southern newspapers. The New Orleans *Bulletin* labeled it *"ill-timed and unwise."* [21] The *North State Whig* of Washington, North Carolina, editorialized: "It was an abandonment of the conservative position hitherto maintained by Whigs of all sections. It was calculated to engender discord, dissolve the ties of an organization, and produce that con-

[16]Toombs to Crittenden, April 25, 1850, in Mary Ann (Mrs. C. C.) Coleman, *Life of John J. Crittenden* . . . (Philadelphia, 1871), I, 365.
[17]Avary (ed.), *Stephens' Recollections*, 26.
[18]Augusta *Chronicle*, December 10, 1849.
[19]*Ibid.*
[20]*Ibid.*; *Daily National Intelligencer*, December 6, 1849, hereinafter cited as *National Intelligencer*; Johnston and Browne, *Stephens*, 237.
[21]New Orleans *Bulletin*, December 19, 1849, quoted in Cole, *Whig Party*, 154.

fusion and disorder which must defeat the hopes of patriotic Whigs everywhere." [22]

On December 3 the House commenced business before jammed galleries. "Every member appeared under a state of excitement," reported an observer, "such as causes men to hold their breath. . . ." [23] After self-examination, Stephens stated: "My Southern blood and feelings are up, and I feel as if I am prepared to fight at all hazards and to the last extremity in vindication of our honor and rights. . . ." [24]

The assembled House numbered 112 Democrats, 105 Whigs, and 13 Free Soilers. It was apparent that if the Northern and Southern Democrats split, the antislavery majority of the Whig party might elect Winthrop, and then proceed on the great strength of the Speaker's office, with the help of Free Soilers and some Northern Democrats, to pass the Wilmot Proviso. Toombs and Stephens determined to prevent this, and, on a broader basis, to bring the North to terms with them on the matter of Southern rights by deadlocking the election.[25] The first ballot showed 103 votes for Howell Cobb, choice of the Democratic caucus; 96 for Winthrop; 8 for Wilmot, the Free Soil candidate; 6 for Meredith P. Gentry, Tennessee Whig and choice of the Whig bolters; and a few scattered. No one received the necessary majority, and so the voting continued day after day and finally week after week.

On December 13, in the midst of the prolonged struggle, Toombs made a powerful impromptu speech which took him for the first time publicly to the brink of disunion. He explained his obstructionist tactics to the House on the grounds that he considered the interests of his section in danger, and consequently was unwilling to "surrender the great power of the Speaker's chair without obtaining security for the future. . . . It is time we understood one another; that we should speak out, and carry our principles in our foreheads." [26] With "his black, uncombed hair standing out from his massive head, as if charged with electricity, his eyes glowing

[22]Washington (N.C.) *North State Whig,* December 12, 1849, quoted in Cole, *Whig Party,* 154.
[23]Milledgeville *Federal Union,* December 11, 1849.
[24]Quoted in Johnston and Browne, *Stephens,* 237.
[25]*Ibid.,* 241.
[26]*Congressional Globe,* 31st Cong., 1st Sess., 28.

like coals of fire, and his sentences rattling forth like volleys of
musketry . . . ,"[27] he said he would make his position clear. If the
South were driven from the territories of California and New
Mexico by congressional legislation or if slavery were abolished in
the District of Columbia, he was for disunion. The territories were
the common property of all the people, and it was the duty of
Congress to insure equal enjoyment of them by slaveholder and
non-slaveholder alike. If guarantees could be given that the rights
of the South would be adequately protected in the future, Toombs
pledged his cooperation in the organization of the House. If not,
he thundered, "let discord reign forever." Toombs' speech was
interrupted several times by loud bursts of applause.[28]

Stephens also spoke on the thirteenth and echoed Toombs' sentiments about disunion if the South were kept out of the territories.
After other impassioned speeches and a near free-for-all following
an altercation between William Duer of New York and Richard
K. Meade of Virginia, the wizened Stephens saw fit to pronounce
it "the most exciting day I ever witnessed in that Hall." [29]

Many congressmen considered the day's events too exciting and
certainly not conducive to the business at hand. Consequently
on December 14 a resolution was adopted making it mandatory
that the balloting for Speaker continue without debate until the
office was filled. When this tactic proved fruitless, Whig and
Democratic caucus committees agreed that another resolution
should be introduced, authorizing a plurality election if three more
ballots proved unsuccessful under majority rule. On the twenty-
second, Frederick P. Stanton of Tennessee rose to present the
plurality resolution which would insure the speedy election of a
Speaker. Within seconds, Toombs was on his feet interrupting
Stanton and claiming the right to be heard on the legal authority
of the House to pass its December 14 order prohibiting debate.
Toombs' delaying tactics aroused a storm of protest in the Hall,
but he stood his ground, maintaining that until a Speaker was
elected and the oaths of office administered to House members,
no rule could be adopted by the House, and so he intended to
speak. Filibuster he did amid jeers, catcalls, and a few shouts of

[27]Benjamin Perley Poore, *Perley's Reminiscences of Sixty Years in the
National Metropolis* . . . (Philadelphia, 1886), I, 360.
[28]*Congressional Globe*, 31st Cong., 1st Sess., 28.
[29]Johnston and Browne, *Stephens*, 240.

"Go it, Toombs," until a jaded House ceased its noise, allowing him to conclude in relative tranquility.[30]

Toombs could not prevent the inevitable, which came shortly after he sat down. On the sixty-third ballot, three days before Christmas, Howell Cobb was declared elected when he received 102 votes to 99 for Winthrop.[31] The House was swept by a brief wave of relief amid congratulations for Cobb, but the homesick Speaker a week later told his wife that he would gladly exchange his "blushing honors" for a "cheerful fireside communion with those dear ones who cluster around my own hearthstone. I have never felt more sick at heart with Washington than I now do," he said, "and never half so determined to retire from public life." [32]

Toombs the obstructionist was uniformly praised back home. The Democratic Milledgeville *Federal Union* stated that the course of Toombs and Stephens in refusing support to Winthrop "has excited in the bosom of every patriotic Georgian, emotions of unmingled gratification." [33] The Whigs of Glynn County adopted resolutions commending the pair for their manly and patriotic course.[34] Not so impressed was the Boston *Courier*, which called Toombs and his little band of Whig supporters "swaggering Bobadils" and "empty-headed brawlers" who "*threaten* mischief, but lack the courage to *do* it. . . . As sure as any real emergency arises where life or limb, property or place encounters a risk, where a true manly heart is required, these will be the first cowards to run." [35] It was not unusual for Northern newspapers at this time to dismiss somewhat intemperate Southern pronouncements on union and disunion as mere bombast. Undoubtedly there was more heat than light in some cases, but often the hard-core determination of Southerners to resist what they termed aggression was not appreciated by the North. Certainly this Boston paper misjudged what Toombs was willing to do, as witnessed by his role in the secession movement of 1860 when he considered the position of the South in the Union hopeless.

[30]*Congressional Globe*, 31st Cong., 1st Sess., 61–63; Phillips, *Toombs*, 72–73; Stovall, *Toombs*, 71–76.

[31]*Congressional Globe*, 31st Cong., 1st Sess., 66.

[32]Cobb to wife, January 1, 1850, in R. P. Brooks (ed.), "Howell Cobb Papers," *Georgia Historical Quarterly*, V (March, 1921), Pt. 3, p. 35.

[33]Milledgeville *Federal Union*, December 11, 1849.

[34]Augusta *Chronicle*, January 6, 1850.

[35]Boston *Courier*, January 2, 1850.

The election of a Speaker did not assuage the bitterness within the two major parties or between sections. The Whigs seemed hopelessly split as Toombs and a few Southerners had refused to the end to cooperate with the party majority. And a handful of Northern Democrats had declined to support Howell Cobb, the party nominee. Between the North and South there existed a set of thorny problems whose solution in an atmosphere of distrust and petty bickering seemed well nigh impossible. California, with Taylor's support, had bypassed territorial organization, drawn up a free-soil constitution, and stood ready for admission into the Union. Southerners said no, unless there were some satisfactory territorial settlement regarding slavery for the rest of the Mexican cession, New Mexico and Utah. Texas and New Mexico were on the threshold of a minor shooting war over a boundary dispute. A long-standing grievance of the South was the lack of effective legislation on the recovery of fugitive slaves whose losses to owners each year, even though small in comparison to the total value of slave property, ran into thousands of dollars. Southerners also found alarming the Northern talk about abolishing slavery in the District of Columbia. There seemed no easy way in sight for closing the lid on Pandora's box of sectional strife.

President Taylor's leadership proved disappointing. His message to Congress backed the admission of California and also that of New Mexico, which was attempting to follow California's procedure of skipping territorial organization by Congress. The other problems Taylor simply left up in the air, suggesting, however, that if Congress kept its hands off the territories, sectional difficulties might be avoided. Most Southerners, including Toombs, regarded the President's approach as highly unsatisfactory to their interests.[36]

Fortunately for the country, Henry Clay, after an absence of nearly eight years, was back in the Senate. An old man now, Clay was still an attractive, persuasive figure, determined as he had been several times in the past to work his magic of healing on the ills that threatened the dissolution of his beloved country. On January 29, 1850, Clay introduced a set of compromise proposals in the Senate designed to settle all controversies of a sectional character. The Kentuckian called for the admission of California as a free

[36]Toombs to Crittenden, April 25, 1850, in Coleman, *Crittenden*, I, 365.

state, the erection of territorial governments in the remainder of the Mexican cession without restrictions on slavery, a satisfactory adjustment of Texas' land claims, the abolition of the slave trade but not slavery in the District of Columbia, a more effective fugitive slave law, and a declaration by Congress that it did not have the authority to interfere with the interstate slave trade.

Clay's "Omnibus Bill," the focal point for debate in the Senate and later in the House, became the hope of moderates in both parties and throughout the country. Toombs, now back in a more familiar role after his harangue of the thirteenth, supported the idea of compromise in the House. The battle here initially centered around an attempt by the supporters of the Taylor plan to get California into the Union without compensation to the South, which stood to lose its equality in the Senate with the admission of the Western state. Leading the fight to block the measure were Toombs, Stephens, and Thomas L. Clingman of North Carolina, who explained that they were opposing the entrance of California only until some settlement were made establishing the principle that Congress could not exclude slavery from the territories. The air was cleared a bit and tensions eased by a conference on the night of February 19 at Cobb's house attended by Toombs, Stephens, Cobb, and Linn Boyd, Kentucky Democrat, from the South, and John A. McClernand, William A. Richardson, both Illinois Democrats, and John K. Miller, Democrat from Ohio, representing the North. It was agreed that the group would strive to resolve the sectional crisis in three ways: by support of the admission of California; by support of the Southerners' stand on the territories; and by blocking any attempt to abolish slavery in the District of Columbia.[37]

The Southern Whigs were anxious to bring the President into accord with their plan of compromise. On February 23, Toombs, Stephens, and Clingman called on Taylor and argued strongly against his "California without compensation" plan. The President refused to budge, and in their frustration the congressmen talked loosely of secession and disunion. Taylor replied wrathfully that if necessary he would place himself at the head of the army to see

[37]Alexander H. Stephens, *A Constitutional View of the Late War Between the States* . . . (Philadelphia, 1868–70), II, 202–205, hereinafter cited as Stephens, *War Between the States;* Stovall, *Toombs,* 80–81; Phillips, *Toombs,* 74–75.

that the laws were obeyed, and that he would not hesitate to hang them if they became involved in rebellion against the United States.[38]

Four days later Toombs continued the battle in the House to protect Southern rights in the territories.[39] It was one of his best efforts. In temperate fashion, he stated that it was the general duty of government to protect the property of its citizens, and that the principle of property in slaves had been established under the constitution. Toombs said the South did not demand that slavery be established in the territories. In fact, he had no quarrel with the right of a people in drawing up a state constitution to exclude slavery. But until that time, he said, "we ask protection against all hostile impediments to the introduction and peaceable enjoyment of all of our property in the territories. . . ." The Georgian acknowledged that in the previous session of Congress he had supported Preston's bill for the admission of the entire Mexican cession as a single state, doubtless to be a free state. But, as he put it, that bill had the "merit of closing the question." This California bill simply would add another non-slaveholding state to the Union, and leave the territorial question "unadjusted." Toombs wanted it settled now before he would support California's admission.

Heating up a bit as he neared the end of his allotted hour, Toombs said:

In this emergency our duty is clear; it is to stand by the Constitution and laws, to observe in good faith all of its requirements, until the wrong is consummated, until the act of exclusion is put under the statute book; it will then be demonstrated that the Constitution is powerless for our protection; it will then be not only the right, but the duty of the slaveholding States to resume the powers which they have conferred upon this Government, and to seek new safeguards for their future security.

A moment later he concluded, "When the argument is exhausted we will stand by our arms."

Toombs' speech was well-received by the press. The editor of the Richmond *Times* called it "able, eloquent, and *moderate*," one

[38]Thurlow Weed Barnes, *Memoir of Thurlow Weed* (Boston, 1884), 176–79.
[39]*Congressional Globe*, 31st Cong., 1st Sess., 198–201.

that "commanded the attention of every member of the House. The effort will cause him to be held in higher estimation than ever." A week later, the *Times* told its readers: "The speech of the session . . . thus far, in the House, is that of Mr. Toombs." [40] The Washington correspondent of the New York *Sun* was also impressed by the statesmanlike restraint of the Georgian, whom he called the "ablest man of either party from the South." The reporter stated that so great was the attention Toombs received that "one might have heard a pin drop from the moment he commenced, until the end of his hour." [41]

Meanwhile, great drama was unfolding in the Senate, where aging political giants were rapidly nearing the close of their public careers. Crowded galleries looked down on Daniel Webster, John C. Calhoun, and Henry Clay appearing together for the last time. Joining the "Great Triumvirate" in debate were younger men, eagerly waiting to replace them as the Senate leaders: Stephen A. Douglas, William H. Seward, Salmon P. Chase, and Jefferson Davis among others. On March 4 the dying and disillusioned Calhoun presented the ultimatum of the Southern extremists who rejected the admission of California, called for equal treatment of the South in the territories, and demanded constitutional safeguards for the rights of the minority South within the Union. Three days later, Webster delivered his famous Seventh of March speech advocating compromise and bucking the prevailing opinion of his native New England. The great orator courageously called on the North to ccasc its antislavery agitation, pointing out that it had already won the battle of the territories since they were ill-suited by nature to the spread of slavery. Webster's effort brought him nothing but vituperation from his own people, but it served, along with Calhoun's death at the end of the month, to lessen the heat of battle and pave the way for eventual compromise victory.

In March, Toombs, in a letter to Governor Towns, indicated publicly to Georgians that he would probably support Clay's compromise package. The Democratic legislature of the state, termed privately by Toombs "the greatest set of scoundrels that even the Democrats ever cursed the country with," [42] had recently passed

---

[40] Quoted in Augusta *Chronicle*, March 6, 14, 1850.
[41] *Ibid.*, March 9, 1850.
[42] Toombs to Linton Stephens, March 22, 1850, in Phillips (ed.), *Correspondence*, 188.

a series of resolutions calling for a state convention to determine the "mode and measure of redress" if the following materialized: the passage of the Wilmot Proviso, the abolition of slavery in the District of Columbia, and the admission of California as a free state together with the continued refusal of the North to return fugitive slaves. Toombs agreed except for the legislature's stand on California, a key part in the Clay program. He stated that the admission of a state was solely a matter for congressional discretion and "would present neither a just nor a sufficient cause for State interposition, or revolutionary resistance." He made it plain that he would vote for or against California as he thought best without reference to the actions of the state legislature, and would oppose convention action on the matter.[43] Since the fire-eaters had howled the loudest about California, it was clear that Toombs was putting himself in the ranks of the moderates by his willingness to accept the Western state into the Union. He was condemned by most of the Democratic press of the state, which was wedded to Calhoun's stand.[44]

In April the Senate referred various proposals for resolving the lingering crisis to a select committee of thirteen, chairmaned by Clay, for the enactment of a master plan. Toombs was optimistic that the work of the select committee would be adopted by Congress. He was also still hopeful that Taylor would come around, regarding him as "an honest, well-meaning man . . . in very bad hands. . . ."[45] In May the committee made seven recommendations within the framework of the Kentuckian's original presentation in January. Around the middle of the month the Senate opened its debate, which saw the moderates arrayed against the extremists, North and South, and an administration which refused to cooperate. The President, under the influence of Seward, a non-compromiser, was still insistent on the passage of his own program, and had come to be very jealous of Henry Clay. It appeared that the White House had solidified in its obstinacy to a solution on any terms but its own.

Although Toombs generally hewed to a policy of sectional rapport in these troubled months, occasionally he lent support to programs somewhat out of keeping with this pattern. In May he and

[43]Toombs to Towns, March 11, 1850, in Augusta *Chronicle*, March 20, 1850.
[44]Shryock, *Georgia and the Union*, 247.
[45]Toombs to Crittenden, April 25, 1850, in Coleman, *Crittenden*, I, 366.

Stephens played a prominent role in the establishment of a news-paper in Washington, the *Southern Press*, designed to be a mouth-piece for reflecting and defending Southern interests.[46] For once, the Augusta *Chronicle* refused to go along with its heroes and registered disapproval. It believed that the *Southern Press* would increase sectionalism when "what we most need to correct the evils of the times, is an enlarged and liberal patriotism, an *Americanism* if we may thus employ the word, which shall be co-extensive with the whole country, and all its great and diversified interests. . . ." [47]

The delaying tactics and amendments of the opponents of com-promise in the early summer built up the tension in Congress once more to a dangerous point. Toombs was caught up in it on June 15 in a debate over the admission of California. He stated again his insistence on the equal participation of the South in the terri-tories. The Georgia congressman, described as a "ferocious looking man, on account of his long black hair and his dark com-plexion," [48] went on excitedly:

I claim the right for her to enter them all with her property and securely to enjoy it. She will divide with you if you wish it, but the right to enter all or divide I shall never surrender. In my judgment, this right, involving, as it does, political equality, is worth a thousand such Unions as we have, even if they each were a thousand times more valuable than this. I speak not for others, but for myself. Deprive us of this right and appropriate this common property to yourselves, it is then your government, not mine. Then I am its enemy, and I will then, if I can, bring my children and my constituents to the altar of liberty, and like Hamilcar, I would swear them to eternal hostility to your foul domination. Give us our just right, and we are ready, as ever heretofore, to stand by the Union, every part of it, and its every interest. Refuse it, and for one, I will strike for *Independence*.[49]

Toombs' "Hamilcar speech" and the excitement it produced in the House were long remembered. His unexpected aggressiveness, which bespoke the fire-eater rather than the compromiser, startled a friend of Howell Cobb's, who wrote the Speaker that "for a great man he [Toombs] is behaving very strangely. I saw a five minutes speech in the papers in which he talked about swearing

[46]Milledgeville *Federal Union*, May 28, 1850.
[47]Augusta *Chronicle*, June 5, 1850.
[48]Milledgeville *Federal Union*, June 4, 1850.
[49]*Congressional Globe*, 31st Cong., 1st Sess., 1216.

his constituents like Hamilcar & all that sort of thing. I never knew of his being drunk but really I began to think something of the kind." [50] The whole episode furnished an interesting insight into Toombs' character. Basically a man of conservative instincts, he could in moments of commotion explode in any direction, after which he would assemble the pieces and resume his former character. But each disassembling doubtless blurred the previous image until under the duress of the secession crisis it disappeared altogether. Stephens seemed to become unglued more slowly, and in this sense was a more stable person than his friend Toombs.

Meanwhile the Taylor administration, in addition to continuing vexations from the compromise struggle, had a first-class scandal on its hands involving several members of the cabinet. The "Galphin claim" dated back to colonial times and concerned debts owed to one George Galphin by Creek and Cherokee Indians. Arrangements were made that Galphin be paid out of the sale of land ceded by the Indians to the Crown, but the Revolutionary War interrupted the transactions. After the war, the land in question came under the jurisdiction of the state of Georgia, and against the state the Galphin claim was then laid. Nothing was done, however, although Toombs became a champion of the Galphins when he entered the legislature, and fought vigorously for the fulfillment of what he regarded as a valid obligation of the state. When Toombs went to Congress he took the claim with him, arguing that the Federal government had inherited the obligations of the British government, and should compensate the Galphin heirs if Georgia would not. In 1848 a bill was passed by Congress authorizing the settlement of the claim. Polk's secretary of the treasury, Robert J. Walker, paid the principal, $43,518.97, but discreetly left the decision as to whether interest should be added to his successor in the new administration.

Since 1833 George W. Crawford of Georgia had been attorney for the Galphin claimants, and on a half-share basis stood to make an enormous amount of money if the interest were paid. When Crawford was appointed secretary of war by Taylor, he did not give up his connection with the claimants, although he hired another lawyer to push the matter for him and did inform the

[50]William H. Hull to Cobb, June 24, 1850, in Howell Cobb Papers, University of Georgia.

President of his situation. The naive Taylor apparently saw no possibility of a conflict of interest in Crawford's course, and so the matter temporarily rested. On the advice of Attorney General Reverdy Johnson, Secretary of the Treasury William Meredith paid the claim for interest, a sum amounting to nearly $200,000, half of which went to his fellow cabinet member Crawford. The press picked up the story in early spring of 1850 and the Galphin claim mushroomed into a scandal of major proportions.

A House investigating committee, asked for by Crawford, made its report on May 17. The secretary of war and his two cabinet colleagues were exonerated from deliberate wrongdoing, but the committee by split vote concluded that the Galphin claim was not a valid one and that the payment of interest was not required by law or precedent. On May 20, Toombs took the floor and gave strong support to the justice of the claim and the integrity of his longtime friend Crawford. Nonetheless, the House, with Toombs and most of the Southern Whigs in the negative, endorsed a set of resolutions upholding the committee findings.[51]

While the President was considering the purge of his tarnished cabinet, a second crisis confronted him—the application for statehood of sparsely populated New Mexico, whose boundaries were hotly disputed by Texas. Taylor determined to back New Mexico, whose precipitous actions he himself had helped inspire, and stood ready to use Federal troops to restrain any hostilities on the part of Texas. His stand was completely unacceptable to all Southerners. They either rallied pugnaciously in support of Texas or viewed the New Mexico statehood proposal as a scheme to block the Compromise.

On July 1 a Southern Whig caucus appointed a three-man committee, Toombs, Charles M. Conrad of Louisiana, and Humphrey Marshall of Kentucky, to remonstrate with the President. Calling on him separately, the congressmen told him that his Southern supporters would be forced into opposition if he persisted in his present posture. Taylor would not be maneuvered, reiterating his endorsement of statehood for California and New Mexico and denying the validity of the Texas land claims. The President fur-

[51]William P. Brandon, "The Galphin Claim," *Georgia Historical Quarterly*, XV (June, 1931), 113–41; Phillips, *Toombs*, 113–29; *Congressional Globe*, 31st Cong., 1st Sess., 628, 1024–27; Brainerd Dyer, *Zachary Taylor* (Baton Rouge, 1946), 327–31.

ther commented that practical politics favored losing the support of twenty-nine Southern Whigs to that of eighty-four Northern party men.[52]

Toombs probably visited Taylor again, and, although the evidence is not clear, it may have been on July 3 in the company of Stephens. As later told by Stephens, one specific complaint made to the President at this time concerned his determination to send Federal troops to occupy the territory in dispute between Texas and New Mexico. Shortly after this, the Georgia congressmen met Secretary of the Navy William B. Preston, in front of the Treasury building, and talked in terms of impeaching the President if troops were sent to Santa Fe. When Preston asked who would impeach him, Stephens replied, "I will if nobody else does." [53]

On the morning of July 3 there had appeared in the *Daily National Intelligencer* a news item suggesting that an armed clash between military forces of Texas and the United States in the Santa Fe area was imminent. The Whig organ, in editorial comment, hoped that the report was wrong, but stated in a mild manner that it was the duty of the Federal detachment to defend Santa Fe if Texas attempted to bring the area under her authority. Stephens objected to this and belligerently wrote the editors, from his desk in the House, that the "first Federal gun that shall be fired against the people of Texas, without the authority of law, will be the signal for the freemen from the Delaware to the Rio Grande to rally to the rescue." [54] The time sequence of events on July 3 is not clear. It is quite likely, however, that Stephens had read the paper and written his rebuttal before he and Toombs called on Taylor. This would help account for the subsequent rash talk about impeachment.[55]

On July 9, after a brief illness, President Taylor died. In the wake of national mourning, the Philadelphia *Bulletin* printed a controversial letter by "Henrico," its Washington correspondent. Henrico charged that Toombs and Stephens had visited the President on his deathbed and had helped hurry his demise by threatening

[52]J. F. H. Claiborne, *Life and Correspondence of John A. Quitman* (New York, 1860), II, 32–33.

[53]Quoted in Avary (ed.), *Stephens' Recollections*, 26; Cole, *Whig Party*, 167; Hamilton, *Zachary Taylor*, 380–81.

[54]*National Intelligencer*, July 3, 4, 1850.

[55]Phillips, *Toombs*, 83, pictures it this way.

a vote of censure against him (if he did not change his stand on California and Texas) for his conduct in the Galphin claim affair. The charge was picked up by other newspapers, particularly the Northern Democratic journals, and given wide circulation. On July 13, Stephens denied the allegation in a letter to the editors of the Baltimore *Clipper*, stating that the interview in question had taken place before the President's illness began, and that nothing had been said concerning the Galphin controversy. Toombs refrained from public comment. Henrico subsequently changed part of his story, but it was some time before the repercussions of the affair died down.[56]

The death of Zachary Taylor broke the political log jam holding back the adoption of a compromise plan. After the accession of Millard Fillmore, handsome New Yorker and professional politician who understood the necessity of compromise in statecraft, events, after one false start, took their natural course. Reflecting the desire of the majority of the American people, Congress moved fairly evenly toward the termination of the national crisis. Meanwhile, the Nashville Convention, assembling with disunion overtones, had adjourned after a tame session which accomplished very little. A second meeting was scheduled following the close of Congress.[57]

Throughout a hot July, the debate in the Senate on Clay's Omnibus Bill continued. On the last day of the month it unexpectedly was defeated. Exhausted, Clay left the scene and his mantle of leadership fell on the strong shoulders of Stephen A. Douglas of Illinois, the ambitious and shrewd "Little Giant." Clay's compromise package was now split into separate bills and a new battle joined.[58]

By the nineteenth of August, with the doughty Douglas in the driver's seat, five bills had passed the Senate over the embittered opposition of Northern radicals and Southern extremists. It was now up to the moderates in the House to see that the task of preserving the Union was carried through to completion. At a caucus of Southern members of the House in early August, a sort of

[56]Phillips (ed.), *Correspondence*, 195; Cole, *Whig Party*, 168*n*; Phillips, *Toombs*, 84–85; Augusta *Chronicle*, July 19, 20, 23, 1850.

[57]Shryock, *Georgia and the Union*, 269–73.

[58]Recent scholarship accords Douglas prime responsibility for the passage of the Compromise. See Holman Hamilton, *Prologue to Conflict: The Crisis and Compromise of 1850* (Lexington, Ky., 1964), 182–84.

watchdog committee on Southern rights was set up, one member from each of the fifteen slave-holding states, with Toombs somewhat surprisingly serving as chairman. Resolutions reported by the committee were projected as minimum demands of the South which must be met. Paramount among them was the division of the country, slave and free, at the old Missouri Compromise line of 36° 30′ if all else failed.[59]

About three weeks were consumed by the House in debate and passage of the compromise measures. Toombs grew weary of it all and longed for his family, who had left Washington in late July for Georgia. He was "lonely as a hermit" he told his wife, and in a burst of youthful passion, the forty-year-old congressman wrote: "I realize almost with pain your exquisite loveliness; do you understand how pleasant recollections produce pain? If you dont just imagine how badly I want to kiss you & cant. Write me every mail, burn this letter, I send you a thousand kisses. I wish you could send me your lips to kiss." [60]

Five days later his ardor had not diminished though his pen had cooled a bit. He wrote his beloved Julia that he believed he was more anxious to see her than save the republic. "The old Roman Antony threw away an empire rather than abandon his lovely Cleopatra, and the world has called him a fool for it. I begin to think that he was the wiser man, and that the world was well lost for love." [61]

Although she missed her husband, Julia Toombs was glad to be home. She wrote Mrs. Armistead Burt, wife of a South Carolina congressman and daughter of John C. Calhoun, that her little village was buzzing with a constant round of parties for the young people. "I hope that I never shall see much more of Washington City again," she said to her friend, who may well have felt the same way. "Give me a life at the south with pure southern hospitality." [62]

Ironically Toombs was brought face to face with one of the problems involved in the sectional crisis shortly after his family's

[59]Augusta *Chronicle*, August 11, 15, 1850; Cole, *Whig Party*, 173.

[60]Toombs to his wife, August 24, 1850, in Robert Toombs Papers, University of Georgia.

[61]Quoted in Stovall, *Toombs*, 82.

[62]Julia Toombs to Mrs. Armistead Burt, August 29, 1850, in Armistead Burt Papers, Duke University.

departure—the loss of runaway slaves. A New York abolitionist and newspaper publisher, William L. Chaplin, was able to entice two slaves away from Toombs and Stephens and conceal them briefly in the capital city. Police were successful, however, in capturing the fugitives as they tried to leave town by carriage.[63] According to the Savannah *Morning News*, the abolitionists in Washington circulated a false report that Toombs offered a reward of $500 for the scalp of his slave.[64]

The Compromise of 1850, on which the House put its stamp of approval by September 17, provided for: the admission of California with a free-state constitution; the creation of two new territories, Utah and New Mexico, with the troublesome slavery question buried under the principle of congressional non-intervention; a payment of $10,000,000 to Texas in return for the surrender of a large area to New Mexico; the abolition of the slave trade but not slavery in the District of Columbia; and a drastic new fugitive slave law. Toombs supported each bill although he voted against the admission of California and did not vote at all on the final passage of the measure to abolish the slave trade in the District of Columbia.[65] He explained that his negative vote on California was not sectional but was because of certain irregularities in her application for statehood.

In his final speech to one of the most momentous sessions in congressional history, Toombs denied that he had betrayed the interests of the South. From the first day to this last hour, he had had but one "ultimatum"—hostility to any legislation by Congress against slave property. "That I have been, now am, and shall ever be ready to resist," he declared. Any concessions that he had made had been for the sake of the public will and "the peace and tranquillity of the Republic. . . ."[66]

It was now over in Congress. A big job still remained for the Compromise supporters—to convince their constituents that they had acted wisely.

With the adjournment of Congress, the Georgia Triumvirate of

[63]Savannah *Morning News*, August 14, 16, 1850; Augusta *Chronicle*, August 6, 10, 1850. These accounts present conflicting statements.
[64]Savannah *Morning News*, August 17, 1850.
[65]*Congressional Globe*, 31st Cong., 1st Sess., 1764, 1772, 1776, 1807, 1837.
[66]*Ibid.*, 1774–75.

Toombs, Stephens, and Cobb headed home. Though travel by rail with its "dust, and smoke, and unpleasant oscillating vertical and horizontal jerkings and eternal clatter" [67] was not conducive to political ponderings, there was much for these battle-fatigued Unionists to consider. Governor Towns, in accordance with resolutions of the legislature which earlier in the year had branded the admission of free-soil California as dangerous to the security of the South, had on September 23 issued a spirited call for the election of a state convention to assemble in Milledgeville on December 10. Georgia was the first Southern state to so act, and with her wealth, population, and strategic geographical location, the "empire state" held the key to the question of union or disunion. It had been all too clear during the Compromise struggle that Georgia's acceptance of Clay's Omnibus Bill would not be easily attained. Mirroring widespread Democratic discontent, the Milledgeville *Federal Union* described the compromise measures as *"surrender bills,"* and castigated Toombs and Stephens for blowing hot and cold on the question of Southern rights. From "Hamilcar" to "submissionist" the paper labeled Toombs' December to September congressional role.[68]

In Georgia the Triumvirate lost no time in creating a coalition of Unionist Whigs and Democrats to stump the state. Cobb proved a very accurate prophet as he wrote a friend that "we shall have a most exciting and angry contest in the state, and in some sections a very doubtful one—though I entertain no doubt that we shall have a large majority of the convention." [69]

Those who stood in opposition to the Unionists preferred to be known as Southern Rights men. From the beginning of the campaign, however, they labored under the stigma of "disunionists" which the Triumvirate somewhat unjustly but effectively called all those who would not accept the Compromise in its entirety. It is true that within the ranks of the Southern Rightists there did exist a small minority of secessionists who were backed by the Columbus *Times,* the Columbus *Sentinel,* and the Macon *Telegraph.*

[67]Augusta *Chronicle,* August 8, 1850.
[68]Milledgeville *Federal Union,* August 20, September 15, October 8, 1850.
[69]Cobb to John B. Lamar, October 10, 1850, in Phillips (ed.), *Correspondence,* 215. Stephens estimated that he traveled 3,000 miles during the contest. Avary (ed.), *Stephens' Recollections,* 27.

A September 17 quotation from the *Telegraph* read: "For our own part, we are for secession, for resistance, open, unqualified resistance." [70] But by the time of the election of delegates in November, practically no paper or speaker was plugging the cause of outright disunion. [71]

Toombs doubtless helped bring about this change in sentiment. He spoke widely and effectively and at least once, in the enemy camp in Columbus, ran the risk of physical harm. The *Times* stated after their departure that Toombs and Stephens had "operated like sparks in a tinder box on this community. They have raised the dander of our people." [72] Within two hours after their arrival, Toombs was hanged in effigy and at a political rally there were blows struck and the drawing of pistols and blades. [73]

On October 9 there appeared in the Augusta *Chronicle* Toombs' address to the people of the Eighth Congressional District. In it, he reviewed his activities during the last session of Congress in methodical, persuasive fashion. Stealing a bit of thunder from the fire-eaters, he pointed out that he, too, on three points had drawn the line against Northern encroachment on pain of dissolution of the Union: the application of the Wilmot Proviso to the territories; the abolition of slavery in the District of Columbia; and the refusal of Congress to provide efficient legislation for the recovery of runaway slaves. That line had not been crossed. He explained that the Compromise had rectified a mistake made by the South in 1820 when she had permitted slavery to be prohibited north of 36° 30′ in the Louisiana Territory. Now, said Toombs, Utah and New Mexico, which extended to the 42nd Parallel, could come into the union with or without slavery as the people therein might determine for themselves. On paper, this argument appeared sound enough, but as Webster had pointed out and as Toombs undoubtedly knew, there was very little likelihood that slavery could ever be rooted in these arid areas. As for Texas, Toombs reiterated his House statement that her claim to the disputed territory was "purely technical. She had never conquered it, nor brought it, nor possessed it."

[70]Quoted in Augusta *Chronicle*, September 20, 1850.
[71]Shryock, *Georgia and the Union*, 310–11.
[72]Quoted in Augusta *Chronicle*, November 9, 1850.
[73]*Ibid.*

Although Toombs had supported the congressional "non-intervention" part of the Compromise, he called it a "political heresy" and told his constituents he was not satisfied with it. Some Southerners regarded it as the only means of assuring safety for Southern rights, for if Congress had the power to legislate on the subject of slavery in the territories it could, of course, prohibit it. Toombs spurned this negative stand, and said he refused to discharge the government from its "first and highest duty"—that of protecting citizens in the enjoyment of their property in the territories. Southerners should work to achieve this, he said. The admission of California, "the master grievance of the day," Toombs called a matter purely within the discretion of Congress. He had opposed it not because of the fact that California would be a free state but because of discrepancies in the application procedure. To be slave or free was the business of Californians, not Georgians. "If we are wise," he said, "we will defend rather than resist this birthright of American freemen, so invaluable to us, so formidable to the enemies of our property, our peace and safety." [74]

During the campaign Toombs was charged with inconsistency in his congressional posture by the Southern Rights, largely Democratic, press. His occasional dashes to the brink of disunion in moments of agitation, such as the "Hamilcar" venture, gave some substantiation to such assertions as the following from the Columbus *Times*: "It is perfectly clear that during the whole of this long session, up to the moment when the omnibus bills were passed, Mr. Toombs was first on the fence, then on both sides of it—seesawing, and dodging, and talking with a forked tongue.—He was all things to all men. . . ." [75] In stronger language, the *Federal Union* called Toombs and his Unionist colleagues the "true Judases of the country." [76]

There was a third, though little supported, approach to what Georgia's attitude toward the Compromise of 1850 should be— the so-called "nonintercourse" plan advocated by Senator Berrien. The elder Georgia statesman, unlike his colleague William C. Dawson, had refused to endorse fully Clay's proposals, voting against

[74]Augusta *Chronicle*, October 9, 1850.
[75]Quoted in Milledgeville *Federal Union*, October 8, 1850.
[76]*Ibid.*, November 12, 1850.

the admission of California and the abolition of the slave trade in the District. Even so Berrien was not an extremist. He wished only to unite the South within the framework of the Union in a program of economic pressure against the North. But this halfway, neither fish nor fowl, position on so explosive an issue was obviously not a good one politically, and Berrien suffered because of it.[77]

On election day in late November, the Unionists rolled to an impressive victory, nearly doubling the popular vote of their opponents. Of the ninety-three Georgia counties, less than twenty elected Southern Rights delegates to the convention.[78] On December 10, 1850, the convention assembled in Milledgeville with 264 delegates in attendance, including Toombs and Stephens. The great work of the convention was the adoption of the Georgia Platform, basically a Unionist document but containing a list of encroachments on Southern rights which the delegates felt would justify the secession of the state. The preamble and the first three resolutions declared Georgia's devotion to the Union and, while not completely approving the Compromise, stated that it was accepted as a permanent adjustment of sectional difficulties. The fourth and fifth resolutions laid down the Georgia ultimatum: disunion if Congress abolished slavery in the District of Columbia (the Compromise of 1850 had only ended the slave trade), suppressed the interstate slave trade, refused to admit a slave state into the Union, prohibited the introduction of slaves into Utah and New Mexico, or modified the Fugitive Slave Law.[79]

Toombs attempted to get the convention to accept all the resolutions as a package deal, but failed. As each resolution was being considered separately, obstructionist tactics were employed by the extremists. One of these, J. L. Seward, after having been accused by the Unionists of a deliberate stall, retorted that Toombs and Stephens had for weeks held up the organization of the House of Representatives and "having got the people of Georgia to the point of resistance, they come home and ask [them] to submit to the injustice done them." [80]

[77]Shryock, *Georgia and the Union*, 267–69.
[78]Montgomery, *Cracker Parties*, 32–33.
[79]Shryock, *Georgia and the Union*, 329–32.
[80]Quoted in *ibid.*, 332; Augusta *Chronicle*, December 20, 1850.

The struggle over the Compromise of 1850, culminating in the Georgia Platform, made shambles out of the traditional Whig and Democratic political alignment within the state. In August at the beginning of the contest, the Southern Rights party consisting primarily of Democrats had been formed in Macon. The Constitutional Union party, though existing imperfectly through the Toombs, Stephens, and Cobb coalition, did not receive a "formal christening" until the time of the state convention.[81] Helping launch the party were Toombs and Stephens, who on the night of the eleventh spoke to the Unionists at the capital and pointed out the "necessity of the organization of a national party for the preservation of the Constitution and the Union upon the basis of the late adjustment of the slavery question by Congress." Two nights later, the Constitutional Union party was created upon the principles of the Georgia Platform. "The right hand of fellowship" was extended to "patriots" everywhere who subscribed to these fundamental tenets.[82]

The Unionists had undoubtedly won a great victory in Georgia, attributed sourly by Southern Rightists to a "conspiracy of circumstances, the most important elements of which were thirteen-cent cotton [prosperity] and wanton misrepresentation of theirs as a secession party." [83] This triumph, together with the ineffectiveness of the second Nashville Convention which had met in November, did much toward the preservation of the Union in 1850. Henry Clay, the old compromiser, wrote a group of Georgians in February, 1851, that their tremendous accomplishment had "diffused inexpressible joy among the friends of the Union throughout the land. It crushed the spirit of discord, disunion and Civil War." [84]

[81]Montgomery, *Cracker Parties*, 25–27, 35.
[82]Augusta *Chronicle*, December 28, 1850.
[83]Quoted in Montgomery, *Cracker Parties*, 33.
[84]Quoted in Shryock, *Georgia and the Union*, 339.

CHAPTER V

Constitutional Unionist

TOOMBS returned to Washington late in December, 1850, for the last session of the Thirty-first Congress. It was a routine session for the Georgian, whose political interests remained at home with the embryonic Constitutional Union party he had helped fashion. He spoke only a few times and then as a guardian of the public treasury, opposing a rivers and harbors measure, a fortifications bill, and an increase in expenditures for the army. Toombs took a swipe at the standing army, as was his custom when given an opportunity, saying that "such a body of men were dangerous to our liberties, and that a standing army should not be maintained except at the lowest possible standard." [1]

The Whig caucuses were shunned by Toombs, although he conferred with Southerners in the party who came to him for advice, and tried to cut them out of the national organization.[2] He kept in close touch with developments in Georgia. On February 15, 1851, he sent a letter to a committee making arrangements for a large Constitutional Union party rally to be held in Macon on Washington's birthday. Regretting that he would be unable to attend, he expressed strong support for the perpetuation of liberty

[1]*Congressional Globe*, 31st Cong., 2nd Sess., 723, 588, 642.
[2]Toombs to Howell Cobb, January 2, 1851, in Phillips (ed.), *Correspondence*, 218–19.

through a constitution-based Union. Toombs did not think either of the major parties was equal to this task, "both having degenerated into mere factions, adhering together by the common hope of public plunder." The safety of the country could only be realized by the merger of sound Democrats and Whigs with Constitutional Unionists into a "United National party." The true policy of the Constitutional Unionists was to "stand by those who agree with us—repudiate those who differ from us." Although beset by enemies both North and South, one should not falter in doing his duty. "The Constitution and Union is worth a struggle," he said.[3] Toombs' letter was read at the celebration along with those from Clay, Cobb, and others.[4]

A few days later Toombs turned down another February 22 invitation to a union rally in New York City. He commended the efforts to "rekindle the national attachment to the Union," and said the support of the Compromise was the first and most important step in that direction. In closing his letter, he offered this toast: "The Federal Government—Omnipotent in the exercise of its rightful powers—impotent in a career of usurpation. May it ever retain both characteristics." [5]

Toombs had planned a European trip for his family when Congress adjourned, but that had to be deferred in favor of his entrance into the state political arena.[6] The battle lines were redrawn between Constitutional Unionists and Southern Rightists as the Georgia gubernatorial contest opened. In May, former Democratic governor and president of the second Nashville Convention Charles J. McDonald was nominated by the Southern Rights party on a platform which indicated a return to the Calhoun principles of 1849 and a departure from the idea of immediate secession. Perhaps the most significant resolution adopted by the Southern Rights convention, however, was one proclaiming the *right* of a state to secede. At one and the same time, it was hoped by the Southern Rightists that this would have an emotional appeal to Southern

---

[3]Phillips (ed.), *Correspondence*, 227–29.
[4]Phillips, *Toombs*, 100.
[5]Toombs to New York Union Committee, February 21, 1851, in Augusta *Chronicle*, March 8, 1851.
[6]Toombs to Crittenden, April 25, 1851, in Phillips (ed.), *Correspondence*, 233.

sentiment and help split their incompatible opponents who nominated Howell Cobb and rallied around the Georgia Platform.[7]

The abstract right of secession did become a major issue in the campaign. Toombs, realizing its danger to his party, advised Cobb to refrain from argument on it and show "its utter immateriality in the contest." [8] Cobb was fairly successful in straddling the issue with remarks that were "marvels of sophistical ingenuity." [9]

Toombs worked hard, carrying a double load as he had done in 1848, for Stephens was sent to the sidelines by illness. Although inactive, Stephens was full of advice for Cobb which he spelled out specifically to his Unionist colleague in a June 23 letter. He warned that the Southern Rightists would "leave no stone unturned no lie untold and no dollar they can raise unspent. You must be up and awake." [10]

There was much at stake for Toombs in this contest—reelection to Congress[11] and the prospect of election to the Senate if his party could obtain a majority in the legislature. It was commonly noised about the state that he had this in mind. As early as March, Iverson L. Harris had told his friend Berrien that his senatorial scalp was in danger of being lifted by Toombs because of his uncooperative stand on the Compromise of 1850, or, in Harris' words, "[his] endeavoring to make the compromise measures honorable to the South." [12] In July a confidant of Stephens asked him if he were aware of Toombs' ambition for the Senate. He suggested that Stephens might properly succeed to the Senate before Toombs, and if he were inclined in that direction it was time for him to make his move.[13] Stephens, probably because of his infirmities, did not so indicate, although he may have been slightly miffed when he was actually passed over in November.[14]

[7]Shryock, *Georgia and the Union*, 350–51; Montgomery, *Cracker Parties*, 39–40; Augusta *Chronicle*, June 5, 1851.

[8]Toombs to Cobb, June 9, 1851, Howell Cobb Papers, University of Georgia.

[9]Shryock, *Georgia and the Union*, 352.

[10]Phillips (ed.), *Correspondence*, 238.

[11]Elections to Congress had been changed to the October before the convening of Congress in December.

[12]Harris to Berrien, March 12, 1851, in Berrien Papers.

[13]A. H. Kenan to Stephens, July 3, 1851, in Phillips (ed.), *Correspondence*, 241.

[14]Phillips, *Toombs*, 105.

The campaign was to a large extent a carbon copy of the previous one in the fall but with more bitterness. The *Federal Union* said it was a question of whether Georgia "shall be governed by an irresponsible and insolent triumvirate, or act for herself in the capacity of a free and independent sovereignty." [15] Shortly before the voters went to the polls, Toombs, Stephens, and Cobb had in this journal's opinion degenerated into "brow-beating, loud-mouthed demagogues, whose only claim to the reputation they now hold, is derived from the skillful management of their automaton constituencies." [16] The Constitutional Union press was just as partisan. The Augusta *Chronicle* called Toombs the "Pitt of America" and "Richard the lion-hearted, with his strong arm and ponderous battle axe." It spoke of the great power of his oratory and the "breathless silence" on the one hand and the "boisterous approbation" on the other with which it was received. And it added, "One thing is certain, the ladies are all with Toombs. . . ." [17]

On October 11, Toombs wrote Cobb: "Don't you hear these howlings rolling over toward the rocky mountains? We have glory enough for one day." [18] Glory indeed, for the Constitutional Unionists had won a smashing victory. Cobb was in as governor by an 18,000 vote majority, the legislature was heavily Unionist, and Toombs and Stephens were on their way back to Congress.[19] Toombs carried every county in his district, defeating his opponent, Robert McMillen, by a vote of 4,704 to 2,538. [20] Similar results occurred in Mississippi, Alabama, and later in the spring of 1852 in South Carolina. Southern acquiescence to the Compromise of 1850 seemed complete.

In November, 1851, Robert Toombs was elected by the Georgia legislature to the United States Senate to succeed Berrien, whose term was to expire in March, 1853. While perfectly legal, it was a maneuver that left the Triumvirate open to serious charges of political chicanery and added to the bitterness and divisiveness in state politics. That Berrien's days were numbered was a foregone conclusion—his age and lack of cooperation with the Triumvirate in Washington during the Compromise struggle and in the contest culminating in the Georgia Platform had signaled the end of his

[15]Milledgeville *Federal Union*, August 26, 1851.
[16]*Ibid.*, September 30, 1851.
[17]Augusta *Chronicle*, August 2, 12, September 14, 1851.
[18]Phillips (ed.), *Correspondence*, 261.
[19]Shryock, *Georgia and the Union*, 354.
[20]Augusta *Chronicle*, October 16, 1851.

career. But, as the Milledgeville *Federal Union* tellingly pointed out, only political expediency called for the election of Berrien's replacement at this time. Not before December, 1853, would a new senator be required to take his seat and by that time another legislature, "fresh from the people" and capable of performing the task, would have convened. Furthermore, this election of Toombs to the Senate plus his October election to the House literally made him independent of the people of Georgia for eight years. Obviously, said the *Federal Union*, the Constitutional Unionists were not willing to trust to the future, fearing a clearing of the "mist and fog that now envelops the politics of Georgia." These men "have combined together to rule the State and divide the spoils." [21]

The Albany *Patriot* commented that "Mr. Toombs made Mr. Cobb Governor, Mr. Cobb made Mr. Toombs Senator, and Mr. Stephens is to have what he calls for at all hours." A "Mutual Insurance Company" the Triumvirate was labeled.[22]

Toombs apparently paid no attention to this barrage of criticism as he prepared to return north for the opening of the first session of the Thirty-second Congress. On the night of November 10, following his election to the Senate, he had spoken to a large audience in the capitol outlining his probable course of action in Washington. He indicated the strong possibility of cooperation with Northern Democrats, whom he considered much more trustworthy on the slavery issue than the Seward-led Whigs. If this failed to materialize, then he would appeal to sound men from both organizations to form a party that would "preserve the institutions of the South . . . and the integrity of the Union." [23]

In Washington, Toombs and Stephens had to accustom themselves to new roles—unaligned mavericks in a two-party legislative system. Along with all the Union men of Georgia, they avoided the organizational caucuses of both parties, and in the balloting for Speaker of the House which saw the election of Democrat Linn Boyd of Kentucky threw away their votes on Junius Hillyer, fellow Georgia congressman.[24]

[21]Milledgeville *Federal Union*, November 11, 1851.
[22]Quoted in Augusta *Chronicle*, December 2, 1851.
[23]Athens *Southern Banner*, November 20, 1851.
[24]Stephens to Linton Stephens, December 10, 1851, in Phillips (ed.), *Correspondence*, 274; *Congressional Globe*, 32nd Cong., 1st Sess., 9–10. Hillyer was one of the brothers with whom Toombs had had a serious altercation at the University of Georgia. Apparently, all had been forgiven and forgotten.

It was the intention of Georgia's Constitutional Unionists, who comprised six out of eight of the state's congressional delegation, to initiate a nationwide party based on their principles. Impractical and visionary, the scheme never really got off the ground, if indeed such veteran politicians as Toombs and Stephens ever believed it could. As early as January 7, 1852, just a few weeks after Congress opened, Unionist Charles Murphy from Decatur wrote Governor Cobb: "As to what we ought to do I am at a great loss but one thing is certain that the old Parties are to remain and no 3rd Party will be formed." He thought Toombs and Stephens were acting as "partisans" and unwilling to align either the Democratic or Whig Party with Unionist principles.[25]

Early in February, the *Federal Union* trumpeted gleefully though a bit prematurely that the Constitutional Union Party was dead. "The Union bubble has burst, and the dead carcase [*sic*] of the Union party lies stinking above ground, with no one to give it a decent burial." Toombs and other Unionists were accused of knocking now on the Democratic door. "Let us watch," it said, "and see what Democrats are willing to open the door and let in these wolves in sheep's clothing." [26]

On February 29 another of the Georgia Unionists, E. W. Chastain, informed Cobb that it appeared Stephens would fall back into the Whig ranks, while Toombs' position was something of an enigma. He said that Senator William C. Dawson, Berrien's colleague, was allied with Stephens and that the three doubtless understood each other. "I think I see breakers ahead but I shall still hope for the best," he concluded.[27]

Meanwhile, Toombs was experiencing an unhappy time. Plagued by rheumatism, which finally drove him from his seat in Congress in March and back to Georgia in April, his participation in House affairs was at a minimum.[28] His one major speech during this period was given at a congressional banquet at Willard's Hotel in commemoration of Washington's birthday. Toombs took this occasion, along with other speakers present, to attack the Hungarian rebel chieftain Louis Kossuth, who was in the United States en-

[25]Charles Murphy to Cobb, in Howell Cobb Papers, University of Georgia.
[26]Milledgeville *Federal Union*, February 3, 1852.
[27]E. W. Chastain to Cobb, in Howell Cobb Papers, University of Georgia.
[28]Julia Toombs to Mrs. Martha Calhoun Burt, May 29, 1852, in Armistead Burt Papers; Augusta *Chronicle*, March 6, 1852.

listing money and support for continuation of the struggle against Austrian domination. In strongly conservative and isolationist terms, he condemned the solicitations of the popular revolutionary, saying Kossuth wished the United States to "turn knight-errant, imitate the knight of La Mancha [Don Quixote], and travel up and down the world, revenging or righting the wrongs of all injured nations." The United States should not, he said, interfere with the institutions of another country, in view of the difficulty it was having agreeing on the proper principles of its own internal policy. Let it look after its own affairs and steer clear of European entanglements. Those nations who desired to be free had only to will it.[29] The New York *Daily Times*, ardent Kossuth champion, deplored the addresses, saying the "mantle of Washington was [being] made to protect the interests and the political crimes of despots of Europe." [30] The Kossuth rage continued for some time in the United States but finally evaporated when it appeared that the Hungarian wanted active intervention by the United States in Europe, something traditional American policy opposed.

The refusal of Toombs and other former Whigs to play ball with the national party also caused the *Times* much annoyance. "Those gentlemen put up the State of Georgia at public auction, and pocketed the price of its sale. They found it very convenient, for their personal purposes, to discard all allegiance to the national Whig party, and to enter the field as the champions of a new faith. They have prospered by it." [31] Toombs was again attacked the next day. The *Times* spoke of how he had "bargained himself" into the Senate two years before any vacancy had occurred.[32]

The political situation in Georgia in the spring of 1852 was characterized by party fragmentation and wholesale confusion, leading eventually to a staggering five electoral tickets in the presidential contest in November. In late 1851, shortly after the gubernatorial election, the Southern Rights party had assumed the Democratic label under the leadership of Herschel V. Johnson, and began to work toward the rehabilitation of the party in Georgia. On March 31, these "Regular" Democrats met in state convention,

[29]Augusta *Chronicle*, March 18, 1852.
[30]New York *Daily Times*, March 17, 1852, hereinafter cited as New York *Times*.
[31]*Ibid.*, April 14, 1852.
[32]*Ibid.*, April 15, 1852.

selected delegates to attend the national party's Baltimore convention on June 1, and prepared an electoral slate.

Beset by the failure of its representatives in Congress to launch a nationwide Unionist party and the basic incompatibility of Whigs and Democrats within its ranks, the Constitutional Union party began to show signs of an early demise. Governor Cobb hoped, before the funeral, to take his coalition party into the Democratic ranks and assume his old-time leadership of Democracy in the state. The Johnson faction was determined, however, that the governor should eat humble crow before any reinstatement should occur.[33]

The Constitutional Union party drifted along ineffectually into April, with its various factions looking for possible escape routes when the structure would finally collapse. Toombs was indisposed through much of the spring and remained inactive politically. From his home he watched the bolting of the Whig congressional caucus in Washington by Southerners after the failure of the caucus to endorse as a finality the Compromise of 1850. [34] He followed with great interest a state convention of the Constitutional Union party on April 22 where a spirited debate ensued over a resolution to send delegates to the Democratic convention on June 1. The debate terminated in a deadlock. On April 23, following convention adjournment, a rump meeting mainly of Cobb-supporting Democrats dubbed "Supplementals" in contrast to the "Regulars," chose a delegation with the understanding that it cling to the principles of the Compromise of 1850 and urge their adoption as a basis for action for the Democratic party.[35] An authority on the kaleidoscopic nature of Georgia politics at this time has written: "The events of April 22 and 23 might be considered as having begun the disintegration of the Constitutional Union party. . . . After April 23, it was simply awaiting a formal death sentence." [36]

Toombs returned to Washington in early May, but within a few days was down again with rheumatism, which kept him incapacitated for several weeks. On the twenty-seventh he wrote Cobb, giving some clarification of his political thinking. He said he had

[33]Montgomery, *Cracker Parties*, 45–47.
[34]Augusta *Chronicle*, April 23, 25, 1852; New York *Times*, April 22, 1852.
[35]Augusta *Chronicle*, April 27, 28, 1852; Montgomery, *Cracker Parties*, 57–59.
[36]Montgomery, *Cracker Parties*, 59.

written a letter to Georgia denouncing the "Fillmore movement" which aimed at having the state represented at the national Whig convention on June 16. Toombs commented favorably to Cobb on the action of the "Supplemental" Democrats in choosing delegates to Baltimore, and gave the impression he would support the Democrats if they nominated a sound man. For the present, he said, ". . . the skies are bright and brightening,"—a very optimistic and confident statement for a politician whose own party was rapidly disappearing and who might soon be looking for a new political home.[37] In spite of Toombs' opposition, a small Whig convention attended by representatives from only sixteen counties was held on June 7 in Milledgeville. Delegates to the party's national convention were chosen bearing the Georgians' preference for Fillmore.[38]

Berrien meanwhile had resigned his seat in the Senate, effective June 1, and Cobb appointed Robert M. Charlton to fill the vacancy.[39] The New York *Times* commented that Berrien had been a creditable senator, although of late narrowly devoted to sectional interests. "Mr. Toombs will bring, perhaps, greater zeal, but far less ability and influence, to the same work." [40]

At the Democratic convention a dark horse, Franklin Pierce of New Hampshire, often called a Northern man with Southern principles, was nominated for the presidency. The party platform explicitly avowed faithful adherence to the Compromise of 1850. Toombs was pleased on both counts, remarking to Cobb that "our principles [were] triumphant," and calling the candidate a "fair, great, upright & sound man without the least objection on the slavery issue." [41]

The Whigs, also in Baltimore, as was expected nominated General Winfield Scott, able soldier, strong Unionist, but inexperienced politically and beset by personal idiosyncrasies. In a triumph of the moderate wing, the Compromise was adopted as a final settlement of sectional problems. The nomination of Scott was received with mixed emotions in the South, principally because of the uncertainty of his attitude on slavery. Ultimately, however, most

[37]Phillips (ed.), *Correspondence*, 297–98; Augusta *Chronicle*, June 5, 1852.
[38]Montgomery, *Cracker Parties*, 63–64.
[39]Augusta *Chronicle*, May 27, 1852.
[40]New York *Times*, May 28, 1852.
[41]Toombs to Cobb, June 10, 1852, in Brooks, "Cobb Papers," V, Pt. 4, p. 52.

state organizations supported their party nominee in November. While Senator Dawson accepted Scott's candidacy and campaigned for him in Georgia, most of the Unionist Whigs, led by Toombs and Stephens, repudiated the general. In a telegram of June 23 to the Augusta *Chronicle*, the Georgia congressmen stated that they did not believe Scott should be supported by the Constitutional Union party. They did, however, pledge to abide by the decision of the party's state convention.[42]

On July 3, Toombs made a lengthy and somewhat disconnected speech in the House in which he denounced Scott's candidacy, pronounced as acceptable the Democratic nominees, and branded the national convention, since 1836 the method for nominating presidential candidates, as conducive to second-rate leaders.[43]

Two days later the attack on Scott continued. There appeared in the *National Intelligencer* a notice signed by nine former Southern Whigs, including Toombs and Stephens, citing reasons why Scott was inimical to the interests of the South. Among them were his refusal to endorse unequivocally the compromise measures either before or after his nomination and the fact that he had been the favorite candidate of the free-soil wing of the Whig party.[44]

It was reasonable to assume at this point that Toombs would cast his fortunes with Cobb's Democrats. He had coupled his public denunciations of Scott with Democratic endorsements, and had written Cobb privately in late June that at the Constitutional Union convention he would use his "best exertions to get them to adopt Pierce & King. . . ." If that seemed inadvisable, he would attempt "to dissolve the party decently & in order." [45] Unionist Democrats were of the opinion that Toombs had no other choice but to support their cause. On July 11, just before their convention, John H. Lumpkin wrote Cobb that Toombs owed this to them because they had been "mainly instrumental in giving him his present position on the ground that he would act with us in favor of the National democratic nominee." [46]

Toombs' friend Stephens was moving in another direction: the formation of a national Constitutional Union party, and the support

---

[42]Quoted in Augusta *Chronicle*, June 25, 1852.
[43]*Congressional Globe*, 32nd Cong., 1st Sess., Appendix, 816–20.
[44]National *Intelligencer*, July 5, 1852.
[45]Toombs to Cobb, June 24, 1852, in Howell Cobb Papers, University of Georgia.
[46]Phillips (ed.), *Correspondence*, 310.

of Daniel Webster. At the convention which opened on July 15, the Cobb Democrats enjoyed a commanding majority, and were able to endorse an electoral slate for Pierce but at the expense of a party split when the Webster-supporting Whigs walked out.[47] It was thought that Toombs was involved in Cobb's victory. The Milledgeville *Federal Union* warned against an alliance with its old enemy. "Like one afflicted with the plague, his embrace is death. Let all democrats who wish to escape a political contagion, as fatal as the plague or cholera, avoid the Toombs party." [48]

The *Federal Union* had nothing to fear, for Toombs in late summer decided to go along with Stephens and the Webster ticket, the so-called Tertium Quid movement. Doubtless their warm friendship and Toombs' great respect for Stephens' judgement accounted for this unexpected alignment. In August and September, efforts were made which would have simplified the hopelessly confused situation by proposed amalgamations of the two Whig factions and two Democratic groups but without success. The struggle for power with great promise of political spoils prevented a harmonious solution to what in reality had become quite farcical.[49] Only one thing seemed sure—the Constitutional Union party was dead. It was so pronounced on August 10 by the executive committee of the party.[50]

Toombs' campaigning for the lost cause of Daniel Webster was infrequent and low-keyed, in contrast to his customary whirlwind technique. On September 7, for example, he spoke in his home town for some two hours, reciting the somewhat worn theme of being willing to support any man who would plant himself upon the broad principles of the constitution. He attacked Scott, recommending that all who thought it a moral duty to free their slaves vote for him. He praised Pierce highly, too much so thought the Webster-supporting Augusta *Chronicle*, but urged his constituents to vote for Webster. History might well remember the Massachusetts senator as "the greatest man on earth, and the greatest President of the greatest Republic on the face of the globe," Toombs grandly claimed.[51]

[47]Milledgeville *Federal Union*, July 27, 1852; Montgomery, *Cracker Parties*, 69.
[48]Milledgeville *Federal Union*, July 20, 1852.
[49]Montgomery, *Cracker Parties*, 72–91.
[50]*Ibid.*, 75.
[51]Augusta *Chronicle*, September 15, 1852.

Apathy reigned on election day among the citizens of Georgia, particularly those of Whig inclinations, as the five electoral tickets polled less than 61,000 votes. The Regular Democrats backing Pierce received 33,843 votes; the Cobb Democrats, sometimes called the Tugalos, 5,733 for their Pierce electors; the Scott Whigs 15,789; the Webster ticket 5,289; and a ticket of Southern Rights extremists 119.[52] The Democrats won nationally by a tremendous electoral margin of 254 to 42, although the difference in popular votes was much less impressive. Scott carried only four states: Kentucky and Tennessee in the South and Massachusetts and Vermont in the North. Ostensibly the strong vote of the nationwide Democratic party and the decline of the sectional Free-Soil party indicated a victory for moderation and a yearning for domestic peace and tranquility. But the rather poor showing of the Whig party, once a vital and adhesive force for union, portended an even greater disruption yet to come.

Shortly after the election Toombs, his wife, and daughters Louisa and Sallie departed for his place near Roanoke in Stewart County in the southwestern part of Georgia. They passed several pleasant weeks in this "wild & out of the way" place away from the turmoil of the political scene, though Toombs was never one to play the country gentlemen when on his plantation. Stephens once described him as

one of the most successful planters from the Potomac to the Rio Grande. His plantation discipline and his treatment of his slaves was on a perfect system of reason, justice, and humanity, looking as much to the welfare of his dependents as to his own pecuniary interests. Notwithstanding his engagements in law and politics, and the fact that his plantation was two hundred miles from his domicile, he held its management under complete control; planned all the crops, and by correspondence kept informed just how matters were going on, and gave directions. His system and its success was wonderful. He would have as overseers only men of sobriety, good sense, and humanity.[53]

On December 15, Toombs wrote Crittenden a short letter com-

[52]Phillips, *Toombs*, 110; Shryock, *Georgia and the Union*, 361–62; Cole, *Whig Party*, 274. Webster died a few days before the election. The Augusta *Chronicle*, the leading Webster organ, then plunked for either Fillmore or John J. Crittenden although it retained Charles J. Jenkins, Georgia Whig, as vice-presidential candidate. October 27, 1852; Montgomery, *Cracker Parties*, 90.

[53]Avary (ed.), *Stephens' Recollections*, 426.

menting on the election and the future of the Whig party. He pronounced the election, in typical overstatement, as one in which the "nation, with singular unanimity, has determined to take a man [Pierce] without claims or qualifications, surrounded by as dishonest and dirty a lot of political gamesters as ever Cataline assembled, rather than the canting hypocrites who brought out Genl. Scott. The decision was a wise one," Toombs thought. The country could never achieve peace and security with the likes of "Seward, [Horace] Greeley and Co." in positions of influence. Unless the Whig party rose to meet the standards of the Democrats, low as they were, it deserved no resurrection and would have none.[54]

Lame-duck sessions of Congress frequently were devoid of either accomplishment or excitement, particularly those before a new administration was ushered in. Toombs would have so pronounced the last session of the Thirty-second Congress. He did not take his seat until January 3 and seldom thereafter raised his voice in debate. His few remarks bespoke his well-known role as a conservative dispenser of Federal funds. "I object to pensions for anybody," he declared on January 28. [55] Throughout his congressional career, no one ever had the slightest reason for charging Robert Toombs with anything less than total devotion to the cause of frugality.

Reluctant though he was to spend the public's money, he could be lavish in the expenditure of his own. The social event of the spring in Washington, Georgia, was the marriage of Louisa Toombs to William Felix Alexander, son of Toombs' longtime neighbor, Adam Leopold Alexander. The handsome bridal gown, the "splendid supper table and provisions enough on it for three hundred people," [56] and the crowding of guests into the stately Toombs mansion reflected the desire of a devoted father to spare no expense in making his daughter's marriage a memorable one. One of the guests was Henry Watkins Allen, later Confederate governor of Louisiana, who was quite impressed with the lavish affair. His host he saw as a "noble fellow—his manners are affable, easy and

---

[54]Phillips (ed.), *Correspondence,* 322. Compare this description of Pierce with an earlier one in a letter to Cobb, page 85.

[55]*Congressional Globe,* 32nd Cong., 2nd Sess., 441.

[56]Louisa Gilmer to her husband, April 30, 1853, in Boggs (ed.), *Alexander Letters,* 186.

elegant—with a genius of the highest order, he is the most popular man in Georgia and one of the most popular men in the United States." [57] "Lou" was described by the bridegroom's sister as the "prettiest bride I ever saw, and she reminded me of some of the romantic descriptions in novels of 'fair and fragile' brides—too fair and frail I am afraid for much of the wear and tear of life." [58] Her observation was prophetically and tragically true, for Louisa Toombs was dead less than two years later, at the age of twenty-one.

Toombs backed another losing cause in Georgia's 1853 gubernatorial contest. By convention time the warring Democratic factions had been united through the willingness of Cobb to come hat in hand over to the camp of the "Regulars." The Democrats in mid-June nominated Herschel V. Johnson, leader of the resurgent party movement. Johnson, a man of balance and perspicacity, proved an admirable choice to head the Georgia Democracy. [59]

The nameless opposition, called by the Milledgeville *Southern Recorder* the "Conservative men of Georgia," [60] met in Milledgeville a week later and nominated Charles J. Jenkins, who had been vice-presidential candidate with Webster on the Tertium Quid ticket. The proceedings were so dominated by Toombs that the hostile *Federal Union* labeled the gatherings the "Toombs Convention." [61] An incongruous set of resolutions declared adherence to the principles of the Georgia convention of 1850, denounced both Whig and Democratic parties as unfit for support, condemned the consignment of public lands by the Federal government to internal improvements in a particular state, and reaffirmed Washington's Farewell Address admonition against entangling alliances. [62] Toombs addressed the convention and sharply criticized the Pierce administration for its abolitionist and free-soil appointments. The *Federal Union* accused the future senator of speaking with a "forked tongue, one way at home and another in the Halls of Congress." [63]

Although Johnson characterized the opposition of Toombs and

[57]Quoted in Vincent H. Cassidy and Amos E. Simpson, *Henry Watkins Allen of Louisiana* (Baton Rouge, 1964), 30.
[58]Louisa Gilmer to her husband, in Boggs (ed.), *Alexander Letters*, 185.
[59]Montgomery, *Cracker Parties*, 99–100.
[60]Quoted in the Augusta *Chronicle*, June 25, 1853.
[61]Milledgeville *Federal Union*, June 28, 1853.
[62]Augusta *Chronicle*, June 25, 1853.
[63]Milledgeville *Federal Union*, June 28, 1853.

Stephens as "zealous, fierce and potent," [64] the campaign was a fairly dull one. The two candidates remained on good terms, sometimes travelling and rooming together as they stumped the state. Election returns in October showed Johnson the winner by a narrow margin of only a few hundred votes. The Democrats also won six of the eight congressional seats. [65] Toombs' attempt to revive Constitutional Unionism had failed.

After the election, several Democratic papers called on Toombs to give up his senate seat (his term had actually begun on March 4, 1853, at the close of the Thirty-second Congress). They charged that when he was elected by the legislature in 1851 he promised to support the Democratic party presidential nominee in 1852, provided the national party convention endorsed the Compromise of 1850 as a permanent solution of the sectional crisis. This he had not done, although it will be remembered that Toombs had given strong indications of swinging behind Pierce before he had joined Stephens on behalf of Webster. As he obviously did not now represent the people of Georgia, he should step aside. [66] If Toombs gave this attack any thought, he did not reveal it. Doubtlessly he regarded it as unworthy of notice.

A few weeks later Toombs did become seriously involved in a nasty little episode which revealed how reckless and heedless of consequences he could become when aroused. During the gubernatorial contest, he had engaged in debate one V. A. Gaskill, a man he had encountered before in public gathering and for whom he had built up a strong dislike. At this particular meeting, Toombs gave Gaskill a "severe but [in his opinion] well-merited castigation" and attacked the policy of the Pierce administration in appointing to office men who were not supporters of the Compromise principles. One of these was Secretary of War Jefferson Davis who, according to Gaskill, Toombs denounced as a "disunionist sitting in the counsels of the nation." [67]

Gaskill, after defending Davis against the Toombs' attack, wrote the Mississippian asking for a statement on the charge. Davis' reply was published in several Georgia newspapers. He denied that he

[64]Quoted in Percy S. Flippin, *Herschel V. Johnson of Georgia: State Rights Unionist* (Richmond, 1931), 55.

[65]Montgomery, *Cracker Parties*, 115.

[66]Milledgeville *Federal Union*, October 25, 1853.

[67]Toombs to editor, Augusta *Chronicle*, November 4, 1853; V. A. Gaskill to editor, Milledgeville *Federal Union*, November 22, 1853.

had been a disunionist either when opposing the Compromise of 1850 or when unsuccessfully seeking the governorship of Mississippi in 1851. Davis admitted he supported the right of a sovereign state to secede but had spoken of it only as the "last remedy." A man who was ready to believe that he would destroy the Union and at the same time hold a place among its leaders after swearing to uphold the constitution could only be "radically false and corrupt," Davis concluded.[68]

Toombs, in his countering letter which was published in the Augusta *Chronicle*, said that Gaskill had misrepresented his remarks; that in his arraignment of the Pierce administration he had stated that the President after professing his support of the Compromise, had filled his cabinet with those who had opposed it. The charge that Davis was a disunionist he had never made. Toombs could have stopped here and charged the whole affair off to Gaskill's distortion and Davis' imprudence. But characteristically he plunged ahead and outdid the secretary in epithets. The usual course for an aggrieved gentleman, he said, was first to inquire of his alleged accuser as to the truth of the purported statement. Only "swaggering braggarts and cunning poltroons" pursued the course followed by Davis.[69]

The affair was seen by several Northern newspapers as a prelude to a duel. Fortunately, such was not the case, although on the eve of Toombs' departure in late December for Washington and the Senate neighbor Adam Leopold Alexander still felt uneasy about what might happen between the two men.[70]

[68]Davis to Gaskill, September 21, 1853, in Griffin *Jeffersonian*, quoted in Milledgeville *Federal Union*, November 1, 1853.

[69]Augusta *Chronicle*, November 4, 1853.

[70]Savannah *Morning News*, November 16, 1853; Adam Leopold Alexander to Edward Porter Alexander, December 24, 1853, in Edward Porter Alexander Papers.

CHAPTER VI

Senator from Georgia

IT was with a new title that Robert Toombs travelled to Washington for the Thirty-third Congress—senator from Georgia. Few
men had more cause for personal satisfaction than the forty-three-
year-old junior senator. He was wealthy, with land holdings in
five counties of the state and $10,000 out at interest.[1] He had
begun his large scale land speculation in Texas in partnership
with former Governor George W. Crawford, which ultimately
netted him over $200,000.[2] Toombs' land fever remained strong
down to the war. In 1856 he bought 320 acres in La Pointe
(later Bayfield) County, Wisconsin, for $12,800.[3] In the spring
of 1857, he carefully examined the Mississippi delta from Memphis
to Vicksburg, "the best cotton country in the world," after which
he purchased approximately two thousand acres in Desha County,

---

[1]Wilkes County Tax Digest, 1850; United States Census Report, 1850, Wilkes
County, Georgia (Microfilm MS in Georgia Archives).

[2]Atlanta *Constitution*, December 16, 1885; Toombs to son of George W.
Crawford, March 25, 1871, in Alexander H. Stephens Papers. Duke University.

[3]Henry M. and Matilda W. Rice to Robert Toombs, October 28, 1856
(Copy of deed in Office of County Clerk, Washburn, Wis.). This land was
sold by Toombs' heirs in 1888, three years after his death, for only $3,000.
See Heirs of Toombs to Isaac H. Wing (Abstract information from deed
in Office of County Clerk, Washburn, Wis.).

Arkansas, about seven miles above the mouth of the Arkansas River.[4]

Politically Toombs was as secure as he was financially. Although adrift without a party, he had a six year lease on a Senate seat and carried with him the general approbation of a large percentage of the citizens of Georgia. Washington had not changed greatly since Toombs entered Congress in 1845. It was still a "shambling, dilapidated, ill-planned town set off by a few fine buildings and squares." [5] But if the exterior of the nation's capital city left much to be desired, its social life in the 1850's often bordered on the spectacular with a continuous round of dinners, dances, and receptions. "A hundred hostesses renowned for their beauty and wit and vivacity vied with each other in evolving novel social relaxations," declared Mrs. Clement C. Clay, an Alabama senator's wife. One of these was Mrs. Toombs, who, according to Mrs. Clay, said she spent $2,000 a month on entertainment. Another hospitable home in Washington belonged to the Howell Cobbs, and was described by Mrs. Clay as a "rendezvous of the epicurean as well as the witty and intellectual." [6]

Toombs' new political home, the historic Senate chamber, was a small semicircular room topped by a low half-domed ceiling. Ionic columns supported a modest Senate gallery. The open fires lent an atmosphere of conviviality and comfort to the surroundings. On cold days many senators made frequent trips to the burning hickory logs, "more interested in the state of the fires than in any State of the Union." [7] The Senate was distinctly a "black broadcloth assemblage, the cut of the coat being a long frock." [8] It possessed more dignity than the House, and maintained a sense of decorum which the larger branch of Congress on the other side of the Great Rotunda lacked. Both houses in 1854, however, exhibited an informality which impressed German immigrant and scholar Carl Schurz, who later wrote:

[4]Toombs to ——— (?), August 27, 1857, in private collection of Toombs letters in possession of Dr. E. Merton Coulter, Athens, Ga.; hereafter cited as Toombs Letters, Coulter Collection; J. L. Erwin, Judge of Desha County, Ark., to author, January 8, 1963.

[5]Nevins, *Ordeal of the Union*, II, 53.

[6]Mrs. Virginia Clay-Clopton (Clement C. Clay), *A Belle of the Fifties* . . . (New York, 1904), 29, 86.

[7]Christian F. Eckloff, *Memoirs of a Senate Page, 1855–1859*, ed. Percival G. Melbourne (New York, 1909), 6.

[8]*Ibid.*

There was an air of genuine naturalness about the looks, the bearing, and the conduct of the members as well as of the proceedings—no artificially put-on dignity; commotion enough, but little affected furor, except with some Southerners, the business being done without much restraint of logic or method. The congressman with bushy chin whiskers, wearing a black dress coat and a satin vest all day, a big quid of tobacco in his mouth, as in these days we sometimes see him as a comic figure on the stage, was then still a well-known type on the floor of the Senate and the House. There was much tobacco chewing with its accompaniments, and much lounging with tilting of chairs, and elevation of feet on desks—much more than there is now in the same places; but then those things seemed more natural, and less offensive than they do now. There were also more evidences of a liberal consumption of intoxicants. I do not mean to say that there were not men of refined presence and bearing in the two houses. There were, indeed, not a few; but the majority struck me as rather easygoing and careless of appearances.

Listening to running debates and to set speeches, I was astonished at the facility of expression which almost everybody seemed to command. The language may not always have been elegant or even grammatically correct; it may sometimes have been blunt and rough; but it ordinarily flowed on without any painful effort, and there was no hemming and hawing.[9]

Such an arena was tailor-made for the convivial, glib, and sometimes sartorially careless Robert Toombs. He immediately found a home in it.

There were no towering figures in the Senate when Toombs became a member. Calhoun, Webster, and Clay were gone, and Toombs through his long and able service in the House was able to assume equal rank with his new colleagues. Among them were: the Little Giant from Illinois, Stephen A. Douglas, whose sentences, "clear-cut, direct, positive . . . went straight to the mark like bullets, and sometimes like cannon-balls, tearing and crashing";[10] the tall, handsome, and arrogant Charles Sumner of Massachusetts; the "slim, wiry figure, the thin, sallow face, the overhanging eyebrows, and the muffled voice of Seward [of New York]";[11] tough, hard-working Ben Wade and the stately Salmon P. Chase of Ohio; John Bell, a man of moderation as befitted a senator from the border state of Tennessee; the smooth, sophisticated Louisianian,

[9]Carl Schurz, *The Reminiscences of Carl Schurz* (New York, 1907–1908), II, 29.
[10]*Ibid.*, 30.
[11]*Ibid.*, 33.

Judah P. Benjamin, whom listening to was "like listening to music . . .";[12] and later, Jefferson Davis of Mississippi, with whom Toombs had already broken a lance.

On the day Toombs belatedly took his seat, January 23, 1854, a bill was introduced in the Senate by Douglas (chairman of the committee of territories) which was to result in the destruction of the Whig party, the birth of the Republican party, and a re-kindling of sectional controversy climaxing in secession and civil war. Douglas' measure called for the organization of two new territories, Kansas and Nebraska, with the question of slavery being left to the territorial inhabitants. The bill specifically called for the repeal of the Missouri Compromise restriction barring slavery north of 36°30' in the Louisiana Territory, declaring it to be incompatible with the non-intervention principle of the Compromise of 1850. A multiplicity of purposes has been suggested for the Little Giant's sponsorship of the Nebraska bill: his presidential ambitions and the need for Southern political support; the pro-motion of a transcontinental railroad west from Chicago with the accompanying enhancement of his real estate in the Chicago area; and the realization that this area of the country needed to be opened for settlement, with "popular sovereignty" being the best solution for determining the status of slavery.[13]

Southern congressmen lined up almost solidly behind the bill, as a furor erupted in the North over the proposed violation of a "sacred compact" (the Missouri Compromise) between the sections. Toombs presided over a caucus of Southern Whig senators which met in worried session after the *National Intelligencer,* considered the Whig voice in Washington, had announced its opposition to the Douglas measure. Fearing that misrepresentation might result from the paper's stand, the senators agreed that George E. Badger of North Carolina, who had the floor, should the next day announce in the Senate that the Southern Whigs were united in favor of the bill.[14]

Toombs years later remarked that had he been able to return

[12]Eckloff, *Memoirs,* 56.

[13]Nevins, *Ordeal of the Union,* II, 100–107; Avery Craven, *The Coming of the Civil War* (New York, 1942), 326–32.

[14]*Congressional Globe,* 33rd Cong., 1st Sess., Appendix 755–56. Senator John Bell of Tennessee, who was to vote against the bill, several months later became involved with Toombs in a nasty little debate over just what had happened at this caucus. Toombs contended that Bell was there and raised no objection to the action taken. Bell denied that any such thing had happened while he was present, *ibid.,* 756–77.

to Washington at the beginning of the session, he would have "crushed the scheme [particularly the repeal of the Missouri Compromise] at its first proposal." [15] Such a course was frought with danger, he thought, because it reopened the controversy over slavery which had been buried in the Compromise of 1850.[16] This may well have been hindsight on his part, for on February 3 he wrote a friend that there could be no doubt "as to the propriety and policy of repealing the Missouri compromise." He denied that any compact had been entered into in 1820, for that measure had been carried primarily by Southern votes without much Northern support. The Compromise of 1850 was, on the other hand, a true compact supported by a majority of both parties and both sections. Its principle of popular sovereignty offered the only possible solution to the dangerous question of slavery in the territories.[17]

On January 24, the day after the presentation of the Nebraska bill, there appeared in the press an article entitled "Appeal of the Independent Democrats in Congress to the People of the United States." Designed by its author, Salmon P. Chase, to arouse widespread Northern fears, it bitterly denounced the measure as a violation of a compact, a betrayal of Northern rights, and a scheme to exclude free soilers from a vast area of the West.[18] The "Appeal" and Douglas' subsequent attack on it opened up one of the most heated debates in congressional history. Out of it came a grouping of all the antislavery elements into a new political organization, the Republican party.

Toombs entered the debate on February 23 with his maiden Senate speech. He built it on four main points: that the Nebraska bill was constitutional and consistent with the true policy of the government; that popular sovereignty was the wisest disposition of the slavery issue; that the Missouri Compromise was neither constitutional nor a compact; and that the founding fathers did not intend that slavery be limited, restrained, and finally abolished as had been asserted in recent speeches. It will be remembered that the bill allowed the territorial inhabitants to determine the status of slavery. Toombs chose to regard this as meaning when a constitution was being drawn up immediately prior to statehood. This

[15]John C. Reed, *The Brothers' War* (Boston, 1905), 262.
[16]Phillips, *Toombs*, 119–20.
[17]Toombs to W. W. Burwell, February 3, 1854, in Phillips (ed.), *Correspondence*, 342.
[18]*Congressional Globe*, 33rd Cong., 1st Sess., 281–82; New York *Times*, January 24, 1854.

was "popular sovereignty" as opposed to "squatter sovereignty" which allowed the decision on slavery to be made at any time during a territory's existence. Obviously if squatter sovereignty were followed, Southerners and their slaves could be excluded immediately from a territory and free-soil status guaranteed when statehood was assumed. There were, then, marked differences of opinion on this point among the supporters of the bill, but its general phraseology allowed each to interpret it as he wished, and the desire for passage kept the troublesome matter swept under the rug.[19]

Toombs' stand now was the same as it had been in 1850—that it was the duty of the government to protect the right of persons with their property to enter freely and enjoy a territory until such time as the territory assumed the sovereignty of statehood. At that time, the state could mold its own institutions as it saw fit.[20]

The Missouri Compromise was unconstitutional, Toombs said, because in prohibiting slavery north of 36°30' in the Louisiana Territory, the principle of the equality of states had been violated. No compromise had been involved, since only a minority of Northern congressmen had approved it. Despite contrary assertions, the history of the United States since its earliest years showed a continuous recognition of the institution of slavery, Toombs continued.

Toombs' speech was hailed with pleasure by the Democratic Athens *Southern Banner*, which called on all Southern Whigs to disengage themselves from the "foul and loathsome alliance with the Sewards, Greeleys and other Northern Whigs" and close ranks with the Democratic party for united support of the Nebraska bill. It twitted Toombs about being a recent convert to popular sovereignty after denouncing it bitterly in the 1848 presidential election campaign. A close examination of Toombs' speeches shows, however, that he had opposed *squatter* and not *popular* sovereignty, although the refinement then was not as clear as he later made it.[21]

The New York *Times*, anti-Toombs since his break with the Whig party, noted that he had spurned Senators Seward and Sum-

[19]*Congressional Globe*, 33rd Cong., 1st Sess., Appendix, 346–51; Cole, *Whig Party*, 288–92.
[20]*Congressional Globe*, 33rd Cong., 1st Sess., Appendix, 347.
[21]Athens *Southern Banner*, March 9, 1854. See pp. 49–50 for his 1848 declarations.

ner, Nebraska bill opponents, when they had attempted to congratulate him on the completion of this his first speech in the Senate. The usually moderate *Times* exploded:

> The conduct of Mr. Toombs in this instance, is that of the class of politicians to which he belongs. The ultra pro-slavery propagandists of the South uniformly resent all opposition to their projects as a personal affront. They no more recognize the right of a Northern man to hold and express opinions on Slavery different from theirs, than they do the right of a slave on their plantations to resist their commands. They are intolerant, domineering and insolent, not occasionally nor by accident,—but habitually and on principle. . . . It is simply bringing the habits of the plantation into the Senate Chamber. It is the slave-driver's lash,—differing a little in shape, and applied to Northern white men, instead of Southern slaves:—but wielded for the same end, the enforcement of their will, and by essentially the same means,— brute force instead of justice and reason.[22]

Early on the morning of March 4 the Senate, after a continuous session of seventeen hours, voted thirty-seven to fourteen in favor of the Kansas-Nebraska bill. It then adjourned at 4:55 A.M. for a three day rest. Toombs was absent because of sickness, but his colleague, Senator Dawson, noted for the record that his vote would have been in the affirmative had he been present. Only two Southerners voted against the bill—John Bell of Tennessee and Sam Houston of Texas. Bell considered the measure mischief-making and of no practical value to the South, for the Kansas-Nebraska area was not suited to slavery; Houston regarded the Missouri Compromise provision a compact which he could not vote to break.

In the House the struggle was fierce and the vote close, but due in large measure to the adroit leadership of Stephens the bill carried by a vote of 113 to 110.[23] The Whig party was now dead. In May, Chase of Ohio, a Whig, declared that the Southern members of the party by banding together in support of the bill had declared war on the institutions of the North. "After this," he said, "I hope to hear no more from them of national parties. They have by their own act rendered such a thing impossible." [24]

The turmoil was now transferred from the halls of Congress to

[22]New York *Times*, March 6, 1854.
[23]Johnston and Browne, *Stephens*, 277; Stephens to J. W. Duncan, May 26, 1854, in Phillips (ed.), *Correspondence*, 345.
[24]*Congressional Globe*, 33rd Cong., 1st Sess., Appendix, 764.

the territory of Kansas where a struggle and later civil war between free-soil and proslavery forces ensued. "Bleeding Kansas"
became a running sore which Congress could not heal as the nation
drifted ominously toward still more tragic events.

In July Toombs joined with other Southerners in the Senate
to block a House-passed Homestead bill granting 160 acres free
to settlers after five years of occupation and cultivation. The general
feeling was that such a measure would drain population out of
the South, cause a deficiency in the treasury that the heavy tax-
paying South would have to make up, and encourage the settlement
of free-soilers in the public domain. Toombs stated that the public
lands were held by Congress in trust for all the people, and that
free, individual allotments were in violation of this. He preferred
a scheme by which a proportionate share might go to every American citizen, as had been done for state lands in Georgia through the
lottery system.[25] Toombs' proposal was obviously impractical, as
he doubtless knew. The main thing was the defeat of the House bill,
and this was accomplished.

The interim period between sessions of Congress found Toombs
in his multiple roles as lawyer, planter, and businessman. His letters
at this time, however, reveal him in a new and unhappy one—that
of a worried father. His daughter Lou, who had been ill for
months, was not improving. Furthermore his daughter Sallie was
courting, and her suitor was not altogether pleasing to the senator.
Toombs wrote his wife from his Stewart County plantation that
they had to find out more about him. "There are some things in
the stock of people I do not like but if I was certain he was all right
himself I should care less for that—Sallie would be very unhappy
with the wrong sort of a man, but," said the father resignedly, "I
suppose she is but little inclined to be advised on such a matter." [26]

The Toombses were called home from Washington before
the close of the second session of the Thirty-third Congress by the
steady decline of Louisa. Toombs had spoken only once up to this
time, opposing unsuccessfully an expansion of the pension system
for widows of army and navy officers. He said he would not have
voted for the original system which he termed a "vicious one" and
certainly would not support any extension of it.[27]

[25]Ibid., 1210–12.
[26]Toombs to wife, November 1, 1854, in Robert Toombs Papers, University
of Georgia.
[27]Congressional Globe, 33rd Cong., 1st Sess., 94.

When Louisa seemed on her way to recovery, Toombs went back to Washington where on February 24 he spoke against several internal improvements bills. Bad news again summoned him home. He was with his daughter when she died on March 4, 1855.[28]

Linton Stephens penned a touching memorial to Louisa Toombs in a letter to his half brother Alec on March 8: "She was so good, so intelligent, so artless, so innocently gay and cheerful of spirit, that it was impossible to know her well without being touched with a tender and a most kindly regard for her. She had the blended virtues of her father and mother, and added a chaplet of gracefulness and quietness, all of her own. Poor Lou! poor Lou!" [29]

Robert Toombs had been without national party affiliation since December, 1850, when the Constitutional Union party had been formed to carry Georgia for the principles of the Compromise of 1850. He had been without any party affiliation since August, 1852, when the Constitutional Union party was officially dissolved amid the confusion of the presidential campaign that saw the election of Franklin Pierce. Without a political base, Toombs had tended to cooperate with the Democrats and late in 1855 closed ranks with them along with Stephens.

Other former Whigs found such an affiliation with old foes repugnant. Some of them drifted into the Know-Nothing or American party, which was gaining momentum on the political scene. The Know-Nothings had originated out of native hostility to the largely Catholic immigration of the 1840's from Ireland and Germany. Operating on a platform endorsing the maintenance of a Protestant America against malevolent foreign influences, various secret organizations had coalesced into a national group which went into politics in the early 1850's. In Georgia, the Know-Nothings movement was initiated in 1854, and by 1855 was well-established enough to be a decisive factor in state politics. Several former Whig newspapers endorsed "Sam" as the party was called, among them the Augusta *Chronicle*, longtime Toombs' mouthpiece.[30]

Toombs was never seriously inclined toward the Know-Nothings, although he spewed forth their type of language and reflected their attitudes briefly in 1853 as he tried to rally the state for guberna-

---

[28]*Ibid.*, 926; James Hillhouse Alexander to Edward Porter Alexander, February 24, 1855, in Edward Porter Alexander Papers.

[29]James D. Waddell (ed.), *Biographical Sketch of Linton Stephens, . . . Containing a Selection of His Letters, Speeches, State Papers, Etc.* (Atlanta, 1877), 123.

[30]Montgomery, *Cracker Parties*, 126–28, 136–38.

torial candidate Charles Jenkins against Democrat Herschel V. Johnson. He railed against the foreign influences in the Pierce administration, calling it "an adjunct of *'German Jews, Red Republicans, and Infidel Scotch.'* " [31]

If there were ever any doubt about his attitude, he cleared it away in a long letter on June 6, 1855, to the editor of the Columbus *Times and Sentinel.* There were many reasons why he was opposed to the Know-Nothing party. It was a secret society in a nation where freedom of speech and liberty of the press were cardinal principles. It required members to carry out party decrees whether approved or not. It promoted religious intolerance. It was a divisive force in Southern politics.

> The true policy of the South is to unite; to lay aside all party divisions. Whigs, Democrats and Know Nothings should come together and combine for the common safety. If we are wise enough to do this, to present one unbroken column of fifteen states united for the preservation of their own rights, the Constitution and the Union, and to uphold and support that noble band of patriots at the North who have stood for the Constitution and the right against the tempest of fanaticism, folly and treason which has assailed them, we shall succeed. We shall then have conquered a peace which will be enduring, and by means which will not invite further aggression.[32]

In 1851 Toombs and his family had planned a trip to Europe, but it had to be postponed because of politics. He had never given up the idea and particularly now, with the death of his daughter, he wanted to get away. He told his wife he wanted relief from the "thousand harrassments [*sic*] of business" and looked forward to the pleasure of "quiet & uninterrupted strolling of you, & I & Sallie over the hills & plains of Europe, where no body knows us. . . ." I wish we could take "our lost darling child," wrote the bereaved father. "Thank God there was rest in heaven." [33]

Definite plans were now made. Toombs worked hard to wind up his law cases, "pretty much speaking all day & studying all night & that too without the benefit of specks which I begin to need," he wrote his wife from Milledgeville where court was in session. He said that he was being avoided by old Whigs who had

---

[31]*Ibid.,* 127.

[32]Toombs to T. Lomax, June 6, 1855, in Phillips (ed.), *Correspondence,* 353.

[33]Toombs to his wife, April 28, 1855, in Robert Toombs Papers, University of Georgia.

joined the Know-Nothings because he had spoken "not softly of the miserable wretches who expect to govern a great country like this with imbecility if they can only cover it with secrecy." [34]

On June 6 the Toombs party, consisting of the senator and his wife, daughter Sallie, son-in-law and widower, Felix Alexander, and George H. Shorter, apparently a friend of Alexander's, sailed from Boston. Shopping and sightseeing in London and on the continent were the prime activities abroad. Toombs was much impressed by the "grandeur and magnificence" of London. He attended several sessions of Parliament. Although he heard, among others, the great Palmerston in action, he told Stephens that the "speaking was poor, very poor, the matter commonplace, and the style perfectly genteel but perfectly insipid." [35] He enjoyed Westminster Abbey and the Tower of London, in each of which he spent a day. The channel crossing from France to England proved a harrowing experience for Toombs. Three hours in the worst sea he ever saw put him prostrate and completely out of action, with "one steward bringing me basin after basin." [36]

By the time Toombs returned to Georgia, the decks had been cleared for action in the governor's race. The Democrats had nominated Herschel V. Johnson; the Know-Nothing or American party as it was now being called, Garnett Andrews; and a third party, the Temperance party, Basil H. Overby. Toombs supported Johnson and Democratic candidates for the legislature. He did not actively campaign, but his Democratic leanings embroiled him in a vitriolic name-calling contest with the Augusta *Chronicle*, American booster. The trouble began when Toombs called the *Chronicle* to task for opening its columns to the abuse of Stephens (an anti-Know-Nothing like Toombs) by one of its correspondents. The newspaper concluded a bitter exchange by commenting that Toombs was acting in very unseemly fashion for a man "who, for fifteen years, has courted our friendship, and during that whole period, has never omitted a convenient opportunity to seek our companionship! Poltroonery could not attain a lower depth." [37]

On October 1, Johnson was elected governor, garnering 53,478

[34]Toombs to his wife, May 18, 1855, in Robert Toombs Papers, University of Georgia.
[35]Toombs to Stephens, June 21, 1855, in Phillips (ed.), *Correspondence*, 354.
[36]Toombs to his wife, June [actually July] 8, 1855, in Robert Toombs Papers, University of Georgia; Stovall, *Toombs*, 125–28.
[37]Augusta *Chronicle*, October 3, September 22, 1855.

votes to 43,222 for Andrews and 6,284 for Overby. In spite of Toombs' known preference for Johnson, Wilkes County was carried by Andrews (a native son) by 349 to 286. The state legislature was substantially Democratic.[38]

In November Toombs attended a fusion meeting of Anti-Know Nothings and Democrats at the capitol in Milledgeville, and made public his conversion to the Democratic party. He had seen the light, he said in a speech of an hour and a half, during the Kansas-Nebraska bill struggle when many Northern Democratic senators had stood faithfully by the South. Duty and patriotism dictated the course he was now taking.[39] The benediction was pronounced by the *Chronicle* when it intoned: "For the future, we shall regard these gentlemen [Stephens was right behind Toombs] as Democrats, and as Democrats we shall treat them." [40]

Toombs was ill with a bad cough and rheumatism in early December, and consequently his return to Congress was delayed. On the eve of his departure he wrote a friend that he would leave home "with great reluctance a little afraid of Washington City climate & caring hardly the snap of my fingers for the course of events. The free-soilers are already whipped & the [presidential] contest I think will only be one of 'spoils' next year in which I do not feel any concern." [41]

Before settling down to work in Washington in the Thirty-fourth Congress, Toombs journeyed to Boston, one of the strongholds of abolitionism, and delivered a lecture on slavery in Tremont Temple on January 24. 1856. He was but one of several well-known public figures who were participating in a series of lectures in the Massachusetts capital designed to present various shades of opinion on the explosive issue.[42] Before a large audience, Toombs spoke from a prepared text in a restrained manner, being "much calmer, and cooler than in his excited harangues in Congress, or on the Georgia stump," according to a New York newspaper.[43] He spoke around two main points: the constitutional

[38]Milledgeville *Federal Union*, October 2, 8, 1855; Augusta *Chronicle*, October 7, 1855.

[39]Milledgeville *Federal Union*, November 13, 1855.

[40]Augusta *Chronicle*, November 15, 1855.

[41]Toombs to Thomas W. Thomas, December 17, 1855, in Robert Toombs Papers, Duke University.

[42]Laura E. Richards (ed.), *Letters and Journals of Samuel Gridley Howe* (Boston, 1909), II, 403–04.

[43]New York *Express*, n.d., quoted in Augusta *Chronicle*, January 30, 1856.

powers and duties of the Federal government relative to domestic slavery; and the influence of slavery upon the slave and American society. In precise, analytical fashion, he showed that slavery was an established fact at the time of independence and that the Constitution clearly recognized its existence. There was not a single clause in the Constitution which gave Congress the right to "abolish, limit, restrain, or in any other manner to impair the system of slavery in the United States. . . ." On the contrary, he said, every clause dealing with slavery "was intended either to *increase* it, to *strengthen* it, or to *protect* it." [44] Toombs stated that Congress did not have the constitutional power to exclude slavery from the territories, a principle affirmed by the Supreme Court a year later. In fact, it was the duty of the Federal government to protect the common enjoyment of the territories by all citizens of the United States until its authority was superseded by a state constitution.

Fundamental to Toombs' consideration of the institution of slavery *per se* was his firm belief, and that of most Southerners, in the superiority of the white race. When the African and Caucasian coexisted in the same society, the subordination of the African was the "normal, necessary, and proper condition, and that such subordination is the condition best calculated to promote the highest interest and the greatest happiness of both races, and consequently of the whole society. . . ." Toombs was not concerned with the question of whether the African should have been removed from his home and placed in bondage. England and the Christian world had already made that an accomplished fact for the Southern states at the time of their independence. It was their duty to devise a practical *modus vivendi* for the various elements of society which would secure the greatest happiness for all concerned. As Africans were "unfit to be trusted with political power, incapable as freemen of securing their own happiness, or promoting the public prosperity," their slave status was recognized and perpetuated. Toombs pointed out the numerous benefits to the slave in the Southern states: protection of life, provision for food, clothing, and shelter, and benevolent treatment when old or infirm. Although not paid in wages, the slave was compensated in kind, "the necessaries and comforts of life," which frequently meant greater compensation

[44]*A Lecture Delivered in the Tremont Temple, Boston, Massachusetts, on the 24th January, 1856 by R. Toombs* (Pamphlet in Emory University Library).

than the free laborer received. Thus the perennial conflict between labor and capital over the division of the earning of labor was avoided. Toombs recounted some of the charges frequently made against the peculiar institution, among them the denial of religious instruction and education to slaves, the non-recognition of slave marriages, and the separation of families. There was need for improvement in these areas, he said, and some states were taking remedial steps.

Toombs denied that slavery was a wasteful, unprofitable system of labor. The wealth and productivity of the Southern states in agriculture belied this. Behind the profitability of slavery was the fact that the "labor of the country is united with and protected by its capital, directed by the educated and intelligent, secured against its own weaknesses, waste, and folly, associated in such form as to give the greatest efficiency in production, and the least cost of maintenance."

Toombs' conclusion presented a near-Utopian South. His Massachusetts listeners heard him say:

No stronger evidence of what progress society may make with domestic slavery can be desired, than that which the present condition of the slaveholding States present. For near twenty years, foreign and domestic enemies of their institutions have labored by pen and speech to excite discontent among the white race, and insurrections among the black. These efforts have shaken the national government to its foundations, and bursted the bonds of Christian unity among the churches of the land; yet the objects of their attacks—these States— have scarcely felt the shock. In surveying the whole civilized world the eye rests not on a single spot where all classes of society are so well content with their social system, or have greater reason to be so, than in the slaveholding States of this Union. Stability, progress, order, peace, content, prosperity, reign through out our borders. Not a single soldier is to be found in our widely-extended domain to overawe or protect society. The desire for organic change nowhere manifests itself. Within less than seventy years, out of five feeble colonies, with less than one and a half millions of inhabitants, have emerged fourteen republican States, containing nearly ten millions of inhabitants, rich, powerful, educated, moral, refined, prosperous, and happy; each with republican governments adequate to the protection of public liberty and private rights, which are cheerfully obeyed, supported, and upheld by all classes of society. With a noble system of internal improvements penetrating almost every neighborhood, stimulating and rewarding the industry of our people; with moral and intellectual surpassing physical improvements; with churches, schoolhouses, and colleges daily multiplying throughout the land, bringing education and religious instruction to the homes of all the people, they may safely challenge the admiration of the civilized world. None of this great improvement and progress have been even aided by the federal government; we have neither sought from it protection for our private pursuits, nor appropriations for our public improvements. They have been effected by the unaided individual efforts of an enlightened, moral, energetic, and religious people. Such is our social system, and such our condition under it. Its political wisdom is vindicated in its effects on society; its morality by the practices of the patriarchs and the teachings of the apostles; we submit it to the judgment of mankind, with the firm conviction that the adoption of no other system under our circumstances would have exhibited the individual man, bond or free, in a higher development, or society in a happier civilization.[45]

Throughout the speech, Toombs' audience remained remarkably polite, occasionally applauding, a few times hissing, but for the most part sitting in "respectful silence." At the end, there were three cheers for the senator from Georgia. There seemed to be a "general expression of approbation towards the lecturer, not of his opinions, but of his candor and bearing," reported the New York *Herald.*[46]

From championing the cause of slavery in Boston, Toombs returned to Washington to become an ardent supporter of another cause. In 1855 Congress, in a burst of reform, had authorized the creation of a fifteen member naval board to inquire into the efficiency of naval officers. Those found incompetent were, after approval by the secretary of the navy and the President, to be dropped from the rolls or put on a reserve list and made ineligible for further promotion. The board performed its task, according to the New York *Times,* "with a promptness and decision which have rarely been equaled and never excelled since the palmy days of the French Republic, when the guillotine was never permitted to stand still." [47] Out of some five hundred officers, 230 involuntarily underwent a change in status. The *Times* calculated that a brief twelve minutes and forty seconds, on the average, was spent on each case.

Prompted by the lamentations and petitions of some of the affected officers and the revelation that the board had neither kept a journal of the proceedings nor given reasons for its decisions,

[45]*Ibid.*
[46]Quoted in Milledgeville *Federal Union,* February 5, 1856.
[47]New York *Times,* January 18, 1858.

several senators including Toombs swung into action. The *Times* found it a pleasant and refreshing sight to see sectional partisanship, so rampant in Congress, thrust aside for the moment. Toombs based his attack on two themes—that the President could not have reviewed the decisions of the board as he was required to do since no records were kept, and that each officer should have been acquainted with the reasons for his dismissal. In a gallery-pleasing speech on February 13, Toombs called for the petitioners to be brought face to face with their accusers. This was a principle, he contended, which had been "engrafted at Runnymede into the charter of British liberties; again and again affirmed and defended by our remote ancestors; engrafted on all of our constitutions and bills of rights and is part and parcel of every living, breathing, American freeman." [48] If these officers, he concluded, were not so treated, he preferred to see every ship in the Navy "towed out into the broad Atlantic, and with their flags nailed to their masts, and with every sail set, given 'to the god of winds, the lightning, and gale.' " [49]

In spite of a stout defense of the board's action led by Senator Stephen R. Mallory, chairman of the Naval Affairs Committee and sponsor of the controversial bill which created the retirement board,[50] Congress followed the demands of the reformers. An act was passed in January, 1857, which permitted those who had been dropped by the board to request an investigation by a court of inquiry, leading to possible restoration to active duty.[51]

Apart from his attempt to see justice done for a portion of the United States Navy, Toombs spent most of his time in the Thirty-fourth Congress on the recurring and troublesome Kansas issue. Soon after Douglas' bill became law in 1854, immigrants in substantial numbers began to move into Kansas. To some extent this was normal frontier expansion. Unfortunately, however, in the violently partisan atmosphere of the day, the rush of settlers became to a large extent an adjunct of the sectional struggle. As the decision over slavery was left to the inhabitants of the territory,

[48]*Congressional Globe*, 34th Cong., 1st Sess., 408.

[49]*Ibid.*, 409. Toombs spoke at some length on May 1 as he reviewed the history of the proceedings and reiterated his charges of unfairness, *ibid.*, Appendix, 506–12.

[50]Joseph T. Durkin, *Stephen R. Mallory: Confederate Navy Chief* (Chapel Hill, 1954), 62, 66, 74–83.

[51]*Congressional Globe*, 34th Cong., 3rd Sess., Appendix, 115–18.

a race developed between North and South to see which could populate and thereby control Kansas. Nebraska, it was recognized, would inevitably be free because climate and soil were not conducive to slavery. The North had all the advantages: a larger, more mobile population; more capital; and easier avenues of travel. From the beginning the free-soil population outnumbered the pro-slavery settlers. But events were not allowed to take their natural course, to the distress of Kansas and the nation.

In March of 1855, elections were held for a territorial legislature. Several thousand Missourians, called by Horace Greeley "Border Ruffians," crossed over into Kansas and helped vote in a proslavery majority. The legislature proceeded to adopt the slave code of Missouri and to limit officeholding to proslavery men. Angered, the free-soilers set up a rival government at Topeka and petitioned Congress for statehood. Kansas trembled on the brink of violence.[52]

In January, 1856, President Pierce in a special message to Congress, denounced the Topeka movement as unconstitutional, threw the weight of his office behind the proslavery territorial legislature, and declared he would use force for the preservation of law and order. On February 28, Toombs upheld the President's hand in debate, calling his pronouncements wise, just, and commendable to patriots everywhere. With remarkable candor, Toombs stated that he believed Kansas would eventually be free. But until that time, the settlers of Kansas should be allowed to legislate for themselves, "unawed and uncontrolled," as envisioned by the principles of the Kansas-Nebraska bill. At all times, they should be protected "against insurrection from within and invasion from without." This meant, of course, Toombs' support for the Southern-oriented government of Kansas which Pierce had recognized.[53]

Stephens called Toombs' speech great, "one of his powerful blasts that brought down the galleries in applause." Toombs was the only senator, he said, who had brought applause from the spectators thus far in the session. "He is," continued Stephens, "unquestionably the ablest debater and most eloquent man now in that body. For originality of thought and power of expression he has no equal." [54]

[52]Alice Nichols, *Bleeding Kansas* (New York, 1954), 7–92.
[53]*Congressional Globe*, 34th Cong., 1st Sess., Appendix, 115–18.
[54]Stephens to Thomas W. Thomas, February 29, 1856, Alexander H. Stephens Papers, Duke University.

The debate on Kansas continued through the spring. Although it was frequently bitter, the Senate chamber was relatively free from personal insult and bad taste until Charles Sumner arose on May 19 to deliver a speech he later entitled "The Crime Against Kansas." [55] The Massachusetts Brahmin was probably the most unpopular man in the Senate because of his enormous arrogance and his penchant for sharp invective, particularly against Southern leaders. On this day and the next one, Sumner reached a high-water mark in outrageous language as he assaulted and insulted Southern society in general and Senators Andrew P. Butler of South Carolina and James M. Mason of Virginia in particular. Douglas of Illinois, author of the Kansas-Nebraska bill, was also castigated in an offensive manner.

On May 22, Congressman Preston Brooks of South Carolina, Butler's nephew, approached Sumner, who was seated at his desk in a nearly empty Senate chamber, and after briefly accusing him of insulting his state and kinsman, beat him over the head with a cane until Sumner fell to the floor. It was all over very quickly. Toombs was one of the witnesses to Brooks' attack. A few days later when the affair was under discussion in the Senate, he stated that he had not attempted to interfere or give assistance to Sumner. Furthermore, he had remarked at the time that he had approved of Sumner's caning.[56] Toombs' almost casual recital of what had transpired evoked an emotional response from Ben Wade, a staunch Ohio free-soiler who said:

I am here in a pretty lean minority; there is not, perhaps, more than one fifth part of the Senate who have similar opinions with my own, and those are very unpopular here; but when I hear it stated on the floor of the Senate that an assassin-like cowardly attack has been made upon a man unarmed, having no power to defend himself, who was stricken down with the strong hand and almost murdered, and that such attacks are approved by Senators, it becomes a question of some interest to us all, and especially to those who are in the minority. It is very true that a brave man may not be able to defend himself against such an attack. A brave man may be overpowered by numbers on this floor; but, sir, overpowered or not, live or die, I will vindicate the right and liberty of debate and freedom of discussion upon this floor, so long as I live. If the principle now announced here is to prevail, let us come armed for the combat; and although you are four to one, I am here

[55]*Congressional Globe*, 34th Cong., 1st Sess., Appendix, 529–44.
[56]*Congressional Globe*, 34th Cong., 1st Sess., 1305.

to meet you. God knows a man can die in no better cause than in vindicating the rights of debate on this floor. . . .[57]

The signs of the times were indeed ominous—not only did the cultured Sumner engage in disgusting epithets and the chivalrous and battle-courageous Brooks initiate a sneak attack, but Toombs condoned Brooks and Wade apparently found no fault with Sumner.

Brooks resigned his seat in the House but was shortly reelected while being flooded with canes from Southern admirers. Sumner remained out of the Senate for over three years, in the Northern mind a martyr to the barbarity of the Southern slave society. Toombs remained convinced that Sumner had justly reaped what he had sown. Jocularly he wrote George W. Crawford at the end of the month that the "Yankees seem greatly excited about Sumner's flogging. They are afraid the practice may become general and many of [their] heads already feel sore. Sumner takes a beating badly. He is said to be ill, tho' I don't believe it." [58]

In June the major party conventions were held, the Democrats meeting in Cincinnati and the fledgling but confident Republicans in Philadelphia. In the background was the eruption of civil war in Kansas, touched off by the "sack" of Lawrence by a proslavery group on May 20 and the cold-blooded murder of five proslavery men and boys on Pottawatomie Creek on May 25. The Democratic convention chose James Buchanan of Pennsylvania in preference to President Pierce, who was willing to run again, and Stephen A. Douglas whose authorship of the Nebraska bill now hung about his neck like a political albatross. Buchanan had been out of the country as ambassador to England during the struggle over Douglas' bill and thus was not a party to any of its partisanship or bitterness. Additionally, Buchanan's conservative views on slavery made him acceptable to the influential Southern bloc in the party. The platform upheld the Kansas-Nebraska Act and the general principles of popular sovereignty, although it did not spell out whether or not a territorial government could exclude slavery before the formation of a state government, a potentially dangerous issue.

[57]*Ibid.*
[58]Toombs to George W. Crawford, May 30, 1856, in Phillips (ed.), *Correspondence*, 365; George Fort Milton, *The Eve of Conflict: Stephen A. Douglas and the Needless War* (Boston, 1934), 236–37, suggests that Sumner's injuries were exaggerated.

Most of the Georgia Democrats preferred Pierce. Toombs did not appear to have had a strong leaning toward any candidate. He considered Buchanan and Douglas the favorites but had "too little interest to speculate upon so uncertain an event" as the nomination.[59] The Georgia delegates had stopped in Washington for a short while before proceeding to Cincinnati. Here along with distinguished Democrats Howell Cobb, Cass, Douglas, and John C. Breckinridge of Kentucky (to be nominated for the vice-presidency on the Buchanan ticket) they enjoyed dinner at the Toombs', who were famous for their often lavish hospitality. Toombs did not go to Cincinnati but spent the time in New York City on business.[60]

The Republicans passed over several party stalwarts, including Seward and Chase, and chose the glamorous John C. Frémont, noted Western explorer and soldier. Their platform called for a repeal of the Kansas-Nebraska Act, the admission of Kansas into the Union with its free-state constitution, and opposition to the expansion of slavery. Earlier in the year the Know-Nothing Party had nominated former President Millard Fillmore as its presidential candidate, but this was only a nominal distraction nationally to the main contest between Democrats and Republicans.

Back in Washington, the Democrats led by Douglas and Toombs tackled the problem of "Bleeding Kansas" again, hoping that a solution would cut down on the bumper political harvest the Republicans were reaping from it. On June 24, the Georgia senator introduced a bill which he hoped would provide a genuine test for determining the attitude of the inhabitants of Kansas toward slavery, thereby putting the matter at rest once and for all. He wanted to give the "professional agitators, and those whose business it is to mislead and delude the people, and madden their passions with false stories of wrongs and outrages, not one solitary inch of ground on which to stand."[61] Toombs' bill provided that a census of the population of Kansas be taken under the supervision of five commissioners appointed by the President; that all white male inhabitants over twenty-one who were bona fide residents

[59]Toombs to George W. Crawford, May 30, 1856, in Phillips (ed.), *Correspondence*, 365.
[60]Waddell (ed.), *Linton Stephens*, 124; Toombs to George W. Crawford, May 30, 1856, in Phillips (ed.), *Correspondence*, 365.
[61]*Congressional Globe*, 34th Cong., 1st Sess., 1438.

be registered as voters; that delegates to a constitutional convention be chosen by these voters in November; and that Congress admit Kansas into the Union immediately under the constitution, free or slave, drawn up by that body.[62]

On July 2, Toombs' bill passed the Senate 33 to 12, but not before some heated debate.[63] The Republicans, as was expected, lined up against it, basing their opposition in part on the untrustworthiness of President Pierce to carry out his part of the measure fairly. Toombs defended the President, saying what he himself did not fully believe, that "no truer, juster, more patriotic, more impartial, or more national man has ever succeeded to the chair of Washington than Franklin Pierce." [64] He scored Seward and Henry Wilson of Massachusetts for offering him a cartridge box after he had tendered them a pure and undefiled ballot box as the panacea for Kansas. He did not believe that they represented Northern public opinion, but if they did, he would not shrink from the challenge. "I am content to accept it whenever the North offers it." [65] He turned directly on Seward, fellow Union College graduate, with great bitterness, accusing him of an unprincipled quest for power through the promotion of treasonable and wicked sectional schemes. To be condemned by the New Yorker was "an honor to be coveted," said Toombs.[66]

Toombs was optimistic about the fate of his bill. He thought it would pass the House and in doing so settle the Kansas question in Congress forever. Even if it did not, it would help the Democrats North and South in the coming elections by making them champions of a "fair settlement." [67] The debate continued in the Senate after the measure had been approved. On July 9, Toombs engaged in a lengthy tussle with several free-soilers, including William P. Fessenden of Maine, Wilson, and Wade. He stuck to his oft-repeated declaration that his bill was simply a means of ascertaining the will of the majority of the people of Kansas, no more no less.[68] Toombs' stand was transparently honest and sincere, but

[62]*Ibid.*
[63]*Ibid.*, 805.
[64]*Ibid.*, 772.
[65]*Ibid.*, 770.
[66]*Ibid.*
[67]Toombs to William C. Rives, July 4, 1856, in William C. Rives Papers, Library of Congress.
[68]*Congressional Globe*, 34th Cong., 1st Sess., Appendix, 869–72.

his bill failed to get through the House of Representatives where the Republican strength was strategically placed. Whether it actually could have relieved some of the pressure of sectionalism bearing so dangerously on the body politic it would be difficult to say. But it certainly merited a try.

Toombs took an active part in the presidential campaign of 1856. He fired a heavy salvo at the Republicans in early July in a widely circulated letter to an Athens friend when he said: *"Our danger is not from abroad, it is at home. The election of Frémont would be the end of the Union, and ought to be. The object of Frémont's friends is the conquest of the South. I am content that they shall own us when they conquer us, but not before."* [69] The New York *Times,* a force for reasonableness in the North, found such statements irresponsible and dangerous. It answered the Georgian's belligerency by saying optimistically that if the American people could rid themselves of the "intermediation of turbulent and inflammatory demagogues, and by direct conference learn to understand each other fairly and frankly on this vexed question of Slavery, agitation of the subject would cease forever; and that so far from resisting the inauguration of Frémont the South would join cordially in his election." [70]

Before he left Washington to take the stump in Georgia for Buchanan, Toombs wrote Judge Thomas of Elberton that the "equality & safety & liberties of the South are indissolubly bound up in the defeat of both Fremont & Filmore." [71] Frémont, of course, stood no chance in any Southern state, but he might well win nationally if Fillmore could dilute Buchanan's strength in the South. So it was primarily the Know-Nothings against whom Toombs armed himself for battle.[72]

The Democratic canvas in Georgia was centered primarily around the theme of a divided South ensuring a Republican victory. It proved effective and served to draw a sizeable number of Know-Nothings into the Buchanan camp before the November election.[73] Toombs found himself as much on the defensive as the offensive, which was not surprising for a politician who had

[69]Quoted in New York *Times,* August 2, 1856.
[70]*Ibid.*
[71]Toombs to Judge Thomas, July 31, 1856, photocopy of original in Archives of Union College, Schenectady.
[72]*Ibid.*; Phillips, *Toombs,* 170.
[73]Montgomery, *Cracker Parties,* 168–84.

twice changed parties. In 1848, Toombs as a Whig had eulogized Fillmore, Taylor's vice-presidential running mate. In 1850 Fillmore's support of the Compromise of 1850 had drawn his warm praise. And in 1852, Toombs had pronounced Fillmore as eminently more acceptable as a Whig presidential candidate than General Winfield Scott. Now he was called on to destroy Fillmore. The Augusta *Chronicle*, former Whig and now American journal, had never forgiven Toombs for his defection from the party of Henry Clay. "Like an officer who makes up his mind to betray his soldiers and carry them over to the enemy, he conducted the old Whig guard through intricate defiles and over bogs and across streams and round and round, far away from their camp and arms, until the propitious moment arrived to deliver them up to the enemy." [74] The *Chronicle* kept up a constant barrage against its former friend, targeting mainly on what it dubbed his shameless inconsistency and untrustworthiness.[75]

On October 23, Toombs clashed in a memorable, open-air debate with Benjamin H. Hill, unsuccessful American congressional candidate in 1855 but probably the best talent in the party. Bearding the veteran in his home town, young Hill fought Toombs at least to a draw and in the opinion of some, "rode away with the laurels of the day." [76] Having no record to defend, Hill hammered away boldly at that of Toombs, calling him a political chameleon, a disunionist, and a traitor to the South for supporting the Kansas-Nebraska bill and its principle of squatter sovereignty. Toombs denied all of these assertions, while reaffirming the popular sovereignty interpretation of Douglas' bill which precluded any hostile action on slavery by territorial inhabitants until the assumption of statehood.[77]

Hill also tangled with Stephens and goaded him to such an extent that the emaciated congressman challenged him to a duel, which Hill declined.[78] Truly a new and formidable force had arisen in Georgia politics in the form of this brilliant and audacious young orator from La Grange.

[74]Augusta *Chronicle*, September 17, 1856.
[75]*Ibid.*, September 13, 14, October 22, 29, 1856.
[76]Stovall, *Toombs*, 152.
[77]*Ibid.*, 144–52; Augusta *Chronicle*, October 29, 1856.
[78]Stephens to Thomas W. Thomas, December 12, 1856, in Phillips (ed.), *Correspondence*, 384.

In November Buchanan carried Georgia by a vote of 56,597 to 42,394 over Fillmore.[79] Nationally, he defeated Frémont and Fillmore, but his popular vote was less than the combined total of his opponents. For the first time out, the Republicans had done remarkably well. The Union had been preserved, but the ominous portent of a strong, sectional party hung heavily in American politics.

Toombs waltzed through the last session of the Thirty-fourth Congress with a minimum of participation. With the Buchanan administration waiting in the wings for the March accession, there was not a great deal that could be accomplished, as was the case in most interregnums. He spoke infrequently; only in his eulogy of the recently deceased Preston Brooks did he become aroused and then to such an extent that he completely broke down. Stephens noted that this was the first time he had even seen his friend shed tears.[80] Toombs' emotional outburst was hinged on more than Brooks' demise, although he was apparently fond of the South Carolinian. The day before, he had heard of the death of Mrs. Linton Stephens, which had deeply affected him and had, perhaps, brought back painful memories of his departed daughter, Louisa, who had died only two years before.[81]

Before Toombs left Washington, he and Jefferson Davis were reconciled and their long standing estrangement dating back to 1853 ended.[82] It was the work of four mutual friends and fellow senators: Butler, Crittenden, Mason, and Thomas J. Rusk of Texas. In a formal little ritual on March 12 the antagonists received identical messages hand-carried to them in the Senate chamber, requesting affirmative answers within an hour to a plea for reconciliation—"that all past controversy shall be no more regarded by either of you—that when you meet, you shall receive, speak to, and treat each other as is common among gentlemen." The proposal was agreed to in writing by both men.[83] The New York Times pronounced the hatchet burying a "treaty of alliance, offensive and defensive, in behalf of the cause of fire eaterism and extreme sectional views." [84]

[79]Augusta *Chronicle*, December 2, 1856.
[80]Johnston and Browne, *Stephens*, 325; *Congressional Globe*, 34th Cong., 3rd Sess., 500–501.
[81]Johnston and Browne, *Stephens*, 325.
[82]See pp. 91–92.
[83]Milledgeville *Federal Union*, March 24, 1857.
[84]New York *Times*, March 18, 1857.

In late spring and early summer Toombs, accompanied by a small party which included his wife's brother and Felix Alexander, made the long trip to Texas to check on his land holdings. Traveling by way of Memphis and New Orleans, he purchased land in the Mississippi delta before moving on to the plains.[85] Stovall states that Toombs had a dramatic parley at Fort Worth with some squatters who had illegally moved in on some of his land, and succeeded in obtaining their agreement to buy what they occupied at fair prices.[86] Just before he left Texas, he was thrown from a buggy and badly sprained an ankle, putting him on crutches for some time.[87]

According to tradition, as Toombs was returning home he was handed a letter which told him of the nomination of Joseph E. Brown for governor by the Democratic state convention. "And who in the devil is Joe Brown?" asked the bewildered senator.[88] Joe Brown out of the North Georgia mountains was a Democrat of Southern Rights vintage who had been in the state senate for several years and since 1855 had served as a circuit judge. Aided by a stalemate among better known candidates, dark horse Brown had secured the nomination.[89] The Know-Nothings selected Ben Hill to carry their standard, and so another lively contest was promised. Toombs had a great deal of interest in the state elections, for he was up for reelection to the Senate and needed a favorable legislature to accomplish this.

National politics dominated the local contest, but it was largely a matter of which party could attack the enemies of the South more vigorously, rather than divided approaches on basic issues. A few days after the inauguration of Buchanan, the Supreme Court in the case of *Dred Scott versus Stanford* had ruled that neither Congress nor, by implication, a territorial legislature could interfere with slavery in the territories. Furthermore, the Missouri Compromise, which had barred slavery in the Louisiana Territory north of 36°30', was unconstitutional. The decision of the Taney-led court had been designed to settle forever the vexing problem

[85]See pp. 93–94.
[86]Stovall, *Toombs*, 153–54.
[87]Toombs to W. W. Burwell, July 11, 1857, in Phillips (ed.), *Correspondence*, 403; William Felix Alexander to Edward Porter Alexander, April 18, 1857, in Edward Porter Alexander Papers; Toombs to his wife, May 3, 1857, in Robert Toombs Papers, University of Georgia.
[88]Quoted in Stovall, *Toombs*, 154.
[89]Montgomery, *Cracker Parties*, 193; Stovall, *Toombs*, 157.

of slavery in the territories. It proved, however, to be an irritant of major proportions, stimulating instead of deadening sectional controversy. Technically the South had won a great victory, but it was one which an enflamed Northern public opinion would not accept. Southern Democratic popular sovereignty had triumphed over Northern Democratic squatter sovereignty but at the cost of destroying the *modus vivendi*, the free interpretation of the issue, between the two wings of the party.

By the time the gubernatorial contest warmed up, the Kansas imbroglio had taken another unfortunate turn. In June delegates to a constitutional convention scheduled for September had been chosen in an election rigged in favor of the proslavery faction and boycotted by free-soilers. Buchanan-appointed territorial governor, Robert J. Walker, interested in fair play in Kansas, urged that the constitution when completed be submitted to the people for ratification or Congress should refuse to admit the territory as a state. In an *obiter dictum*, he declared that climatic conditions dictated a future free-soil status for Kansas. Southerners bridled at this as officious meddling and a violation of the established doctrine of congressional non-intervention in the territories. Toombs also thought Kansas would eventually be a free state. But he was more concerned at the moment with the settlement of the problem than with the result, and believed Walker's pronouncements trouble making and ill-timed. It was really none of his business, he thought.[90]

Georgians became quite agitated over Walker's opinions. In fact, Governor Walker in Kansas threatened to become the central issue of the governor's race in Georgia. Ben Hill and the Know-Nothings linked Walker with the Buchanan administration and declared a plague on the entire perfidious Democratic house. Howell Cobb, in a difficult position as secretary of the treasurer in Buchanan's cabinet, tried to minimize the significance of Walker's statements and, above all, keep the President and the Democratic administration in the good graces of his constituents at home. Brown surprised his backers by his adroitness and composure, and rode out the Kansas storm by contesting Hill in the making of anti-Walker statements while refraining from attacking the President.[91]

[90]Toombs to W. W. Burwell, July 11, 1857, in Phillips (ed.), *Correspondence*, 403–404.
[91]Montgomery, *Cracker Parties*, 189–200.

Toombs spoke all over the state, following a pattern of condemning Walker and disapproving his retention by the Buchanan administration, but advising a "strong and active adherence to the Democratic organization" because of the "utter untrustworthiness" of the Know-Nothings on any question.[92] He succeeded or failed acccording to the particular newspaper account of his oratory which Georgians happened to read. The Macon *Journal and Messenger* called one effort a "rehash from the debris of old issues and slanders, which were presented in quite an ungraceful and unsenatorial style, as insulting to the intelligence, as it was unsuited to the taste of a Macon audience." [93] The Savannah *Morning News* found an address in that city before a rapt audience "one of the most powerful and convincing arguments in vindication of Southern rights as maintained by the National Democracy, that we have ever heard." [94]

The Democrats swept to nearly total victory in October. Brown defeated Hill by some 10,000 votes, and six out of eight congressional seats were retained, although one casualty was Linton Stephens.[95] In November Toombs was reelected to the Senate by the Democratic legislature, his new term to commence in March, 1859. His vote was 169 to 74 for the American candidate, Eli H. Baxter, while ex-governor Charles J. McDonald picked up four.[96] "I found no difficulty whatever in my election," Toombs later said.[97]

[92]Toombs to Stephens, August 15, 1857, in Phillips (ed.), *Correspondence*, 421.

[93]Quoted in Athens *Southern Watchman*, September 17, 1857.

[94]Savannah *Morning News*, September 25, 1857.

[95]Montgomery, *Cracker Parties*, 201; Howell Cobb to Alexander H. Stephens, October 9, 1857, in Phillips (ed.), *Correspondence*, 424.

[96]Athens *Southern Watchman*, November 12, 1857.

[97]Toombs to W. W. Burwell, November 20, 1857, in Phillips (ed.), *Correspondence*, 425.

CHAPTER VII

The Storm Gathers

THE grim specter of Kansas continued to haunt the nation as the Thirty-fifth Congress began its sessions in December, 1857. It was laid to rest within a year but at the expense of a serious rift within the Democratic party that presaged its split in 1860 and that of the Union in 1861.

In September the constitutional convention meeting in Lecompton, Kansas, had drawn up a proslavery document that was to be submitted to popular vote but in a restricted manner. The territorial inhabitants were not free to pass on the constitution as a whole, but could only signify whether the future admission of slaves was to be permitted. Regardless of how they voted on this, the slave property already in Kansas was to be protected. In December, with the free-soilers largely abstaining, the constitution "with slavery" was approved by a vote of 6,143 to 569. Despite the fact that another referendum in January, 1858, on the constitution as a whole revealed an unfavorable vote of 10,226 to 162, Buchanan chose to uphold the unpopular document. He did so, says his latest biographer, simply because "he was a legalist," and the legality of the Lecompton constitution was without question in his mind. The fact that his stand favored Southern interests was merely coincidence, not subservience to Southern extremists.[1]

[1]Philip S. Klein, *President James Buchanan: A Biography* (University Park,

Looming large in the minds of administration Democrats was the chance through Lecompton to end the whole messy affair on which the Republicans had capitalized so effectively.

Douglas felt that the Lecompton constitution did not represent the wishes of the majority of the people of Kansas, and thus was contrary to the basic principles of popular sovereignty. He consequently broke with the administration and waged a vigorous fight against its acceptance by the Senate. Toombs spoke several times in support of Buchanan's policy, against a backdrop of disunionist sentiment in Georgia. On February 9 and again on March 26, Governor Brown wrote Stephens that the rejection by Congress of Kansas and the Lecompton constitution would, under the terms of the Georgia platform, compel him to call a state convention to evaluate Georgia's status in the Union.[2]

On February 2, Toombs stated his conviction that the Lecompton constitution came from a regularly constituted, legal government and should be approved.[3] Several weeks later, with patience wearing thin, he told the Senate that the whole business of the country was becoming subordinate to the Kansas issue. He accused the opposition of deliberately stalling through dilatory tactics. With great warmth and amid applause from the galleries, he declared: "Sir, the country has rights. The majority have rights, and they have duties; and one of those duties is that the business of this country shall be done decently, and in good order, and in due time; and I trust there is fidelity enough to themselves, and to their principles, and to their country yet in the majority of the Senate, to stand at all hazards, and crush this faction." [4]

The debate climaxed on March 22 in an able, three-hour speech by the ailing Douglas before a crowded and excited Senate chamber. He was followed by Toombs who reiterated the legality of it all, and denied the assertion that a majority in the Senate was trying to cram a slavery constitution down the throats of Kansans. He accused some of the Northern senators of playing the hypocrite since they had consistently supported the Wilmot Proviso

---

Pa., 1962), 308. For a brief discussion of less favorable interpretations, see *ibid.*, 303–308.

[2]Governor Brown to Stephens, February 9, March 26, 1858, in Phillips (ed.), *Correspondence*, 431, 432.

[3]*Congressional Globe*, 35th Cong., 1st Sess., 524–27.

[4]*Ibid.*, Appendix, 101.

which called for prohibiting slavery forever in the territories. "That means," said Toombs, "that you can cram freedom whether the people want it or not, but take care how you cram slavery." [5] On a note of practicality Toombs concluded by saying that after admission Kansas would be a free, sovereign, and independent state to make constitutions and laws at its own pleasure, to right its wrongs, and redress its grievances. The implication was obvious: Kansas by its own hand could make itself free once a member of the Union.[6]

Under heavy pressure from the administration, the bill passed the Senate on May 23 by a vote of 33 to 25 over Republican, anti-Lecompton Democratic, and American (Know-Nothing) opposition. Crittenden of Kentucky and Bell of Tennessee, prominent Southern nationalists, voted nay, an action regarded by Toombs with "shame and indignation. . . ." [7]

Shortly after the Senate vote was taken, Toombs went home for a short period to attend to some legal affairs. He wrote Stephens: "All well in Geo. The weather is delightfull, trees and flowers in full bloom and nature looks charming." [8] Things were not going so well in Washington. Stephens, floor manager for the administration forces, was having rough sledding in pushing the Lecompton constitution through the House. "I am wearing out my life for nothing," he lamented to his brother Linton early in the fight.[9] On April 1 the House rejected the Senate bill and passed a substitute plan, earlier proposed by Crittenden but voted down in the Senate, which called for the resubmission of the entire constitution to a popular referendum in Kansas. The House bill was turned down by the Senate on April 2.

The compromise machinery of Congress eventually ground out an acceptable bill, named for one of its sponsors, Representative William H. English of Indiana, a pliable, ambitious, anti-Lecompton Democrat. Largely the brainchild of the sick Stephens, who worked vigorously to extract the administration from an almost hopeless position, in essence it proposed another referendum on Lecompton. If this were rejected, Kansas would have to wait for statehood

[5]Ibid., 202.
[6]Ibid., 204.
[7]Toombs to Stephens, March 28, 1858, in Phillips (ed.), Correspondence, 433.
[8]Ibid.
[9]Quoted in Johnston and Browne, Stephens, 330.

until its population equaled the number required for a congressional district: over 90,000. Acceptance meant early admission plus a liberal donation of Federal lands. Republicans at the time branded the proposal as a bribe, although it was customary for Congress to make such donations; and the offer to Kansas was no larger than that made to Minnesota when it joined the Union in 1857. Nonetheless, it was a curious arrangement which seemed less than straightforward.[10]

Toombs' role in breaking the congressional deadlock was less significant than that of Stephens, but his influence was felt. He worked closely with Stephens, polling congressional opinion on occasion for him, and kept the nervous Buchanan informed of developments.[11]

On April 30 the Senate passed the English bill 31 to 22 with Douglas, Bell, and Crittenden in opposition. The same day the House concurred by a vote of 112 to 103. On August 2 the Lecompton constitution was rejected by a vote of 11,812 to 1,926; Kansas was destined to remain a territory until January, 1861, when the secession of Southern states opened the doors to statehood. As Kansas faded from the public eye, in its backwash there remained an unfortunate legacy of increased sectional ill-will and party schism that could only weaken the structure of the nation.

After Congress adjourned, the nation followed the doughty Douglas to Illinois where he engaged Republican nominee Abraham Lincoln in memorable battle over the retention of his Senate seat. Out of a series of joint debates came his famous Freeport Doctrine in answer to Lincoln's question as to how he could reconcile squatter sovereignty with the Dred Scott decision. Douglas said that despite the court's prohibition of the exclusion of slavery from a territory, by unfriendly legislation or lack of local support slavery could be effectively driven out. Douglas succeeded in winning the election but further alienated the South.

In other action in the first session of the Thirty-fifth Congress, Toombs clashed with Jefferson Davis, chairman of the Military Affairs Committee, over the Mississippian's proposal to increase

[10]Henry H. Sims, *A Decade of Sectional Controversy, 1851–1861* (Chapel Hill, 1942), 98; Allan Nevins, *The Emergence of Lincoln* (New York, 1950), I, 296–98; Roy F. Nichols, *The Disruption of American Democracy* (New York, 1948), 167–72, 175.

[11]Toombs to Buchanan, April 18, 1858, in Phillips (ed.), **Correspondence**, 433; Nichols, *Disruption*, 170.

and reorganize the army. The debate was waged while newspapers kept the American public informed of friction in Utah where a showdown between Mormons and Federal authority was threatened. Toombs, as usual, was unalterably opposed to any measure which enlarged the military establishment. "I know that it is just as impossible for the Ethiop to change his skin, or the leopard his spots," he said, "as for a regular army to be the friend of liberty." [12] A wide variety of reasons attracted enough opposition to send the bill down to defeat.

Somewhat paradoxically, Toombs, the winter anti-militarist, became a roaring exponent of jingoism in the spring of 1858. Early in the year the British had begun the search of American merchantmen in Caribbean waters in quest of suspected slavers. Several had been fired upon. In some quarters, American indignation rose to dangerous proportions, and in late May, Toombs delivered some irresponsible remarks on the situation. Although not spelling out the reason, he said that for the last ten years the United States had had cause for war with England, and that it was a scandalous thing that we had not fought. He thought that at present a fleet should be sent to the Gulf, the offending British vessels seized and either sunk or brought to port, and the officers in charge hanged.[13]

The New York *Times* called Toombs' blast "nonsensical bombast." Satirically thrusting at him and the South in general, it said:

There are several splendid things which could be effected in a war with England. We could reopen the Slave-trade, for the benefits of the Gulf States. An immense amount of money would necessarily be divided among public men and their friends. A national debt of five hundred millions would be rolled up in an incredibly short space of time, to be eventually paid by the industry of the country—that is to say, of the North. The South despises industry, as only fit for the 'mud-sills of society.' We do not, however, for a moment suppose Mr. Toombs to be influenced by such considerations, or by any motive less potent than his own warlike disposition. He is 'ready for war,' and don't care who knows it. Even his antagonist, the British lion, is freely welcome to the intelligence. That toothless old beast will be somewhat astonished when Mr. Toombs gets hold of him. But we greatly apprehend the timorous creature will shrink back, and that we shall see no fight, after all. Mr. Toombs is of few words. Like all really

[12]*Congressional Globe*, 35th Cong., 1st Sess., 455–56.
[13]*Ibid.*, Appendix, 447.

formidable men, his utterances are mild. Providence wisely ordains that such should be the case. For if courage and bold talking were combined, greatness would be oppressive beyond the endurance of the common crowd.

Let us rejoice in Mr. Toombs. If nobody else would be prepared for war, *he* is ready.[14]

In June, through the quiet channels of diplomacy, Anglo-American accord was reached when the British foreign secretary refuted any right of search during peacetime.

Between sessions of Congress, Toombs' third and only surviving child, Sallie, married Dudley M. DuBose, an aspiring young Georgia lawyer. Although a happy marriage, it proved to be an ill-fated one, for like her sister Louisa and infant brother Lawrence, Sallie went to a premature grave.[15]

The second session of the Thirty-fifth Congress, December, 1858–March, 1859, was held in new quarters in the recently completed wings of the Capitol. After a valedictory address by Senator Crittenden in the old chamber, the solons moved into the new hall, called by one observer "capacious and elegant." [16] It was a strong group—Douglas, Seward, Davis, Crittenden, Bell, Wade, Houston, and Benjamin—but tragically barren of accomplishment in this next to the last session before the dissolution of the Union. The senior senator from Georgia, Robert Toombs, bowed to none of his colleagues in talent. A glimpse of the powerful Toombs at this time was given by the Washington correspondent of the Milledgeville *Federal Union*:

To the left of the Vice President's seat, upon the range next to the outside seats, just in front of Seward, Hale, and Wilson, attired in a neat, black, well adjusted suit, sits the famous and formidable Toombs. His partially grey, but thick hair, hangs bushily upon his head. I had an opportunity the other day to hear him speak. His subject was the Tariff, which, though of itself, dry, was made deeply interesting under his masterly touch. He has a powerful voice—it filled the hall, every nook and corner completely. Bold and fearless, conscious of his giant resources, he handles his subject with a giant's power. Fair, and free from sectionalism, he embraces the whole country in his heart—if he demolishes a system, one better is suggested and urged. Toombs is

[14]May 27, 31, 1858.
[15]William Felix Alexander to Edward Porter Alexander, July 26, 1858, in Edward Porter Alexander Papers.
[16]Milledgeville *Federal Union*, March 1, 1859.

built for an orator, tapering like a wedge from his shoulders, which support a round, well developed head, to his feet; with arms and hands moving gracefully in gesticulation his oratory and its accompaniments attract the stranger so much that often the depth to which he is diving is unnoticed. It is best for him not to have exceeded ten minutes in preparation before he speaks, for then all the glow and fire of his nature arises in him. . . . He is not so good and entertaining in advancing a scheme, as in defending an established one when assailed.[17]

Free from sectionalism Toombs was not. But despite occasional emotional outbursts, he seemed far less partisan at this critical juncture in his career than many of his associates in Congress. He and Stephens did not want Douglas read out of the party for disloyalty, a stand Toombs was to explain at some length in the state political battles later in the year.[18] At a Democratic caucus at the opening of Congress, Toombs opposed without success a move to strip Douglas of his chairmanship of the important Committee on Territories.[19]

The picture for the administration forces was not a happy one. The summer and fall congressional elections in the North and West had largely shown a repudiation of the Buchanan regime, and the House of the Thirty-sixth Congress would likely be controlled by an anti-administration coalition. In an effort to unite the badly divided Democratic party, Buchanan, in his annual message to Congress, presented a program designed to arouse national pride and enthusiasm. It centered around a vigorous foreign policy, including the purchase of Cuba, and the building of a transcontinental railroad. An upward revision of the tariff was recommended to shore up the treasury. But the efforts of this deadlocked Congress were largely negative.

Toombs took a particular interest in Cuba. The Pearl of the Antilles in the hands of impotent Spain had long dangled alluringly before the eyes of acquisitive Southerners who saw it as a potential slave state. On January 10, John Slidell of Louisiana introduced a bill for the appropriation of $30,000,000 to be used in negotiating the purchase of Cuba. Two weeks later the bill was reported favorably out of the foreign relations committee. On January 24, 1859, Toombs stated on the floor of the Senate that the "only

17 *Ibid*
18 Johnston and Browne, *Stephens*, 347–48; Howell Cobb to Stephens, September 8, 1858, in Phillips (ed.), *Correspondence*, 442–44.
19 Nevins, *Emergence of Lincoln*, I, 425.

question of foreign policy which is worthy of the consideration by American statesmen, is the tropical empire lying at our feet . . . ." It should be, he said, the "American policy to unite, as fast as it can be fairly and honestly done, all the tropics under our flag." [20] He discounted any sectional implications in such a policy, saying that the annexation of Cuba would benefit the entire country, especially the Northern states. Cuba would be the best customer in the world for New England manufacturers, and in return could supply tropical fruits, sugar, and coffee. All of this would be carried on under the benign aegis of "internal free trade." The South would not be benefited as much, he thought. But Toombs' latent Southern nationalism was evident as he concluded his address with this ringing declaration: ". . . Cuba has fine ports, and with her acquisition, we can make first the Gulf of Mexico, and then the Caribbean sea, a *mare clausum*. Probably younger men than you or I will live to see the day when no flag shall float there except by permission of the United States of America. That is my policy." [21]

The purchase of Cuba, which was opposed strenuously by the Republicans, became involved in the attempts by Northern senators to enact a homestead bill. Each side accused the other of demagoguery and needless obstruction. After such a charge by Toombs, Ben Wade of Ohio came back with this classic and scornful rejoinder: "The question will be, shall we give lands to the landless, or niggers to the niggerless?" [22] Neither became a reality in the Thirty-fifth Congress.

On February 23, Toombs listened with disfavor to a hot debate between radical Southerners led by Davis and A. G. Brown of Mississippi and Douglas over the old question of slavery in the territories.[23] The Mississippians, with an eye on the "unfriendly legislation" phrase of Douglas' Freeport Doctrine, demanded that the Federal government enact laws to protect slave property in the territories. Douglas responded by denying the necessity and practicality of this extreme view. He warned that such a platform, if embraced by the Democratic party, would cause it to lose every Northern state in an election. Here in miniature was a preview

[20]*Congressional Globe*, 35th Cong., 2nd Sess., 542–43.
[21]*Ibid*., 543.
[22]*Ibid*., 1353–54.
[23]*Ibid*., 1242–59.

of the 1860 Democratic national convention. Toombs was aware of the dangers implicit in Davis' stand. Although he had spoken many times of the right of citizens to enjoy their property unmolested in the territories, he had a "clear appreciation of the fact that every point scored against Douglas was cleaving the Democratic party in twain." [24] Most Southerners had abandoned the senator from Illinois at this point. Toombs clung doggedly and hopefully to the Little Giant as a key figure in the preservation of the party and hence the nation.

The New York *Times* found this new stand by radical Southerners a bit unsporting and lacking in common sense. "Finding that the doctrine of Congressional non-intervention injures Slavery [the rejection of Lecompton by Kansas], they have abandoned it, and now assert the right and the duty of Congress to legislate *for the protection* of Slavery in the Territories." The only salvation for the South, thought the *Times*, lay in the formation of a *"conservative national party,*—which shall not ignore Northern rights nor Northern sentiment, but hold both in subordination to the Constitution and the preservation of the Union." [25]

Toombs was one of the leading figures in the tariff battle which took place in this Congress. In 1846 as a Whig, he had opposed the Walker Tariff which had lowered duties. Now as a Democrat, he opposed a measure which would have raised duties and increased protection, particularly for the iron and woolen industries. Two years before, in 1857, Toombs had supported a tariff reduction because of the great surpluses built up by the Walker Act. Shortly thereafter the country had been hit by a severe panic and depression, and the surpluses became deficits. The condition of the treasury caused a cry for more revenue to meet government expenditures, and the hard times led to demands for more protection.

Toombs denied the need for additional revenue, claiming the government could meet its expenses for the next year if its income were properly husbanded. He then proceeded to lecture the administration on economy in government, one of his favorite themes. The postal service could be made self-sustaining, he said. In fact, if Toombs had had his way, he apparently would have abolished the Post Office Department altogether. Postal service was not in his estimation a duty of government. "It is of no more importance

24Stovall, *Toombs*, 164.
25New York *Times*, February 26, 1859.

to the people of the United States that this Government should carry my cotton than that it should carry my letters." [26] No regular army, no mail service—so thought the frugal senator from Georgia. Toombs additionally called for the sale of public lands as a revenue measure before tariffs were raised. Summing up his approach to the problem of money for government expenses, Toombs said simply, "You must retrench." [27]

A little speech on protection revealed the emergence of a free trading, laissez-faire Toombs who had departed considerably from his earlier role as a Clay protectionist:

Forty years ago the country was young, was poor; our manufactures were few and feeble; we wanted capital; we wanted skill; we imposed our taxes in such manner as greatly promoted our manufacturing industry. We nursed them; we built them up, whether wisely or unwisely the fact is accomplished; and they will go on increasing and prospering in spite of croakers, in spite of convulsions, and in spite of tariffs. All the great branches of our national industry are on a firm basis; they are daily increasing and gathering strength; they will be subject to fluctuations, to adverse times and prosperous times; that is the law of human industry, but the result of it all is still progress. Small men tie themselves on to the one or the other of these great interests, affect to be its peculiar friends for their own advantage. We have education, skill, experience, capital, labor, food, and raw materials lying all around, and millions of active, producing consumers, and free Government. These are the imperishable elements of our material prosperity. Strike down your customs duties to-morrow, and you will not thereby extinguish your furnace fires, nor shut up your factories or workshops, but they would survive it, and still flourish, perhaps all the better, for standing on industry rather than fluctuating legislative enactments.[28]

The Southern bloc stood immovable with Toombs on the tariff, and it failed to pass.

Other proposals were defeated by "strange combinations of vengeful and frustrated lawmakers." [29] So petty was the political partisanship that on the day before adjournment, routine appropriations bills had not been passed by Congress. In fact, adjournment came on March 4 with no funds provided for the operation

[26]*Congressional Globe*, 35th Cong., 2nd Sess., 1452.
[27]*Ibid.*, Appendix, 190.
[28]*Ibid.*
[29]Klein, *Buchanan*, 331.

of the Post Office. Barren of accomplishments, the members of the Thirty-fifth Congress headed for home.

Toombs went back to Georgia intending to stay out of the state political battles in the summer and fall. His law practice was demanding, and he was required at home a good bit after his wife broke her leg in a carriage accident.[30] But, as he said later, he found it "necessary to put in." [31]

The Democratic party in Georgia had been divided by recent national events into two factions: pro-Douglas and pro-administration. Stephens and Toombs sided with the Illinois senator; Secretary of the Treasury Cobb and Governor Brown espoused the cause of Buchanan. Stephens had startled the state by declining to be a candidate for reelection to Congress, although he did not withdraw from the political arena. The pact between Cobb and Brown was largely a mutual back-scratching one, involving a second term for Brown and control of the Georgia delegation at the 1860 national convention for presidential hopeful Cobb.[32]

Cobb was anxious to preserve harmony with his fellow politicians, for a disunited Georgia Democracy would have been an insurmountable obstacle on the road to the White House. In May one of his lieutenants, Congressman James Jackson, sounded out Toombs and Stephens in Athens at a supreme court session. He reported to Cobb that Toombs would support a qualified endorsement of the Buchanan administration by the forthcoming state party convention. "I haven't a doubt his heart is with you," Jackson wrote. About the introverted Stephens he could say nothing.[33]

Three months later, Tom Cobb was pumping Toombs for his and Stephens' feelings toward his brother's nomination. Toombs stated that he and his friend both agreed that Howell Cobb was "the best man in the nation for the office." Tom was careful to deny that his brother was actually a candidate; he said that in talking with Toombs, he simply represented friends who did not want any obstacle to arise in the state delegation in case Cobb's name were suggested at the national convention. Toombs felt

[30]Toombs to Stephens, April 16, 1859, in Alexander H. Stephens Papers, Emory University.
[31]Toombs to Stephens, August 27, 1859, Phillips (ed.), *Correspondence*, 447.
[32]Montgomery, *Cracker Parties*, 222.
[33]Jackson to Cobb, May 30, 1859 (?), in Brooks (ed.), "Cobb Papers," VI, 240–41.

that the delegation should support Cobb. Any other candidate would be unworthy of the state. Tom Cobb informed his brother that he was satisfied that the senator was "candid and sincere." But he was far less sure of Stephens' attitude.[34]

As was expected, Brown was renominated by the Democratic convention meeting without Toombs in Milledgeville in June. A resolution endorsing the national administration ran into trouble but was carried by a vote of 374 to 34. The "Opposition Party," constructed around a nucleus of former Know-Nothings, nominated Warren Akin, little known lawyer from Cass County. Ben Hill was in the ranks of the Opposition, and, in surprising contrast to his unionist sentiments in 1861, fired heavy salvos for Southern Rights extremism.[35]

Toombs campaigned vigorously and widely for the Democratic nominees. Just as vigorously did the Opposition press sail into him. "The burly blusterer, Bob Toombs, who disgraces the State of Georgia by the occupancy of a seat in the Senate," he was called by the Athens *Southern Watchman.* "While professing Whiggery, his violent abuse of Democracy provoked the Democratic press to skin him unmercifully; and since he has sold out to the Democrats, his insulting defamation of his former associates has compelled the press of that party [now the Opposition] to denounce him as he deserves." [36]

On September 8, Toombs delivered an important speech at Augusta. It was in a sense his high-water mark as a moderate statesman, a compromiser for the sake of union. Rarely after this did he reach such heights. He pointed out how the South had gained major victories (in reality hollow ones) through the repeal of the Missouri Compromise, the popular sovereignty interpretation of the Kansas Nebraska Bill, and the Dred Scott decision. He disagreed strongly with the advocates of squatter sovereignty, most prominent of whom was Douglas. And yet, he continued,

I do not belong to those who denounce him. The organization of the Democratic party leaves this an open question, and Mr. Douglas is at full liberty to take either side he may choose, and if he maintains his ancient ground of neither making nor accepting new tests of political

[34]T. R. R. Cobb to Howell Cobb, August 24, 1859, in Brooks (ed.), "Cobb Papers," VI, 242–43.
[35]Montgomery, *Cracker Parties,* 226–32.
[36]Athens *Southern Watchman,* September 8, 1859.

soundness I shall consider him a political friend and will accept him as the representative of the party whenever it may tender him; and in the meantime if he should even wander after strange gods, I do not hesitate to tell you that with his errors I prefer him and would support him tomorrow against any opposition man in America. We are told that we must put a new plank in the platform of the Democratic party, and demand the affirmance of the duty of Congress to protect slavery in a territory where such territory may fail to discharge this duty. I reply, I do not think it wise to do the thing proposed. . . . No; I shall prescribe no new test of party fealty to Northern Democrats, those men who have hitherto stood with honor and fidelity upon their engagements. They have maintained the truth to their own hurt. They have displayed a patriotism, a magnanimity rarely equaled in the world's history, and I shall endeavor in sunshine and in storm, with your approbation if I can get it, without it if I must, to stand by them with fidelity equal to their great deserts. If you will stand with me we shall conquer faction in North and South, and shall save the country from the curse of being ruled by the combination now calling itself the opposition [the Republicans]. We shall leave this country to our children as we found it—united, strong, prosperous and happy.[37]

Toombs' moderation aroused the wrath of the Augusta *Chronicle* which pointed out how years before he had made vigorous protests against Cass' support of squatter sovereignty. "The fiery and eloquent young Hotspur of 1848 has gently as a sucking dove bowed the knee to Black Douglas in 1859." Hitting him again, the *Chronicle* declared: "Southern Democratic *Doughfaces strike hands* with the base, cruel, black-hearted, deceitful, treacherous enemies of the South, for the sake of a corrupt party organization." [38] Wailed the Athens *Southern Watchman*, "Oh, Mr. Toombs, Mr. Toombs! What a fall was that, my countrymen!" [39] The Macon *Citizen* editorialized: "We do not say that Senator Toombs is an Abolitionist in feeling or principle—we do not say that he has any Freesoil propensities—we do not believe but that he loathes and detests them. But we *do* say—and say it deliberately—and we believe it when we say it—*that he is an unprincipled traitor to the rights and interests of the South in the Territories of the United States*." [40]

Privately, Toombs' hopes for the future were less sanguine than

[37]Milledgeville *Southern Recorder*, September 13, October 4, 1859, quoted in Phillips, *Toombs*, 177-78.
[38]Augusta *Chronicle*, September 11, 1859.
[39]Quoted in Augusta *Chronicle*, September 21, 1859.
[40]*Ibid.*, September 22, 1859.

his public pronouncements. On December 4, he wrote Stephens that unless the Democrats could win the election in 1860 with "some sound, reliable Southern Democrat . . . the future is gloomy enough." If the Republicans triumphed, "I see no safety for us, our property and our firesides, except in breaking up the concern." In phraseology he was to use in the Senate within a few weeks, he stated that "we should prefer to defend ourselves at the doorsill rather than await the attack at our hearthstone." [41]

Normally Christmas was a gay season in Washington, D.C. Toombs wrote his friend, Stephens, however, on December 28, 1859, that everything had been "dull and stagnant" during the holidays. "The social intercourse between North and South, or rather between Dems. and Reps. seems almost wholly to have ceased and all sides seem sullen and ill-natured." [42]

The animosities that disrupted the city's social life were amply reflected in the Capitol where the first session of the Thirty-sixth Congress was getting underway. Never had the political situation been as grim. In October, John Brown's raid on Harpers Ferry with the avowed purpose of fomenting a slave uprising had horrified the South. Although he was condemned by responsible Northern leaders, including Abraham Lincoln, his martyrdom was growing, feeding as it were on the emotionalism of the slavery issue. Southerners were repulsed by what appeared to be an endorsement of a deranged abolitionist.

The Senate had a solid Democratic majority, but the House showed a Republican plurality. The election of a Speaker would depend upon the voting of the twenty-six Know-Nothings and the one Whig who held the balance of power in this traditionally turbulent chamber. For some two months the House, many of whose members were armed, wrangled over the Speakership amid fisticuffs, barroom language, and cries of dissolving the Union. Focal point for much of the uproar was the endorsement by the Republican candidate, John Sherman of Ohio, along with a sizeable number of other Republicans, of a recent publication, *The Impending Crisis*, by Hinton Rowan Helper. A representative of the North Carolina yeoman class, Helper had attempted to show

[41]Toombs to Stephens, December 4, 1859, in Phillips (ed.), *Correspondence*, 450.
[42]Toombs to Stephens, December 28, 1859, in Phillips (ed.), *Correspondence*, 453.

statistically the burdensome nature of slavery on the Southern
economy and the non-slaveholding whites. Although it was not
for the most part inflammatory, it was considered extremely dangerous by Southern congressmen. Finally Sherman stepped aside
in favor of a compromise choice, William Pennington, New Jer-
sey Whig, who was elected on February 1 after forty-four ballots.
The fight was over, but the wounds of battle still rankled.

Toombs felt that he had blocked Sherman's election by a powerful speech he made in the Senate on January 24. Shortly after
Christmas, he had told Stephens that he was preparing an address
in which he proposed to review calmly the state of the union,
"making a clean breast of it," and withholding nothing "because
it may be unpalatable or even dangerous to anybody or any
section." At the time of his letter he was not optimistic about
the future. He considered Sherman a certain victor, and called
Buchanan and his cabinet petty, partisan politicians who were "as
rabid and imbecile as ever and much more profligate . . . ." He
noted the interest of many of his colleagues in the upcoming party
conventions, saying that the "old fogies in the Senate are all candidates for the Presidency from highest to lowest, and are as silent,
sanctimonious and demure as a wh__e [sic] at a christening." [43]

Toombs' speech, solemnly and deliberately delivered, lasted about
an hour and a half, and was directed primarily at the Republican
party, which he felt was endangering the Union through its policies.[44] He described the party as a coalition of abolitionists and
"waifs and strays—deserters of all former political parties" which
had "but one living, animating principle or bond of union, and
that is hatred of the people and institutions of the slaveholding
States of this Union." Specifically he charged the Black Republicans with three things: annulling that part of the constitution
and the congressional statutes of 1793 and 1850 (which called for
the deliverance of runaway slaves) by the passage in many Northern states of personal liberty laws making the recovery of fugitives
extremely difficult; depriving slaveholders of their rights in the
territories as recently set forth in the Dred Scott decision and, in
addition, undermining the Supreme Court itself; and inciting servile insurrection in the Southern states.

[43]Toombs to Stephens, December 28, 1859, in Phillips (ed.), *Correspondence,* 452.
[44]*Congressional Globe,* 36th Cong., 1st Sess., Appendix, 88–93.

For these reasons, said Toombs, "I maintain that this coalition is unfit to rule over a free people; and its possession of the Federal Government is a just cause of war by the people whose safety is thereby put in jeopardy." He called on Southerners to put aside differences and unite with all good men everywhere against the Republicans. Particularly did he extend the hand of friendship to Northern Democrats, most of whom he still regarded as trustworthy and honorable, though frequently in opposition to the Southern pattern of action.

Toombs made it quite plain that a Republican victory in November would irrevocably rend the fabric of union. In reality, he declared, the war against Southern institutions and firesides was already underway. "Listen to 'no vain babblings,' to no treacherous jargon about 'overt acts;' they have already been committed. Defend yourselves, the enemy is at your door; wait not to meet him at the hearthstone—meet him at the doorsill, and drive him from the temple of liberty, or pull down its pillars and involve him in a common ruin."

The Georgia senator's "doorsill speech" provoked considerable and mixed comment. Stephens, now at home instead of in Congress, said it was "exactly on the right line," showing more statesmanship and less impulse and passion than any speech he had ever made.[45] The Savannah *Morning News* stated that Toombs had put the cards of the South on the table—that it was up to the North to adhere to its duty and responsibility if the two sections were to avoid open collision.[46] For the anti-Democratic Augusta *Chronicle*, the speech was a source of painful amusement. Toombs was blowing hot again after having told Georgians last September in his pro-Douglas oration that things did not look too bad. It was the same old Toombs, "neither looking behind nor before him." Sneeringly the *Chronicle* said: "We can see him foaming and chafing, the lightnings flashing from those usually dull brown eyes, the lion's mane all tangled like the billowy sea, while from out the large voluptuous mouth, 'leaps the live thunder.'" It was ridiculous to talk about dissolving the Union in case of Republican victory, thought the *Chronicle*. If they were public enemies, then we should make war on them now, and not go into an election determined

[45]Stephens to J. Henly Smith, February 4, 1860, in Phillips (ed.), *Correspondence*, 460.
[46]Savannah *Morning News*, January 30, 1860.

beforehand to disregard the popular decision if it be against us.[47]

The New York *Times* saw Toombs' address as too well-planned to smack of genuine passion. It was, the *Times* fancied,

a pure threat—a cool, calculated, pre-determined menace, not forced to the lips by the pressure upon the soul of an intolerable grievance, but the studied rhetorical display of one who has his assigned part to fill. It seems to be produced according to a preconcerted programme, and if we had the book of stage directions we should expect to find in it, 'Enter Toombs, breathing forth fire and slaughter.' . . . The play is put upon the stage for performance till November next, when the curtain is to drop, and *exeunt omnes* for four years.

The speech of Mr. Toombs, when regarded in this light, must be owned to be rather an impudent and impotent piece of dictation.[48]

Calculated Toombs' speech was—an empty threat it was not.

Horace Greeley's New York *Tribune*, appraised by Toombs as the "general receptacle of all falsehoods," [49] failed to see anything Machiavellian about the Georgian's speech. It was typical Southern bombast, in this case a particularly insulting piece of "volcanic oratory." The *Tribune* denied that the nation was in serious trouble. In what was undoubtedly the misstatement of the year, it said that "there is no nation in existence whose disorders are so trivial as our own." The only disturbing question was slavery in the territories, and this was no cause for any great convulsion. The Republican party in the interest of freedom and civilization said simply that its expansion should be checked.[50] In the months before the election of Lincoln, the Republican party and newspapers reflecting Republican opinion consistently regarded secession as a "mere rhetorical weapon, devised to frighten the electorate, but not for a moment seriously intended to be used, except by the most ultra of the fire-eaters." [51] Even after Lincoln's triumph in November and new evidences of danger, they were not immediately aroused. It was a tragic miscalculation.[52]

Early in the session, the senators from Mississippi, Brown and

[47]Augusta *Chronicle*, February 14, 1860.
[48]New York *Times*, January 26, 1860.
[49]*Congressional Globe*, 36th Cong., 1st Sess., 838.
[50]New York *Tribune*, February 2, 1860.
[51]David M. Potter, *Lincoln and His Party in the Secession Crisis* (New Haven, 1942), 16, hereinafter cited as Potter, *Secession Crisis*.
[52]*Ibid.*, 19.

Davis, returned to the disturbing theme which had produced such dissonant chords in the Thirty-fifth Congress. Resolutions were introduced by them calling for territorial legislatures or, if necessary, Congress to insure adequate protection for slavery in the territories, and denying the right of a territorial people to decide for or against slavery until statehood was attained. This demand for a slave code was an unnecessary and provocative move. By 1860 it was clear to most that slavery and Western territories were basically incompatible; that, as Webster had suggested in 1850, the laws of nature had limited its existence to the South. But extremists such as Brown and Davis insisted on keeping alive an artificial issue to the point of disunion if necessary.

Toombs regarded their intransigence with extreme displeasure. He wrote Stephens that "hostility to Douglas is the sole motive of movers of this mischief." Although he did not disagree in principle with Davis, it was the "very foolishness of folly to raise and make prominent such *issues now.*" Toombs himself had made the protection of Southern rights in the territories a point in his January speech, but he had never pressed for the passage of a slave code either by a territorial legislature or by Congress. He was content to ride along pragmatically on the Dred Scott decision, which to him was all the South needed at the moment. Toombs told Stephens that Davis' course could only lead to the alienation of Northern Democrats. The Georgia senator wanted Douglas defeated at the convention in Charleston, but he did not want him and his supporters "crippled or driven off. Where are we to get as many or as good men in the North to supply their places? . . . It is naked folly to turn out a quarter of a million at least of such men on such pretenses." Toombs stated that he would "resist . . . to the last extremity" the adoption of Davis' resolutions at the next Democratic caucus.[53] Nevertheless, a modified version of the Mississippian's resolutions was adopted over some Southern opposition, including that of Toombs, at the meeting, which was boycotted by Douglas Democrats. It would remain, however, for the national convention to write the platform of the party.[54]

Toombs spoke again on February 27, making a long, detailed exegesis of the main points of his January speech and once more

[53]February 10, 1860, in Phillips (ed.), *Correspondence*, 461.
[54]Nevins, *Emergence of Lincoln*, II, 180; Nichols, *Disruption*, 284; Milledgeville *Federal Union*, May 29, 1860.

charging the North with infidelity to the constitution.[55] March 7 witnessed a debate between Toombs and Ben Wade on the same issues. The Ohio senator, not a popular speaker according to the New York *Times* but one whose "battle-axe style" attracted attention,[56] charged Toombs with contradiction and needless emotion. According to the Georgian, the South had never been so prosperous and yet, said Wade, even with the North out of power politically, Southerners continually shouted about the dangerous aggressions of that section which were threatening the very pillars of government. "In one breath they are all boast and glory; in the next it is all despair and destruction." How could this be, he asked. Wade pointed out how Toombs had spoken of the insecurity of slave property because of the personal liberty laws, and then waxed eloquent over how few slaves had fled Georgia; and how the Georgian had charged the North with perjury and disloyalty to the constitution, and then followed with the statement that Republic victory in November would be the signal for Southern secession.

Wade did not deny a lack of enthusiasm in the North for the enforcement of the fugitive slave acts. But he contended that Ohio's personal liberty law was for the purpose of protecting citizens of Ohio from kidnapping, not obstructing the Federal statutes. He claimed that the court in the Dred Scott case had overstepped its bounds for the purpose of effecting a political object, and that hence the decision was of no validity. Wade said the Republican party was not a threat to the South. It stood for only two things: the limitation of slavery and a homestead bill. He believed that the territories belonged not to the states but to the people, and that Congress as a trustee of the people could fashion legislation for them. As long as he was a member of Congress, "in the vast Territories of this nation I will allow no such curse to have a foothold." [57]

It was apparent from Toombs' rebuttal that he and his Northern colleague were poles apart in viewpoint, and were not likely to find common ground for compromise. Particularly so when Toombs said:

Sir, I have taken an oath to support the Constitution here as a Senator, in all my official action. . . . I am bound to support it every-

[55]*Congressional Globe*, 36th Cong., 1st Sess., 888–94.
[56]New York *Times*, March 8, 1860.
[57]*Congressional Globe*, 36th Cong., 1st Sess., Appendix, 150–54.

where, while it exists; but when revolutions begin, constitutions end. My first, my only allegiance is due to Georgia. When she pronounces for new safeguards for her liberties, duty, honor, and patriotism require me to stand by her colors. I shall then vacate my seat here, and shall no longer be bound by a compact which your party has annulled and disregarded, even when acting under its obligations. If by such a course that Senator thinks I violate my oath to the Constitution, I am quite sure he and I can never agree upon the nature of such an obligation. Sir, I was not educated in the school of passive obedience. I will not maintain the Union when the Constitution is overthrown. Obedience to such a Union is treason to the Constitution. The cry of Union by those who subvert the Constitution is simply adding hypocrisy to treachery.[58]

In defense of his section, Toombs stated that over the years the South had asked nothing in the way of assistance from the Federal government. Southerners had paid their taxes, fought their country's battles, and wanted only the "peaceful enjoyment of the fruits of their own honest toil." Conversely, since 1789, there had been a continual cry from the non-slaveholding states for "protection, prohibition, and bounties. Give, give, give, had been the steady cry of New England; the middle States of the North have been equally urgent." [59]

Much of what had been said in this first session of the Thirty-sixth Congress had reflected the coming party conventions and the allurement of the big prize in November. Toombs noted in the middle of March that the "strife here runs 'fast and furious' between the friends of the different candidates. It looks to me very much like the officers of ships being engaged in cheating one another at 'three-up' in the forecastle while the vessel is labouring among the breakers." [60] Along with Toombs, the nation watched apprehensively as many Democrats left Washington for Charleston and the party convention. A great deal depended on what they would do.

As early as December, 1859, Georgia had begun its preparations for the Charleston gathering in April. A state Democratic convention, controlled by Cobb supporters, met, endorsed the secretary as a nominee, and chose a slate of delegates to the national party convention. As the action had been hasty and somewhat irregular,

[58]*Ibid.*, 156.
[59]*Ibid.*, 157.
[60]Toombs to Stephens, March 16, 1860, in Phillips (ed.), *Correspondence*, 464–65.

there was much opposition to it in the state. Consequently, the party's executive committee summoned another convention in March. A bitter fight ensued between the pro-Cobb and anti-Cobb factions, leading to a temporary secession of the anti-Cobb delegates, who elected their own slate for Charleston. The convention finally reassembled, whereupon an agreement was reached to combine this ticket and the pro-Cobb delegates as a single unit and rescind the previous endorsement of Cobb. The harpooning of the rotund cabinet member had been brought about, to some extent, by his former ally, Governor Brown, and by Stephens, who had opposed him since the break between Douglas and the Buchanan administration.[61] Although he was not technically precluded from consideration at Charleston, this loss of face caused Cobb to write a public letter of withdrawal on March 20 to the president of the state convention. He was doing so, he said, in the interest of harmony, for there had to be union against the common enemy.[62]

Toombs apparently played no part in the "stop Howell Cobb" movement. In fact, about the only feelings he expressed at all about the convention were the gloomy ones that regardless of the nominee, the Democrats would probably lose in November.[63] If he ever had a candidate it was Robert M. T. Hunter of Virginia, but three days before the convention opened, Toombs wrote Stephens that he did not think he could be nominated because he was an honest man and hence unacceptable to the North. Douglas, whose nomination Toombs opposed though not bitterly, would be defeated, he said, because his enemies were "numerous, vindictive and remorseless." [64]

The ten-day convention in Charleston was in sharp contrast to the languid, springtime beauty of the elegant city. The stormy session climaxed in a split over party platform, and set in motion a complex series of events that led ultimately to dual Democratic presidential candidates. Toombs sat out the convention in a "pretty well vacated" [65] Washington, D.C., interposing infrequently in its activities. When he heard that platform making would precede the

[61]Montgomery, *Cracker Parties*, 237–38; Phillips, *Toombs*, 188–89.
[62]Milledgeville *Federal Union*, March 27, 1860.
[63]Toombs to James Madison Spullock, March 17, 1860, in James Madison Spullock Collection, Georgia Archives.
[64]Toombs to Stephens, April 20, 1860, in Phillips (ed.), *Correspondence*, 467–68.
[65]*Ibid.*, 467.

nomination of the party's candidate, something he regarded as a tactical error on Douglas' part, he telegraphed the Georgia delegation "to get a good one and a Southern man on it or bolt." [66]

The majority report of the platform committee stated that it was the duty of the Federal government to protect the rights of persons and property in the territories and wherever else its constitutional authority extended. The minority report, or Douglas platform, recognized that a difference of opinion existed within the party over slavery in the territories, and therefore resolved that the party should abide by Supreme Court decisions on questions of constitutional law. Despite an impassioned speech by William L. Yancey of Alabama for the acceptance of minimum Southern demands as embodied in the majority report, the excited convention by a vote of 165 to 138 substituted the minority for the majority report. A bolt of the cotton states followed, with their delegates reassembling in another building in the city. Twenty-six of the thirty-six man Georgia delegation joined the seceders.

In Washington, Toombs heard that the main convention had then adopted the "Tennessee platform," a compromise measure which attempted to reconcile the majority and minority proposals; whereupon he advised the seceding Georgians to "go back and stand on it." [67] But Toombs' information was erroneous. The convention went through fifty-seven ballots in a futile attempt to select a nominee. Although Douglas led in every voting, he did not secure the necessary two-thirds majority. So, on May 2, the convention recessed until June 18 when it would try again in Baltimore. The bolters' convention, somewhat taken back by the adjournment, also recessed, to meet in Richmond on June 11.

While the Democrats were picking up the pieces from the Charleston debacle, two other party conventions were held, with more successful results. In early May at Baltimore, the conservative Constitutional Union party nominated John Bell of Tennessee as presidential standard bearer, and drew up a platform calling for the preservation of the Union and the constitution, and the enforcement of the laws. In the middle of the month, the jubilant Republicans, at Chicago, passed over several leading men, and chose Abraham Lincoln as their nominee. A broad platform, aimed

[66]Toombs to Stephens, May 5, 1860, in Phillips (ed.), *Correspondence*, 468.
[67]*Ibid.*

at diverse interests, asserted that neither Congress nor a territorial legislature could legalize slavery in any territory, and also included proposals for a homestead act, a protective tariff, and a transcontinental railroad.

Following the Charleston convention, a group of citizens from Macon, Georgia, asked for the views of some of the leading Democrats in the state on the course of action that should now be followed. Stephens and former governor Hershel V. Johnson regretted the split, called for a return to the old Southern doctrine of non-intervention (that Congress should pass no law upon the subject of slavery in the territories), and favored participation in the Baltimore convention. Governor Brown supported the principles of the majority report but thought the insistence upon them at the convention ill-advised. He also was in favor of attendance at Baltimore. Onetime presidential hopeful Cobb approved the secession of Southern delegates at Charleston, but hoped for Georgia's participation in both of the forthcoming conventions and the healing of party dissensions.[68]

Toombs' response was inflammatory in comparison to the tone of the others. Although it may not have been prudent to push Southern constitutional rights so vigorously at Charleston, he said, once done the seceding delegates acted "with manly firmness" in standing by them, and he approved what they did. Even so, he counseled joining the convention at Baltimore and the postponement of the Richmond meeting until later. Toombs reaffirmed his belief that there was no rightful power anywhere which could exclude slave property from the territories. Georgians were surrounded by danger, he warned, but the greatest was not the dissolution of the Union. "Our greatest danger today is that the Union will survive the Constitution. . . . Look to the preservation of your rights." [69]

This May 10 letter marked a fateful change in the thinking of Robert Toombs concerning the overriding question of slavery in the territories on which the Democratic party had floundered at Charleston and the nation was to flounder in a few months. Although in the past he had contributed his share of provocative

[68]Phillips (ed.), *Correspondence*, 471; Johnston and Browne, *Stephens*, 357–64; Phillips, *Georgia and State Rights*, 189–90.
[69]Toombs to Robert Collins and others, May 10, 1860, in Phillips (ed.), *Correspondence*, 475–77.

and emotional outbursts about the sancitity of Southern rights, he had never quite shut the door on the notion that there could be honest differences of opinion within the Democratic family. In September, 1859, in his much-condemned speech in Augusta, he had kept the door open for Douglas and the Northern Democrats. As late as February, 1860, he had written Stephens that it was extreme foolishness for Davis to insist on a debate in the Senate on slavery protection just before the convention, for it might lead to the estrangement of Northern Democrats. Now he was not sure. On May 16, he wrote Stephens that while he had no objection to "non-intervention" as interpreted from the Southern standpoint, it meant "squatter sovereignty" to Douglas' people, and this he could not accept in view of the Dred Scott decision. "Therefore," he said, "I think it due to truth and fair dealing in the party and to the rights of the South that we should understand one another." [70]

Five days later, Toombs joined the debate in the Senate over the long-pending Davis resolutions which he had not supported previously. The fifth resolution was the crux of the matter: "Resolved, that if experience should at any time prove that the judicial and executive authority do not possess means to insure adequate protection to constitutional rights in a Territory, and if the territorial government should fail or refuse to provide the necessary remedies for that purpose, it will be the duty of Congress to supply that deficiency.[71]

Toombs stated that he had originally opposed this, but now, because of changing circumstances and the enunciation of doctrines adverse to the South, he approved every word of it. A basic issue was before the country and had to be resolved. It was folly to shirk this duty. He still would have no slave code as desired by the Mississippians, for men who disregarded the obligations of the constitution would just as easily ignore a law passed in pursuance thereof. What he demanded was the same kind of protection that extended under the constitution to any property anywhere. If that protection were not forthcoming, he would do what he could "to build up new systems, better suited to perform the great ends of all human government, the protection of life, liberty,

[70]Toombs to Stephens, May 16, 1860, in Phillips (ed.), *Correspondence*, 478–79.
[71]Quoted in Phillips (ed.), *Correspondence*, 481.

and property." Toombs still hoped that the Democrats could get together at Baltimore, "against an enemy ever watchful who denies all of our rights, and seeks to overthrow the Constitution. Drive off no sound man who is against the enemy," he said in a brief flashback to his earlier stand, "even by pressing upon him undeniable political truth; trust something to time." In a rhetorical flourish typical of the day and the hour, he concluded: "Unite and let the shout go forth from every city and town, every hamlet and fireside, every mountain top and every valley, from the Atlantic to the Pacific, from the Lakes to the Gulf, 'The country is in danger; ho! every freeman to the rescue!'" [72]

For the first time in several years, the Augusta *Chronicle* commented favorably on the gentleman from Wilkes. "He has come up like a man," it editorialized, "fully and fairly meeting the great issue of the day." Said the Columbus *Times* of his speech: "Whoever reads it, will rise from its perusal with the conviction that squatterism and antiprotectionism have about as much vitality as a wad of 'chawed' cotton seed." The Milledgeville *Federal Union* noted that Toombs' oratory was powerful and took some Douglas men by surprise. [73]

During the debate on the Davis resolutions, a group of leading Southern Democrats, with radicalism temporarily muzzled, issued an address to their constituents in which they advised participation in the Baltimore convention and postponement of the Richmond meeting. Realizing that a split party would enhance chances of Republican victory and probably spell the end of their own power in Congress, they apparently hoped to capture control of the convention through union with a portion of the Northern Democracy, and nominate a Southern candidate on the basis of the majority report at Charleston. Signatory legislators included the future President of the Confederate States, Jefferson Davis, and four of his cabinet members: Toombs, Benjamin, Hunter, and John H. Reagan of Texas. [74]

Acting on this advice, most of the Southern states returned their

[72]*Congressional Globe*, 36th Cong., 1st Sess., Appendix, 338–45. Davis' fifth resolution passed the Senate, 42 to 2. The Republicans, with two exceptions, abstained from voting. See Toombs to Stephens, May 26, 1860, in Phillips (ed.), *Correspondence*, 481.

[73]Augusta *Chronicle*, May 26, 1860; Columbus *Times* quoted in *ibid.*, June 19, 1860; Milledgeville *Federal Union*, May 29, 1860.

[74]Nichols, *Disruption*, 311; Milledgeville *Federal Union*, May 29, 1860.

bolting delegations to Baltimore. The Georgia state Democratic convention, meeting in Milledgeville on June 4, registered its approval of the Charleston secession, and reappointed the same delegation with instructions to walk out again if the Baltimore meeting failed to provide protection for slavery in the territories. Its adamant stand caused a group led by Herschel V. Johnson to bolt and elect a rival slate with less rigid instructions.

In Washington, D.C., a pessimistic Toombs observed that the condition of the party was such that no one could be elected by it; even its success would not gain much. "I have ceased to interest myself further than to give my decided opinions to all who ask for them," he told Stephens.[75]

Toombs' pessimism was well taken. He watched in person as Baltimore turned into another Charleston, with even more tragic results, for there was no tomorrow for the Democrats. When the Alabama and Louisiana delegations led by Yancey and Slidell were denied seats by the Douglas-controlled convention, the banner of secession was again raised, and out of the Front Street Theater streamed a large group of bolters, including Georgia's original Charleston slate. While the remaining delegates nominated Douglas, in another part of the city the bolters chose Vice-President John C. Breckinridge of Kentucky as their presidential nominee and Senator Joseph Lane of Oregon as his running mate.[76] The platforms of the two parties were approximately the same as those of the majority and minority at Charleston. When the Richmond convention, a few days later, endorsed the work of the secessionists, the Democratic fiasco was over.

The presidential election in Georgia, says a student of Cracker State politics, "resolved itself into a repetition of the old arguments, the tedious queries, the trite explanations, and the conventional expressions of sanguine hopes and gloomy forebodings." [77] Most of the powerful politicians backed Breckinridge; the most notable exceptions were Stephens, who supported Douglas, and Benjamin H. Hill, who worked for Bell and the Constitutional

[75]Toombs to Stephens, June 9, 1860, in Phillips (ed.), *Correspondence*, 481.
[76]Nominated at this time as Douglas' running mate was Benjamin Fitzpatrick of Alabama. When Fitzpatrick declined, Herschel V. Johnson of Georgia was selected by the Democratic National Committee to take his place.
[77]Montgomery, *Cracker Parties*, 241.

Union party. Hill attempted to parley the state's latent unionism into a fusion of conservatives, but deep-seated bitterness precluded any success. Despite the preponderance of talent in Breckinridge's favor, the Kentuckian failed to carry Georgia by a majority vote. His total of 51,893 was exceeded by Bell's 42,886 and Douglas' 11,580. Bell carried Wilkes County, Toombs notwithstanding. As no candidate received a majority of the popular vote, the state legislature was obliged to make a choice. In view of the certainty of Republican victory, Governor Brown advised no action at all, but the legislature chose Breckinridge electors anyway. The militant chief executive then sent a special message to the lawmakers in which he reviewed the history of Northern aggressions toward the South, asked for $1,000,000 to put the state on a military footing, and recommended the calling of a state convention to consider secession from the Union.

At the request of the legislature, several influential citizens came to Milledgeville to speak their views on secession. On November 12, Tom Cobb, as yet little known in politics although a prominent lawyer, called for immediate secession. This same Cobb had written his wife a month earlier that Northerners and Southerners were different peoples, and that separation was desirable. Subscribing to a widely held belief concerning the future, he said to his spouse: "If all the South would unanimously say 'we separate,' it would be as peaceably done as a summer's morn." [78]

The next night it was Toombs' turn. Yielding to the excitement of the hour, he advanced, for the moment at least, to the front rank of Southern fire-eaters. The South, he said, could no longer safely remain in the Union. Heretofore the warfare against her institutions had been waged on a state level, but now the Federal government would be in hostile hands after March 4. The rising sun on March 5 should find the South out of the Union. "Then strike, strike while it is yet time." [79] Toombs' speech revealed once more that fatal flaw in his political character which denied him the stature of greatness—a tendency under pressure and commotion to slide into the role of extremist which he could play so ef-

[78]Cobb to his wife, October 11, 1860, "The Correspondence of Thomas Reade Rootes Cobb, 1860–1862," *Publications of the Southern History Association*, XI (May, 1907), 156, hereinafter cited as "Correspondence of T. R. R. Cobb."
[79]Quoted in Phillips, *Toombs*, 201.

Miniature of Robert Toombs at age nineteen. Toombs was a law student at the University of Virginia in 1829.

Portraits of Senator and Mrs. Robert Toombs, 1858. Courtesy of Mr. and Mrs. Bolling S. DuBose, Athens, Georgia.

A recent photograph of the Toombs house in Washington, Georgia. Toombs spoke from this porch on the occasion of the first election of Grover Cleveland.

Alexander H. Stephens, Toombs' lifelong friend and political ally.

Howell Cobb, who, along with Toombs and Alexander H. Stephens, was a member of the Georgia Triumvirate.

Photograph of Toombs from a daguerreotype of uncertain date, but probably from the 1850's, when he was in the Senate. Joseph Emerson and Elizabeth Grisham Brown Collection, University of Georgia.

An 1861 engraving showing the inauguration of Jefferson Davis at Montgomery, Alabama.

The first Confederate cabinet. President Davis is seated at the table with a map in front of him. Vice President Alexander H. Stephens is seated at his right and to his left, at the end of the table, is Secretary of State Robert Toombs.

Toombs in 1885, the year of his death. He was seventy-five.

fectively with his spread-eagle oratory and commanding appearance. It was his explosive and undisciplined temperament which dictated this course, not his desire to curry popular favor, for Toombs probably listened as little to the grass roots chorus as any politician of his day.

On the fourteenth, Stephens, in an impressive speech which attracted attention throughout the country, called for moderation. He was constantly heckled by Toombs, who was sitting on the platform. The warm friendship between the two men had cooled since they had taken divergent stands in the presidential campaign, and Toombs seemed to relish baiting the frail ex-congressman. Stephens thought the secession of a state following a constitutionally held election would itself be a violation of the constitution and national obligations. Furthermore, Lincoln in the White House was prohibited by constitutional checks from doing any harm to the South. Stephens pointed out that the South had prospered greatly under the present system of government, and cautioned against pulling down and destroying what had served so well. Toombs had called for the sword, he said, but his great ardor would fade. Let the people express the popular will through a state convention. "My position then, in conclusion, is for the maintenance of the honor, the rights, the equality, the security, and the glory of my native State in the Union if possible; but if these cannot be maintained in the Union, then I am for their maintenance, at all hazards, out of it." [80]

When Stephens finished his speech, Toombs jumped up and proposed three cheers for his estranged friend, "one of the brightest intellects and purest patriots that lives." On being complimented for his seemingly magnanimous gesture, Toombs replied, "I always try to behave myself at a funeral." [81]

Toombs' ardor did moderate as Stephens prophecied, but not immediately. The day after his secession speech, he sent this telegram to Lawrence M. Keitt, South Carolina congressman and a leading advocate of disunion: "I will sustain South Carolina in secession. I have announced to the legislature that I will not serve under Lincoln. If you have power to act, act at once. We have bright prospects here." [82]

[80]Entire speech quoted in Johnston and Browne, *Stephens*, 564–80.
[81]Quoted in Avary (ed.), *Stephens' Recollections*, 58.
[82]Quoted in Phillips, *Toombs*, 203.

Following the speeches, the state legislature called for the election of a convention on January 2, 1861, to meet in Milledgeville on the sixteenth for the consideration of redressing Georgia's grievances. A million dollars was appropriated as a military fund, and Governor Brown was authorized to set in motion the raising of a force of 10,000 men.

Before Toombs returned to Washington for the second session of the Thirty-sixth Congress, he wrote a letter to a citizens' committee of Danburg, Georgia, in which he prescribed a pattern of action which temporarily furled the banner of disunion for one last attempt at reconciliation. After a justification of secession, mainly on the basis of the threat of the Republican victory to the institution of slavery, he suggested that amendments be proposed to the Constitution which would guarantee full and ample security for Southern rights. If the Republicans would support them in good faith, they could be carried in Congress. He felt that it would then be reasonable and fair to postpone any final action until the Northern states had had an opportunity to act on the amendments. If the results proved adverse to the South, then he was for secession not an hour later than March 4, the day of Lincoln's accession to the presidency.[83]

For his conciliatory posture, secessionist hot-heads in Augusta, called "minute-men" by Stephens, proposed to vote Toombs a "tin sword." Noting that Toombs had changed overnight from hero to traitor in the secessionist press, Stephens wrote his brother Linton on December 22 that "these are but the indications of the fury of popular opinion when it once gets thoroughly aroused. Those who sow the wind will reap the whirlwind."[84] In another letter on the same day to a lawyer friend, he viewed Toombs' latest efforts as a scheme, a "master-stroke to effect his object" of taking Georgia out of the Union. Pied-piper like, he would lure conservatives into his camp, and then lead them into disunion when his proposals were rejected, as he doubtless expected them to be.[85] Toombs may have been many things, but one thing he seemed not to be was devious. Undoubtedly, this appraisal was blurred by the

[83]Toombs to E. B. Pullin and others, December 13, 1860, in Phillips (ed.), *Correspondence*, 519–22.
[84]Quoted in Johnston and Browne, *Stephens*, 370.
[85]*Ibid.*; Phillips, *Toombs*, 205.

pair's alienation, for no one knew the impetuous senator better than Stephens.

On December 3, 1860, with Toombs still at home, the chaplain of the United States Senate prayed that "here, and in the House of Representatives, counsels of wisdom and moderation, of peace and conciliation, of truth and justice, of patriotism and piety, may prevail. . . . Oh, hear us in Heaven," he implored, ". . . and heal our land." [86] The early wrangling in Congress seemed to make a mockery out of the clergyman's invocation. The House created a Committee of Thirty-three to work out a plan of sectional compromise, but it was soon apparent that its efforts would be unavailing. Thereupon, a Southern caucus on December 15 adopted a frankly secessionist manifesto, stating that all hope of preserving Southern rights through committees, legislation, or constitutional amendments was extinguished. A Southern confederacy was the only answer. Twenty-three representatives and seven senators, including Davis and Brown of Mississippi, Benjamin of Louisiana, and Iverson, Toombs' colleague from Georgia, signed the document which was intended to influence the South Carolina convention soon to meet. Toombs was not yet in Washington, and so did not participate. At the time, however, it was asserted by some that he would have endorsed the manifesto; this is doubtful, for his Danburg letter with its olive branch implications was being read by Georgians at the same time.

South Carolina left the Union on December 20. On the same day, a Senate Committee of Thirteen was named by Vice-President Breckinridge to tackle the worsening national crisis. It was a strong group with Toombs and Davis from the lower South, and Hunter of Virginia, Lazarus W. Powell and Crittenden of Kentucky from the upper South. Douglas, William M. Bigler of Pennsylvania, and Henry M. Rice of Minnesota represented the Northern Democrats. Five Republicans filled the remaining posts: Seward, Wade, Jacob Collamer of Vermont, James W. Grimes of Iowa, and James R. Doolittle of Wisconsin.

The most important Republican, Seward, did not attend the early meetings of the committee. Having been tapped for service in Lincoln's cabinet, he desired to know the President-elect's mind

[86]*Congressional Globe*, 36th Cong., 2nd Sess., 1.

on compromise. He had left Washington for consultation with Republican politician Thurlow Weed, who was visiting Lincoln in Springfield. Not until the twenty-fourth did Seward return, bearing Lincoln's refusal to accept any expansion of slavery. This, in reality, spelled doom for the Committee of Thirteen.

The committee met for the first time on December 21, and after "an informal conversation," it adjourned. At the outset of business on the twenty-second, the committee adopted a Davis-sponsored rule that no proposal would be considered as adopted unless it were agreed to by a majority of the Republicans and a majority of the other senators. It was a reasonable rule, for it would have been fruitless to present any plan to the Senate which the Republicans would not accept.

Three sets of resolutions were then introduced by Toombs, Davis, and Crittenden. Toombs' proposals, in the form of constitutional amendments, called for: equality and full protection of all citizens with their property in the territories; extradition of persons committing crimes against slave property; protection of slave states against insurrection; enforcement of the Fugitive Slave Act of 1850, prohibition of Federal laws relating to slavery without the consent of a majority of senators and representatives from slaveholding states; and prohibition of the alteration of any constitutional provision pertaining to slavery without the unanimous consent of the slaveholding states. Davis' proposition would have placed slavery, by constitutional amendment, on the same footing with all other property.[87]

Next, the resolutions of the venerable Kentucky senator were presented and considered by the committee. Earlier they had been introduced on the Senate floor, arousing widespread and enthusiastic public support. The fate of a nation seemed to be riding on their acceptance now. Most important among the Crittenden proposals was the extension of the Missouri Compromise line, 36° 30', through the Federal territories to the Pacific. Slavery was prohibited north of the line and recognized and protected south of it. New states from the territories were to be admitted to the Union with or without slavery as their constitutions provided. The key vote of the Committee of Thirteen was registered on this proposal. The four Republicans present voted no. Toombs and Davis, al-

[87]"Journal of the Committee of Thirteen," *Senate Reports*, 36th Cong., 2nd Sess., No. 288, pp. 2–3.

though favoring the proposition, then cast negative votes as they had declared would be their policy on any resolution which the Republicans failed to support. Seward, returning later, also voted in the negative, giving a final tabulation of six for and seven against. By any measurement, the resolution had failed. The other parts of Crittenden's package plan were then defeated by solid Republican opposition. Crittenden said it was "the darkest day of his life." [88]

The next day, Sunday the twenty-third, Toombs dispatched a telegram to his "Fellow Citizens of Georgia" which was published on Monday in several newspapers. In it he reviewed the rejection of the Crittenden resolutions by the committee. He declared that a test had been made fairly and frankly. "Now I tell you," he continued,

upon the faith of a true man that all further looking to the North for security for your constitutional rights in the Union ought to be instantly abandoned. It is fraught with nothing but ruin to yourselves and your posterity.

Secession by the fourth of March next should be thundered from the ballot-box by the unanimous vote of Georgia on the second day of January next. Such a voice will be your best guarantee for liberty, security, tranquillity, and glory.[89]

The Committee of Thirteen continued its sessions through the thirty-first, but no general plan for presentation to the Senate was agreed upon. On the twenty-fourth, Seward made a Republican counter proposal: the guarantee of slavery in the states where it already existed, the amendment of the Fugitive Slave Act of 1850 to include jury trial, and the repeal of personal liberty laws. It failed

[88]New York *Times*, December 24, 1860; "Journal of Committee of Thirteen," 5–6; Potter, *Secession Crisis*, 172; Nevins, *Emergence of Lincoln*, II, 397; Phillips, *Toombs*, 207. Toombs and Davis, somewhat inexplicably, voted affirmatively for the remaining five of Crittenden's resolutions. Phillips suggests that the rule requiring a majority vote from both Republicans and Democrats for the passage of a proposal may have come, in time sequence, *after* the first vote on Crittenden's plan. Under it, regardless of how the two cotton senators voted, Republican opposition would have killed any resolution anyway. Realizing this and, perhaps, wishing to show that they actually favored the plan though voting negatively on its first part, Toombs and Davis voted affirmatively from here on. See also Potter, *Secession Crisis*, 205, fn49.

[89]Phillips (ed.), *Correspondence*, 525.

of adoption as did Toombs' plan, parts of which were voted down on the same day and the rest on the twenty-sixth.[90] On December 28, the committee voted to report that it had "not been able to agree upon any general plan of adjustment," and adjourned subject to the call of the chairman, Senator Powell. On the last day of the month, in pathetic anti-climax, six members convened, heard and approved the reading of the journal, and adjourned for the last time. Toombs was not present.

History has generally put the blame for the failure of the Committee of Thirteen on the Republicans. It is impossible to say, however, whether any success would have been the necessary panacea for the ills of the hour. For some years, Republican supporters tried to saddle part of the responsibility for the failure of compromise on Toombs and Davis in their negative vote on Crittenden's first resolution. But it seems quite clear that the pair would have voted affirmatively if the Republicans had done so. In any event, under the rule adopted, technically it would have made no difference how they voted as long as the Republicans remained in opposition.[91]

Events were now moving swiftly. On January 1, Toombs sent a telegram to the Augusta *True Democrat:* "The cabinet is broken up, Mr. [John B.] Floyd, Secretary of War, and Mr. [Jacob] Thompson, Secretary of the Interior [both Southerners], having resigned. Mr. [Joseph] Holt of Kentucky, our bitter foe, has been made Secretary of War. Fort Pulaski [at the mouth of the Savannah River] is in danger. The Abolitionists are defiant." [92] His warning, coming on the heels of the refusal of the Federal government to give up Fort Sumter to South Carolina, led Governor Brown to order the seizure of Fort Pulaski in the name of the state. It was rumored in Washington, a city beset with wild stories, that Buchanan's cabinet considered having Toombs arrested on the charge of treason for his message to Georgia about the fort. Although the rumor was groundless, Toombs' action did incense the administration.[93]

The news of his election as a delegate to the mid-January Georgia convention brought home to Toombs the fact that his days in Washington were doubtlessly numbered. He began thinking of a

[90]"Journal of Committee of Thirteen," 10–13.
[91]Potter, *Secession Crisis*, 204–206.
[92]Phillips (ed.), *Correspondence*, 528.
[93]Savannah *Morning News*, January 9, 1861.

speech to the Senate—perhaps it would be his last one. In the midst of his preparations, a caucus of Southern senators was held which he did not attend, but whose resolutions he reportedly signed. The embattled Southerners declared that each slave state should secede as quickly as possible; that a convention of the seceded states should meet not later than February 15 at Montgomery; that the members of Congress from the South should request instructions on how long they should remain in Washington; and that Senators Davis, Slidell, and Mallory be appointed a committee to promote the purposes of the meeting. The resolutions were to be sent to the governors of the states represented for their guidance in the forthcoming conventions.[94]

Toombs took the Senate floor on January 7. His speech was an incendiary one that left little room for sectional reconciliation. He did not care to discuss the legality of secession at this late hour. It was already an accomplished fact, legal or not, he declared. The South through the years had asked for nothing except that the North abide by the Constitution. This had not been done. What bothered Toombs more than anything else was the threat to slavery posed by the recent triumph of the Republican party. "We want no negro equality, no negro citizenship; we want no mongrel race to degrade our own . . . ," he declared. "We will tell you when we choose to abolish this thing; it must be done under our direction and according to our will; our own, our native land shall determine this question, and not the Abolitionists of the North.[95]

The Georgia senator said that he would have been willing to accept Crittenden's proposal of dividing the territories at 36°30', but the Committee of Thirteen had turned it down. He now listed his own compromise plan, also rejected by the committee, as the ultimatum of the South and the last hope of adjustment.

Restore us these rights as we had them, as your court adjudges them to be, just as all our people have said they are; redress these flagrant wrongs, seen of all men, and it will restore fraternity, and peace, and unity to all of us. Refuse them, and what then? We shall then ask you, 'let us depart in peace.' Refuse that, and you present us war. We

[94]C. C. Clay, Jr., to A. B. Moore, January 7, 1861, in *The War of the Rebellion: A Compilation of the Official Records of the Union and Confederate Armies* (Washington, 1880–1901), Ser. IV, Vol. I, 28–29, hereinafter cited as *Official Records*.
[95]*Congressional Globe*, 36th Cong., 2nd Sess., 270–71.

accept it; and inscribing upon our banners the glorious words, 'liberty and equality,' we will trust to the blood of the brave and the God of battles for security and tranquillity.[96]

The close of Toombs' speech was greeted with a prolonged storm of hisses and applause,[97] symbolizing the apparent hopelessness of sectional rapport. The longtime defender of national union had at last slammed shut the door of compromise.

On January 10, three days before he left Washington, Toombs attended a dinner party where he became involved in an altercation with General Winfield Scott, commander-in-chief of the army. A topic of conversation was the *Star of the West*, a steamer carrying troops and supplies which President Buchanan had recently dispatched for the relief of Fort Sumter. Word had been received in Washington that the ship had been fired on by South Carolina shore batteries. Toombs remarked that if the ship had been sunk, he wished that those who had ordered her to Charleston had been on board. This brought a sharp rejoinder from Scott to which Toombs replied in strong language. A near fight was averted by others present.[98]

It was all over for Toombs and many of his Southern colleagues. As they prepared to leave, "a dull, vague unrest brooded over Washington, as though the city lay in the shadow of a great pall or was threatened with a plague." [99]

Robert Toombs had entered Congress in 1845 with the moderate political philosophy that temperate and understanding men both North and South should be able to live together within the framework of the Constitution. Although capable of partisan sectionalism in moments of stress, he maintained through various crises a fairly constant adherence to this nationalistic creed. To some extent he was motivated by a strong desire to preserve the Whig party as a national organization. But undoubtedly he was also deeply devoted to the Union. Even with his departure from Whig ranks and the increasing sectional rancor over slavery, Toombs remained relatively dispassionate in his judgments. He saw, or hoped he saw, in the national Democratic party the good men who might yet resolve the sectional strife.

[96]*Ibid.*, 271.
[97]New York *Times*, January 8, 1861.
[98]*Ibid.*, January 12, 1861; Savannah *Morning News*, January 12, 1861.
[99]T. C. DeLeon, *Belles Beaux and Brains of the 60's* (New York, 1907), 40.

Not until 1859 and his growing fear of a Republican victory was his faith in an enduring union seriously shaken. Toombs was convinced that the sectional Republican party, in spite of its professions to the contrary, was a threat to the people, the social order, and the institutions of the South. He saw absolutely no chance for the slightest rapport with such "miscreants," whose "one living, animating principle" was hatred for the South. As Republican strength and influence increased, Toombs in the spring of 1860 moved correspondingly toward support of the extreme Southern demand for Federal protection of slavery in the territories, something the Republicans adamantly opposed. It was an impractical stand, as Toombs himself had in effect said earlier. But it had become a matter of principle, a point of honor, to many Southerners. Perhaps this was reflective of the unrealities of antebellum Southern civilization—a slave society in a world where slavery had nearly vanished; an agrarian economy in the era of the Industrial Revolution; and an Old World code of conduct in a nation being transformed by democratic processes. Once in the camp of the extremists, Toombs bowed to no one in his defense of their stand. A proud and sensitive Southerner did not easily retreat from a principle. Toombs was willing to dissolve a union rather than do so.

CHAPTER VIII

Confederate Secretary of State

O N Sunday morning, January 13, 1861, Robert Toombs left Washington and headed home to attend the state convention which would determine Georgia's course of action in the secession crisis. Confident that his state would leave the Union, he wrote a former South Carolina congressman that "we shall soon be by your side to share your evils, dangers & honors." [1] The day before he departed, Toombs had sent a telegram to the Augusta *Constitutionalist*, hoping thereby to close all avenues of compromise. He said he had found unacceptable Seward's speech of January 12, commonly regarded as embracing the Republican plan of reconciliation, and told the people of Georgia that the New York senator had put "an end to all hope of adjustment." [2]

On January 16 the state convention at Milledgeville began its proceedings. Crowded and excited galleries looked down on what was, perhaps, the most prestigious political gathering in Georgia's long and colorful history. On the floor as delegates were eight former United States congressmen and two former United States senators, two ex-governors, one ex-cabinet member, and every important public man in the state with the exception of Governor

[1]Toombs to Lawrence M. Keitt, January 11, 1861, in Francis W. Pickens Papers, Duke University.
[2]Quoted in Savannah *Morning News*, January 14, 1861. For Seward's speech, see *Congressional Globe*, 36th Cong., 2nd Sess., 341–44.

Joseph E. Brown, former speaker of the House of Representatives, Howell Cobb, and former gubernatorial candidate, Charles J. Jenkins, who were tendered seats by the convention.[3] The popular election of delegates on January 2 had resulted in a slight victory for the immediate secessionists, who held a thirty-odd seat majority at the convention. Union supporter Alexander H. Stephens termed stormy January 2 "the worst day for an election I ever saw in Georgia." He believed that the weather cost the small farmer-backed "Conservative cause" at least 10,000 votes, for the planter-merchant coalition of secessionists was less adversely affected in going to the polls.[4] The opponents of the immediate secessionists, generally and loosely called "cooperationists," represented widely differing opinions, ranging from secession in cooperation with the other Southern states to outright Unionism.[5]

After the opening sessions, the convention conducted its business behind closed doors. The first test of strength came on January 18 when two resolutions were proposed by Judge Eugenius Nisbet, former Unionist turned secessionist, to the effect that it was Georgia's right and duty to secede and that a committee be appointed to draft an ordinance of secession. Cooperationist ex-governor Herschel V. Johnson, playing for time against the secessionist steamroller, offered a substitute resolution declaring it to be Georgia's desire to preserve the Union without injury to herself, and calling for a convention of delegates from all of the slaveholding states to meet in Atlanta on February 16 to consider their relationship to the Union. After a long discussion in which Toombs played a prominent part, Nisbet's proposals were adopted by a vote of 166 to 130. A committee of seventeen, which included the still estranged Toombs and Stephens, was appointed to draft an ordinance of secession.

Following this initial victory for the secessionists, the convention adopted a resolution proposed by Toombs endorsing the action of Governor Brown in seizing Fort Pulaski on January 3. This tangential and provocative move by the delegates was in reply to a New York legislative resolution which had pledged support in men

---

[3]Ralph Wooster, "The Georgia Secession Convention," *Georgia Historical Quarterly*, XL (March, 1956), 24.

[4]Johnston and Browne, *Stephens*, 378–79.

[5]Wooster, "Georgia Secession Convention," 23–24. The vote in Georgia was 50,243 in favor of "immediate action candidates" to 37,123 for those opposed. See T. Conn Bryan, *Confederate Georgia* (Athens, 1953), 5.

and money to President-elect Abraham Lincoln for upholding the authority of the Federal government.

On January 19 the committee reported its ordinance of secession. Benjamin H. Hill, cooperationist, immediately moved that Johnson's resolution be substituted for the ordinance, but his stalling tactics were beaten down 164 to 133, the "key vote in the Georgia convention." [6] Shortly afterwards, with many cooperationists crossing over, the convention voted 208 to 89 in favor of secession.[7]

The climactic moment arrived at 2 P.M. when former governor George W. Crawford, the president of the convention, mounted the stage in the low-ceilinged House assembly hall and stated solemnly to the hushed and tense delegates that it was his "privilege and pleasure to declare that the State of Georgia was free, sovereign, and independent."[8] A few minutes later a cannon fired from the capitol lawn conveyed the news to the state. Amid the cheers of a throng of some 2,500 gathered around the capitol steps, the Stars and Stripes were hauled down. Up fluttered the flag of Georgia, a single red star mounted on a white field. Throughout the afternoon and into the night the city of Milledgeville, and much of the rest of the state, revelled in the intoxication of independence.[9] The daughter of prominent Unionist Judge Garnett Andrews resignedly noted in her journal that her father had done his best to keep Georgia in the Union, "but he might as well have tried to tie up the northwest wind in the corner of a pocket handkerchief." [10]

The convention continued in session until January 29, for the most part creating a framework of government for Georgia as an independent state. In anticipation of a Southern confederacy, Toombs as chairman of the "Committee on Foreign Relations" recommended that ten delegates be chosen to attend the convention of seceded states in Montgomery on February 4. Toombs and Howell Cobb were selected delegates at large, along with Stephens, Ben Hill, Tom Cobb, Francis S. Bartow, Martin J. Crawford,

[6]Wooster, "Georgia Secession Convention," 33.

[7]Allen D. Candler (ed.), *The Confederate Records of the State of Georgia* (Atlanta, 1910), I, 229–60; Wooster, "Georgia Secession Convention," 30–33; Bryan, *Confederate Georgia*, 7–9; Phillips, *Georgia and State Rights*, 202–203. In the final vote Hill sided with the secessionists. Stephens and Johnson opposed secession through the last ballot.

[8]Candler (ed.), *Georgia Confederate Records*, I, 260.

[9]Savannah *Morning News*, January 22, 1861.

[10]Eliza Frances Andrews, *The War-Time Journal of a Georgia Girl, 1864–65* (New York, 1908), 176.

Eugenius Nisbet, Augustus Wright, and Augustus H. Kenan from congressional districts. Georgia's representation was a balance between immediate secessionists and moderates, a mode of action generally followed by the seceded states.[11]

The last major work of the convention was the adoption of a report written by Toombs stating the reasons for Georgia's separation from the Union. The longstanding antislavery policy of the North was advanced by the former senator as the chief cause of secession. With the government now committed to Republicans "whose avowed purpose is to subvert our society, and subject us, not only to the loss of our property but the destruction of ourselves, our wives, and our children and the desolation of our homes, our altars, and our firesides . . . ," Georgians were forced, Toombs asserted, to "seek new safe-guards for our liberty, equality, security and tranquility." [12]

Toombs reached Montgomery on a rainy Sunday, the day before the convention began. His arrival had been delayed two hours by an accident some three miles outside the city, when a rail, laid that morning, had broken, causing the train to leave the track. Remarkably little damage had been done in what Tom Cobb described as an "awful smash up," and what Mary Boykin Chesnut, wife of the former United States senator from South Carolina, saw as the result of traveling on Sunday.[13]

Picturesque Montgomery, located in the heart of the fertile Black Belt, perched on high bluffs overlooking the Alabama River. Small, pleasant, and planter-dominated, it was doubtless agreeable to most of the incoming delegates. Between the river and the capitol were the town's two hotels, Montgomery Hall and the more pretentious Exchange, which housed the leading government figures. "Nightly," wrote observer, "the corridor of the Exchange Hotel was a pandemonium; its every flagstone a rostrum." [14] The rapid and heterogeneous influx of visitors, which doubled the population in two weeks, considerably altered the small-town atmosphere. "Montgomery seemed Washington over again," it was noted, "but

[11]Candler (ed.), *Georgia Confederate Records*, I, 283–84, 294–95.

[12]*Ibid.*, 360–61. The convention reassembled on March 7, ratified the Confederate constitution on March 16 by unanimous vote, and adjourned *sine die* on March 23. See *ibid.*, 381, 458, 615.

[13]T. Cobb to his wife, February 3, 1861, in "Correspondence of T. R. R. Cobb," XI, 159.

[14]DeLeon, *Belles Beaux*, 50.

on a small scale, and with the avidity and agility in pursuit of the spoils somewhat enhanced by freshness of scent." [15]

At noon on Monday, February 4, with six states in attendance, the distinguished Montgomery convention began the business of creating a new nation.[16] Howell Cobb was chosen president of the convention by acclamation. In closing his brief statement of acceptance, he seemed to reflect the spirit and purpose of the delegates as he said: "With a consciousness of the justice of our cause, and with confidence in the guidance and blessing of a kind Providence, we will this day inaugurate for the South a new era of peace, security, and prosperity." [17]

Working swiftly to usher in the new era, the convention within four days framed and adopted a constitution for a provisional government. Patterned after the Federal constitution, it legalized the convention as the national lawmaking congress until a permanent constitution and government could be created.

Next came the important task of selecting a provisional President and Vice President. Robert Toombs may well have been the first choice of the majority of the Montgomery delegates. Giant-sized intellectually and physically, a pre-secession figure of great significance, and a front-runner in the secession movement, he seemed to possess the vigor and boldness necessary for a successful revolutionary experiment. But events on the night of February 8, the night before the balloting, gave the top political post in the new government to Jefferson Davis of Mississippi who, ironically, preferred high military office.

Stephens later explained that largely through "misapprehension" Toombs failed to be tendered the presidency. Georgia's delegation, he said, met for consultation on the matter on the morning of the election, and Toombs was the unanimous choice of those present. Tom Cobb and Bartow, however, told the group that in the caucuses of Florida, South Carolina, and Louisiana held the preceding night Davis had been agreed upon. Stephens noted that "Mr. Toombs seemed very incredulous of this, and his manner indicated some surprise." Crawford was made a committee of one to verify the

[15]*Ibid.*, 48; Savannah *Morning News*, February 7, 1861.
[16]The delegation from Texas arrived several days late.
[17]"Journal of the Congress of the Confederate States of America, 1861–1865," *Senate Documents*, 58th Cong., 2nd Sess., Doc. 234, p. 16, hereinafter cited as "Confederate Journal."

report. If substantiated, the delegation would then support Stephens for the vice presidency instead of Toombs for the presidency. Crawford's inquiry eliminated Toombs. Stephens said he later found out that some of the delegates thought Howell Cobb was Georgia's preference. Unwilling to support Cobb because of "past Party conflicts" and not desiring to offend Georgia by selecting the apparently bypassed Toombs, for the sake of harmony they agreed to back Davis. Stephens observed that while he would gladly have backed either Cobb or Davis, "Mr. Toombs was by far the best fitted for that position, looking to all the qualifications necessary to meet its full requirements." [18]

Tom Cobb, a strange blend of piety, prejudice, and passion, gave a different and gap-filled story to his wife. Well-known lawyer but fledgling politician, Cobb disliked Toombs and Stephens, and until his death at the battle of Fredericksburg in December, 1862, was their constant critic. The Athens lawyer said that on the night before the election an informal canvas—a "counting of noses"—was conducted, revealing Alabama, Mississippi, and Florida for Davis, Louisiana and Georgia for brother Howell, and South Carolina divided between the two. To close the ranks and, perhaps, to spite Toombs, Howell "immediately announced his wish that Davis should be unanimously elected." Apparently only the Cobb brothers and possibly Bartow from the Georgia delegation were present for this pre-election gambit. Cobb's account of the events of the next morning paralleled that of Stephens', but his editorial comment was unique. In his opinion, *"Toombs was much mortified"* by what transpired even though he said he did not want to be president. The ultimate election of Stephens as Vice President was termed by Cobb "a bitter pill to some of us but we have swallowed it with as good grace as we could." [19]

Other explanations have been offered as to why Toombs failed to get what he wanted at Montgomery. Stovall says that "at the eleventh hour, [Democratic] party lines were drawn against Robert Toombs," former Constitutional Unionist whose party colleagues in Mississippi had helped defeat Democrat Davis in the governor's race in 1850. [20]

[18]Stephens, *War Between the States*, II, 329–33.
[19]T. Cobb to his wife, February 9, 11, 1861, in "Correspondence of T. R. R. Cobb," XI, 168, 171–72.
[20]Stovall, *Toombs*, 218; Johnston, *Autobiography*, 125

Stephens wrote his brother on February 23, 1861, from Montgomery that "it was his drinking to excess" that had ruined Toombs' chances. Although not mentioning this in his later account, Stephens said at the time that Toombs "was in the habit of getting tight every day at dinner. One day in particular about two days before the election he got quite tight at dinner and went to a party in town *tighter* than I ever saw him—too tight for his character and reputation by far. I think that evenings exhibition settled the Presidency where it fell." [21]

This incident is also noted in Stovall's biography, although with a certain degree of skepticism. There is, however, no reluctance on the part of Toombs' Boswell to state with firmness that drinking was the Georgian's "great fault." If college folklore can be believed, Toombs started drinking in his early teens at the University of Georgia. It appeared at this time to be a part of a not unusual college behavioral pattern for untamed planter youth. Not until the convention at Montgomery, many years later, does one find substantial evidence that his drinking was done to excess with any degree of regularity. Toombs did not have to drink much in order to get drunk. "He was easily affected by the smallest indulgence," says Stovall. "When he measured himself with others, glass for glass, the result was distressing, disastrous." [22] Toombs' drinking continued during the war years, particularly in periods of frustration and idleness when he found himself, like Saul, off the main stage of action. In the post-war period, largely out of step with a changing South and beset by family tragedy, he cast aside restraint until his drinking became an unbreakable habit.

Jefferson Davis added another chapter to the story of the Confederate presidency in later years after Stephens' account minimizing his popular esteem at Montgomery had appeared in print. Apparently miffed at the "misapprehension" concept, Davis in his *The Rise and Fall of the Confederate Government* included excerpts from letters of persons in attendance at Montgomery to show that there was strong sentiment for him from the beginning among several states. [23] A distinguished Southern historian, familiar with all of

[21]Stephens to his brother, February 23, 1861, in Alexander H. Stephens Papers, Southern Historical Collection, University of North Carolina.
[22]Stovall, *Toombs*, 365.
[23]Jefferson Davis, *The Rise and Fall of the Confederate Government* (New York, 1881), I, 236–41.

the conflicting evidence, has seen the "excessive zeal [of the Provisional Congress] for unanimity and harmony" as perhaps the best explanation for the elevation of Jefferson Davis instead of Robert Toombs to the presidency.[24] This would appear to be the most likely post-mortem on the biggest disappointment in Toombs' political career.

The bare-bones *Confederate Journal* recorded the election of Davis on February 9 as follows: "The vote being taken by States for President, the Hon. Jefferson Davis, of Mississippi, received all the votes cast, being 6, and was duly declared unanimously elected President of the Provisional Government." [25]

Had the mantle of leadership fallen on Toombs, the course of events probably would not have changed. In the final analysis, events in the executive office in Richmond were not paramount in the determination of Southern independence. But it might have been a more interesting struggle with the dynamic, daring Georgian in the saddle instead of the restrained Mississippian. Perhaps the only hope for Confederate victory was one bold throw of the dice early in the conflict. Toombs, always impatient with the pedestrian routine of office work, doubtless would have been willing to make the gamble.

On the same day as the election, the Provisional Congress appointed a committee of twelve men, two from each state, to draw up a permanent constitution. From Georgia, Toombs and T. R. R. Cobb served, "a post of honor" in Cobb's eyes.[26] Toiling long hours in the evening after the close of the regular congressional sessions, the committee, on February 26, reported a completed document. On March 11, after two weeks' debate, the constitution was adopted by Congress and subsequently by state secession conventions or legislatures.[27]

---

[24]E. Merton Coulter, *The Confederate States of America, 1861–1865* (Baton Rouge, 1950), 23.

[25]"Confederate Journal," 40.

[26]T. Cobb to his wife, February 11, 1861, in "Correspondence of T. R. R. Cobb," XI, 172; "Confederate Journal," 41–42.

[27]"Confederate Journal," 87, 851–96. The Savannah *Morning News*, February 16, noted the unusual fact that within thirty days Toombs had traveled more than 1,500 miles, had served under three governments—the U. S. Senate, the Georgia secession convention, the Provisional Confederate Congress—and was in the process of helping to create a fourth—the permanent Confederate government.

The Confederate constitution, not unexpectedly, closely resembled its Federal counterpart. The chief differences lay in its emphasis on the sovereignty of the states, protection for the institution of slavery, and concern for a careful husbandry of public funds. Toombs and Stephens were anxious to pierce the traditional American wall between cabinet and congress which prohibited dual office holding in government. This separation of powers, it was believed, had led in the past to ministerial irresponsibility and government inefficiency. Failing to carry his point in committee, Toombs tried to push it through on the floor of Congress, but was unsuccessful. As a token gesture, there was written into the constitution a clause to the effect that Congress could grant seats on the floor of either house to heads of departments for the purpose of discussing measures pertaining to the departments.[28]

Toombs' zeal for safeguarding the national treasury was reflected in constitutional prohibitions against extra compensation to public contractors beyond the original contract, against appropriations for internal improvements except for certain specified purposes, and against general congressional appropriations except by two-thirds vote of both houses, unless specifically requested by a department head. It is thought that Toombs also authored the provision that the Post Office Department was obligated to live off of its own revenues after March 1, 1863.[29]

Toombs was called back to Georgia on the evening of February 18 by the serious illness of his daughter Sallie (Mrs. Dudley M. DuBose), following the birth of a child. Tom Cobb told his wife that the news "completely unnerved him and he left immediately." [30] That afternoon Jefferson Davis, amid much pageantry, had been inaugurated provisional President of the Confederate States. Toombs was doubtless an observer of the impressive ceremonies witnessed by enthusiastic thousands.

While he was away, Davis, on February 21, submitted his name to Congress for approval as secretary of state. Congress confirmed

[28]Stephens to Linton Stephens, February 17, 1861, in Johnston and Browne, *Stephens,* 386; "Confederate Journal," 853, 863; Phillips, *Toombs,* 228-29; Stovall, *Toombs,* 219-20; Charles Robert Lee, Jr., *The Confederate Constitutions* (Chapel Hill, 1963), 96-100.

[29]"Confederate Journal," 913-15; Phillips, *Toombs,* 229; Stovall, *Toombs,* 220; Lee, "Confederate Constitutions," 100.

[30]Cobb to his wife, February 19, 1861, in "Correspondence of T. R. R. Cobb," XI, 183.

the appointment unanimously.[31] It was not a happy situation for either man. Davis had preferred to tender the post to Robert W. Barnwell of South Carolina, an old and esteemed friend from senatorial days. But before he could make his wishes known, the South Carolina delegation pressed upon him another of its members, Christopher G. Memminger, for the office of secretary of the treasury, and the ultimate selection of Memminger precluded another cabinet member for that state. Davis, who wanted Toombs as secretary of the treasury, then offered the Georgian the post in the state department, a place, as Davis said later, "for which others believed him to be well qualified." [32]

Toombs was in Augusta with his daughter when Davis broached the matter to him. At first he declined to serve. In a follow-up letter to the telegram of refusal, Toombs gave his reasons for not wishing to enter the cabinet permanently, although he agreed to serve temporarily until the position could perhaps be filled by someone from a border state. He told Davis he believed he could better serve the country from a legislative position, and that the illness of his daughter would require his presence at home for periods inconsistent with executive duty.[33]

In the next few days Toombs changed his mind. Sallie improved, and Stephens was able to persuade him that he should enter the cabinet. He returned to Montgomery on February 24, and three days later was sworn into office.[34] Thus was Toombs drawn into a position to which he was ill-suited by nature and into a closer relationship with a man whom he had never particularly cared for.

The executive offices of the Confederacy were crowded together in the Government House, just across the square from the Exchange Hotel. "A great, red brick pile, originally built for ware-

[31]"Confederate Journal," 73.

[32]Davis, *Rise and Fall*, I, 242.

[33]Toombs to Davis, February 20, 1861, in Charles C. Jones, Jr. (collector), Autograph Letters and Portraits of the Signers of the Constitution of the Confederate States, Duke University.

[34]T. Cobb to his wife, February 25, 1861, in "Correspondence of T. R. R. Cobb," XI, 240; Phillips, *Toombs*, 228. Toombs took this oath of office: "I Robert Toombs Secretary of State for the Confederate States of America do solemnly swear that I will well and faithfully execute the duties of said office, and will support the Constitution for the Provisional Government of the Confederate States of America." See Pickett Papers, Box 142, Confederate States of America Archives, Library of Congress.

houses and countingrooms," [35] it became the scene of unprecedented activity with the expansion of the Confederate government. The Exchange Hotel likewise felt the pressure of a burgeoning population. Homesick Tom Cobb, quartered here along with many other public officials, noted sourly that it was "becoming horrible in its filth and astounding in its bills." [36]

Toombs' official duties as secretary of state were first prescribed by an act of Congress on February 21, 1861, and later enlarged by statute on May 6. In addition to his responsibilities in the realm of foreign affairs, the secretary was required to publish all acts and resolutions of Congress, handle applications for letters of marque and reprisal, collect one copy of every copyrighted book, and affix the great seal of the Confederate States to all civil commissions. Toombs' staff included an assistant secretary of state, one chief clerk, a clerk, and a messenger.[37]

Never an office man and rarely a cooperative subordinate, Toombs did not find his rather prosaic and Davis-guided tasks in the department appealing, and spent as little time there as possible. He was fond of saying that he carried the business of the department around in his hat.[38] A frequent visitor to the executive offices observed that "Toombs had nothing to do but talk politics, tell stories and say some very clever things." [39]

The objective of the Confederate State Department's foreign policy was largely threefold: the peaceful separation of the Southern states from the Union; recognition of the Confederacy's independence by Europe; and the promotion of commercial relations with other nations. To carry out the first objective, President Davis, on February 25, appointed Martin J. Crawford of Georgia, John Forsyth of Alabama, and André B. Roman of Louisiana as a commission to represent the Confederate States in Washington. Toombs apparently had nothing to do with their selection. In accordance with a Congressional resolution, their purposes were the negotiation of friendly relations between the two governments

[35]T. C. DeLeon, *Four Years in Rebel Capitals* . . . (Mobile, 1892), 37.
[36]T. Cobb to his wife, February 22, 1861, in Thomas Reade Rootes Cobb Letters (Typescript), University of Georgia, I, 42, hereinafter cited as T. R. R. Cobb Letters.
[37]James M. Matthews (ed.), *The Statutes at Large of the Provisional Government of the Confederate States of America* (Richmond, 1864), 29, 42, 52, 100–104, 157–61.
[38]*Southern Historical Society Papers* (Richmond, 1876–1910), XXIX, 346.
[39]DeLeon, *Belles Beaux*, 83–84.

and the settlement of all disagreements "upon principles of right, justice, equity, and good faith." [40] Particularly was the Confederacy interested in obtaining possession of Fort Pickens, near Pensacola, and Fort Sumter, guarding the entrance to the Charleston harbor, both still in Federal hands. Their official instructions were given them by Toombs on February 27, one of his first acts as secretary of state.

Hanging disconcertingly in the atmosphere of the Northern capital was the seeming indecisiveness of incoming President Abraham Lincoln toward the Fort Sumter issue. His secretary of state, William H. Seward, who regarded himself as the dominant personality of the new government, had no such doubts as to his own course. He hoped for a peaceful reunion of the states through voluntary reconstruction, and viewed the evacuation of Fort Sumter as the removal of a source of irritation, particularly necessary since Major Robert Anderson, the fort's commander, had recommended it from want of provisions.

The Confederate commissioners were unable to obtain a formal meeting with Seward, but were assured by him around the middle of March through an intermediary, Supreme Court Justice John A. Campbell of Alabama, that Sumter would be evacuated.[41] Seward, however, was forced into a position of duplicity as Lincoln began to take hold of the reins of government and move against concession on the issue of the forts. Lincoln's stand was dictated to a large extent by Northern public opinion, the President fearing that the abandonment of Sumter would seriously damage the prestige of his administration already accused of appeasement by its lack of direct action.

For several weeks the commissioners waited in Washington, confident that Seward would carry out his pledge and hoping for negotiations with him that would lead to recognition of the Confederacy. They were in constant touch with Toombs, who was serving largely as an intermediary between them and the Davis cabinet. Their telegrams in this period mirror the changing scene in Washington as the "war party" under Lincoln assumed control:

[40]"Confederate Journal," 55.
[41]James D. Richardson (ed.), *A Compilation of the Messages and Papers of the Confederacy Including the Diplomatic Correspondence 1861–1865* (Nashville, 1906), I, 93–96, hereinafter cited as Richardson (ed.), *Confederate Correspondence.*

March 20—"If there is faith in man we may rely on the assurance [Seward's] we have as to the status." March 22—"We have the highest assurances that the delay in the evacuation of Fort Sumter shows no bad faith[—]that it will be done as soon as possible." March 28—"The senate has adjourned sine die. There is a dead calm here." April 2—"The war wing presses on the President; he vibrates to that side." April 3—"Much activity to-day in the War and Navy Departments." April 5—"The movement of troops and preparations on board vessels of war . . . are continued with the great activity. . . . Having no confidence in the administration, we say, be ever on your guard." April 7—"We believe a hostile movement is on foot and part of it sailed against the Confederate States [the Sumter relief expedition departed on the sixth]. If Seward's reply [to the demands for recognition] is not satisfactory, we shall consider the gauntlet of war thrown down and close our mission." April 8—"This Government politely declines in a written paper to recognize our official character or the power we represent." April 10—"Our mission is closed." [42]

Lincoln's decision to provision Fort Sumter, peaceably if possible, forcibly if necessary, was received by South Carolina authorities on April 8 and immediately relayed to the Davis government in Montgomery. On April 9 a cabinet meeting was held, with the fateful decision of peace or war hanging in the balance. Toombs was late and on arrival was handed the telegram from Charleston. After reading it, he stated, "The firing upon that fort will inaugurate a civil war greater than any the world has yet seen; and I do not feel competent to advise you." [43] But as the discussion continued, according to biographer Stovall, Toombs suddenly ceased pacing the floor, whirled to face Davis and said forcefully: "Mr. President, at this time, it is suicide, murder, and will lose us every friend at the North. You will wantonly strike a hornet's nest which extends from mountains to ocean, and legions, now quiet, will swarm out and sting us to death. It is unnecessary; it puts us in the wrong; it is fatal." [44] If Stovall wrote accurately, then Toombs and Seward,

[42]March 20—Pickett Papers, Box 3; March 22—*ibid.*; March 28—*ibid.*; April 2—*Official Records of the Union and Confederate Navies in the War of the Rebellion* (Washington, 1895–1929), Ser. I, Vol. IV, 256, hereinafter cited as *Official Records, Navies*; April 3—*Official Records*, Ser. I, Vol. I, 286; April 5—*ibid.*; April 7—*Official Records, Navies*, Ser. I, Vol. IV, 258; April 8—*ibid.*, 259; April 10—*ibid.*, 260.

[43]Quoted in Samuel Wylie Crawford, *The Genesis of the Civil War: The Story of Sumter, 1860–1861* (New York, 1887), 421.

[44]Quoted in Stovall, *Toombs*, 226.

two Union College graduates and rival secretaries of state, were reluctant to make Fort Sumter the beginning of a civil war.

Toombs was overruled. On April 10, Davis, reflecting the general feeling of the South that the intended relief of Sumter was a "threat, a challenge, and a breach of faith," [45] set in motion the chain of events that led to the Confederate attack on the fort early on the morning of April 12 and its surrender the next day. On April 14, as the Northern states were girding for war, Mrs. Toombs, speaking for most Southerners, wrote Alexander H. Stephens that "every heart beats with delight at the result in Charleston yesterday." [46]

During the bombardment of Fort Sumter, a Confederate commission was aboard ship en route to Europe to secure recognition and treaties of commerce and friendship from the principal continental powers, especially Britain. The three-man commission, William L. Yancey of Alabama, Pierre A. Rost of Louisiana, and A. Dudley Mann of Virginia ("about the poorest choices possible") [47], had received detailed instructions from Toombs on March 16 concerning the nature and objectives of their mission.[48] They were to stress the legality and permanence of Southern secession, the ability of the Confederacy to maintain itself if war came, and the possibility of the South as a buyer of European manufactured goods. Of great importance, to be alluded to delicately, was the "condition to which the British realm [and the other nations to be visited] would be reduced if the supply of our staple [cotton] should suddenly fail or even be considerably diminished." Here was the trump card of Confederate diplomacy—the belief that the dependence of European governments on Southern cotton would force recognition and the breaking of a Federal blockade if such were imposed. That cotton was king few Southerners denied. But by 1863, for a variety of reasons, the invincibility of King Cotton diplomacy had been shattered, and with its demise perished much of the hope for Confederate recognition.[49]

---

[45]James G. Randall, *The Civil War and Reconstruction* (Boston, 1937), 239.
[46]Mrs. Toombs to Stephens, April 14, 1861, in Alexander H. Stephens Papers, Emory University.
[47]Frank Lawrence Owsley, *King Cotton Diplomacy: Foreign Relations of the Confederate States of America* (2nd rev. ed.; Chicago, 1959), 51.
[48]Richardson (ed.), *Confederate Correspondence*, II, 3–8.
[49]For a convenient summary of the reasons for the failure of King Cotton diplomacy, see Thomas A. Bailey, *A Diplomatic History of the American People* (New York, 1950), 360–62.

Earlier writers have pictured Toombs in opposition to this policy of the Davis government, asserting that he would have preferred to base the quest for recognition not on coercive King Cotton but on the granting of generous commercial privileges to foreign powers. As far as the utilization of cotton was concerned, he is quoted as saying "he would have mortgaged every pound of cotton to France and England at a price sufficient to remunerate the planters as well as to get the aid of the navies of England and France." [50] If these were Toombs' views, he uncharacteristically kept them pretty much to himself. It *is* a matter of record that he did believe in the efficacy of King Cotton, whether he thought it the best policy under the circumstances or not. On June 21, 1861, he wrote Stephens that England and France were "very friendly, assure us they will buy our cotton this fall at all hazards, will observe strict neutrality for the present and acknowledge us formally as soon as either time or our decided success gives assurance of our power to maintain ourselves." [51] Again, on July 5, he told Stephens that France and England would recognize the independence of the Confederacy in the fall. "Simply holding things as they are will secure that, any decided success would hasten it." [52]

The Yancey-Rost-Mann mission ended in early 1862 without positive results. In May of 1861, Britian and France did recognize the belligerency of the Confederacy, though not its independence. But this came as a consequence of Lincoln's formal proclamation of a blockade of the South, and Toombs and the commissioners had little or nothing to do with it. [53]

As its representative to the Juarez government in Mexico, the Confederacy dispatched John T. Pickett, onetime United States consul at Vera Cruz and secretary of the late ill-fated commission to Washington. On May 17, Toombs gave him his instructions. It was particularly important for the South to maintain friendly relations with Mexico, for it could be used as a legal highway for supplies needed by the Confederacy. Pickett's mission was a com-

---

[50]James M. Callahan, *The Diplomatic History of the Southern Confederacy* (Reprint; Springfield, Mass., 1957), 89, 84–88; Stovall, *Toombs*, 234–35; Rembert W. Patrick, *Jefferson Davis and his Cabinet* (Baton Rouge, 1944), 82–83.

[51]Avary (ed.), *Stephens' Recollections*, 67–68.

[52]Toombs to Stephens, July 5, 1861, in Robert Toombs Papers, Duke University.

[53]The correspondence between Toombs and the commission can be read in Richardson (ed.), *Confederate Correspondence*, II.

plete fiasco, as his crude, undiplomatic conduct, culminating in a brawl, resulted in imprisonment and disgraceful exit from the country.[54]

During Toombs' brief tenure as secretary of state he also issued credentials to and maintained contact with Charles J. Helm in the West Indies and Juan A. Quintero in the border Mexican state of Nuevo Leon.[55] On March 4, 1861, a resolution offered by Toombs in Congress led to the dispatch of a Confederate agent to the Indian tribes west of Arkansas. Davis appointed to the post Albert Pike who acted under Toombs' guidance until the latter's resignation.[56]

Toombs spent a good deal of time in examining applications for letters of marque and reprisal.[57] On April 17, President Davis by proclamation had initiated privateering, or service in "private armed vessels," as a weapon of the Confederacy.[58] Privateering had been abolished by international agreement in the Declaration of Paris in 1856, but the United States had refused to sign the document. Nonetheless, Lincoln chose to regard privateers as pirates. Davis threatened retaliation, but the issue never became a matter of great significance as privateering disappeared after 1861, largely because of the blockade.[59]

In May, 1861, the Confederate Congress voted to remove the seat of government from Montgomery to Richmond. This was done largely in deference to the upper South, particularly Virginia, which had left the Union after Lincoln's call for volunteers. Toombs accompanied Davis on the trip north, along with former Texas Senator Louis T. Wigfall and his family. Because of Davis' ill-health, the journey was designed to be made as quietly as possible, but the crowds along the route through Atlanta, Augusta, Wilmington, and Goldsboro insisted on seeing and hearing the dignitaries aboard the presidential train. Toombs and Wigfall attempted to leave the spotlight to Davis, but were frequently forced to speak

[54]*Ibid.*, 20–26; Owsley, *King Cotton Diplomacy*, 87–103; Callahan, *Diplomatic History*, 71–76; Samuel B. Thompson, *Confederate Purchasing Operations Abroad* (Chapel Hill, 1935), 105–107.

[55]Richardson (ed.), *Confederate Correspondence*, II, 46–48; Owsley, *King Cotton Diplomacy*, 113–33; *Official Records, Navies*, Ser. II, Vol. III, 101, 104–105; Callahan, *Diplomatic History*, 76–77.

[56]"Confederate Journal," 105.

[57]*Official Records, Navies*, Ser. II, Vol. 1, 329–74.

[58]*Ibid.*, Ser. I, Vol. V, 796.

[59]The standard work on this subject is William Morrison Robinson, *The Confederate Privateers* (New Haven, 1928).

after the President had concluded his remarks. "The frank and open manner [of Toombs] came home to the hearts of all," noted the *Daily Richmond Enquirer*.[60] Mrs. Wigfall wrote her daughter that the Virginia countryside seemed "like a military camp—the cars crowded with troops, & all as jubilant as if they were going to a frolic instead of a fight." [61]

Richmond, "green and tree-bordered, [with] the May sun gilding white homes and tall spires," [62] was an impressive sight to the presidential entourage. Its leisurely way of life was changing rapidly, however, as it assumed its new role as the capital of a nation at war. A large transient population of government officials, military personnel, office-seekers, and undesirables caused some of the Virginia aristocrats to feel "as the Roman patricians might have felt at [the] impending advent of the leading families of Goths." [63]

The President's offices and state and treasury departments were located in a large granite structure originally known as the Federal Custom House and now as the Treasury Building, situated at the northeast corner of Tenth and Main streets and facing Capitol Square. Nearby was Mechanics' Hall, which housed most of the other executive departments. President Davis, along with some of his cabinet, stayed at the Spottswood Hotel at Eighth and Main, until housekeeping quarters in the city could be found. Mrs. Toombs soon followed her husband to Richmond and remained until 1862. She stayed busy, ministering to the sick, entertaining Georgians, and participating in the blossoming Richmond society.[64] In early June, the Toombses were joined by Sallie and her family.

The last few weeks that Toombs spent as secretary of state were restless, unhappy ones for him. He became increasingly critical of the policies of the administration. "Davis works slowly, too slowly for the crisis," he wrote Stephens.[65] Toombs regarded Secretary of the Treasury Memminger as wanting in action and experience, and incapable of seeing that the "revolution must rest on the

[60]*Daily Richmond Inquirer*, May 30, 1861.

[61]Mrs. Wigfall to her daughter, May 30, 1861, in Wigfall Family Papers, Library of Congress.

[62]DeLeon, *Belles Beaux*, 58.

[63]*Ibid.*, 59.

[64]Edward Porter Alexander to his wife, June 4, 21, 1861, in Edward Porter Alexander Papers; T. R. R. Cobb Letters, I, 176, II, 42, 59–60.

[65]Toombs to Stephens, June 21, 1861, in Avary (ed.), *Stephens' Recollections*, 67.

treasury." [66] He was particularly upset with the South Carolinian for not pushing vigorously the Produce Loan Act of May 16, whereby citizens could pledge to the government the proceeds of the sale of agricultural and manufactured goods in return for high-interest bearing bonds. The government was to use the proceeds to establish foreign and domestic credit. Toombs himself pledged 100 bales of cotton following a speech in his home town by Vice-President Stephens.[67] If this scheme failed, thought Toombs, then "nothing but [a] high hard rigid tax can save us" and that would bring discontent.[68]

Secretary of the Navy Mallory was classified by Toombs as "good for nothing but to squander public money." The Georgian was of the opinion that an active man in his position "could have cleared half the ports of the confederacy of the blockading ships." [69] In turn, Mallory, a loyal supporter of Davis, was suspicious of the general loyalty of Toombs toward the administration.[70] Toombs regarded Secretary of War Leroy P. Walker as a bumbling incompetent, strangling on red tape, and unable to meet the challenge of girding the nation for war with ample troops and arms.[71] Since Montgomery days, Toombs had been an ardent advocate of "taking the initiative and carrying the war into the enemy's country. . . . He was most emphatic in the advocacy of his policy," reported J. B. Jones, War Department clerk, "and bold almost to rashness in his denunciation of the merely defensive idea." [72] Changing the seat of government from Montgomery to Richmond, a hundred miles from the enemy capital, served to increase the ardor of Toombs' desire for offensive war and his dissatisfaction with the continuation of a defensive posture.

[66]Toombs to Stephens, July 5, 1861, in Robert Toombs Papers, Duke University.

[67]Atlanta *Southern Confederacy*, June 12, 13, 1861; Coulter, *Confederate States*, 164–65.

[68]Toombs to Stephens, July 5, 1861, in Robert Toombs Papers, Duke University.

[69]*Ibid.*

[70]Durkin, *Stephen R. Mallory*, 228.

[71]Toombs to Stephens, July 5, 1861, in Robert Toombs Papers, Duke University; Toombs to Governor Joseph E. Brown, July 12, 1861 (copy), in Telamon Cuyler Collection, University of Georgia; J. B. Jones, *A Rebel War Clerk's Diary at the Confederate States Capital* (New York, 1935), I, 39–40.

[72]Jones, *War Clerk's Diary*, 39–40.

Obviously, Toombs' cabinet days were numbered. He told Governor Brown that he was merely a "looker on" in a government whose business was absorbed by the War Department which was run solely by Davis, Walker, and the generals. The rest of the cabinet had "little more to do with [it] than ordinary outsiders." [73] On July 5, Toombs wrote Stephens that he would get out of the government within a short time, but that he wanted to do it as "quietly & inoffensively as possible." He felt he was of no use in his capacity as secretary of state "but to divide the responsibility of measures [?] I do not approve." [74]

And so on July 24, 1861, after five months as secretary of state of the Confederacy, Robert Toombs resigned his office, determined to serve his country directly on the field of battle. He soon entered the army as a brigadier general, ushering in a new chapter in his life that was to end in frustration and bitterness.[75]

[73]Toombs to Brown, July 12, 1861, in Telamon Cuyler Collection.

[74]Toombs to Stephens, July 5, 1861, Robert Toombs Papers, Duke University.

[75]Davis' message to Congress containing the notice of Toombs' resignation and the nomination of Robert M. T. Hunter of Virginia was dated July 24. It was presented to Congress on the twenty-fifth and Hunter's nomination was confirmed at this time. "Confederate Journal," 282. On August 1, Toombs' appointment as brigadier general was presented to Congress by Davis. It was referred to the Committee of Military Affairs but there is no record in the Journal of either the committee's or Congress' action on it. It is assumed that confirmation took place on August 2. See *ibid.*, 307. The following dates are given in the Robert Toombs Staff File, National Archives, Washington, D.C.: "Register of Appointments, Confederate States Army. Date of appointment: July 19, 1861. Date of confirmation: August 29, 1861. To take rank: July 19, 1861. Date of acceptance: July 20, 1861. Remarks: Resigned March 4, 1863."

CHAPTER IX

Confederate Soldier

T HE metamorphosis of Robert Toombs from civilian to soldier was generally received with misgivings. His family was concerned over his ability to withstand the rigors of military life. Even after Toombs had entered the service, his brother Gabriel wrote Stephens, imploring him to use his influence to effect a resignation. Good judgment in the matter had been blinded by his zeal, said Gabriel, and furthermore his health had deteriorated from a recent attack of rheumatism.[1] Tom Cobb wrote his wife that Mrs. Toombs had wept when speaking to him of her husband's entrance into the army. But she was proud of him, said Cobb, "more proud of this act than any of his life," [2]

Within the official Confederate family, there was an absence of enthusiasm. Mallory, who from the beginning of the war had been distrustful of Toombs, saw the resignation as a part of a "spirit of opposition to the Prest & administration growing up in Congress,

[1]Toombs to Stephens, July 31, 1861, in Phillips (ed.), *Correspondence*, 573.
[2]Cobb to his wife, July 27, 1861, in T. R. R. Cobb Letters, I, 118. Julia Toombs soon became reconciled to her husband's decision. Cobb told his wife that he and brother Howell had dined with the Toombses on July 31, and that Mrs. Toombs had become "very cheerful about it." At the same dinner Toombs jocularly remarked that his wife "had failed to furnish him with a son for the war and he was consequently compelled to go himself," August 1, 1861, T. R. R. Cobb Letters, I, 128.

instigated only by envy and ambition. . . ." [3] Jefferson Davis was concerned about Toombs' lack of military training, but, desiring to preserve harmonious relations with the important Georgian, he acceded to the change. On July 24, he wrote Toombs:

> I receive with great regret your resignation as Secretary of State; but cannot complain that the same patriotism which induced your entrance into my cabinet in that position, now prompts your withdrawal for another field where you believe your services to be more useful to the country.
>
> The intercourse between us all has indeed been pleasant and this but increases the reluctance which I feel in parting from you. I reciprocate most cordially your kind personal feelings, and trust that the same benefit to your country will result from your services in the field as has been received from your counsels in the cabinet. [4]

Newspaper comment varied. The Richmond *Examiner* labeled Toombs' decision, along with similar ones by the Cobb brothers, "an error of generosity," and gently deplored the gaps left in civil leadership by their departure. [5] The Richmond *Dispatch* commented that "the services of one of the ablest men in the Confederacy" had been lost. It added that "Mr. Toombs was of a temper to prefer the active duties of a soldier, in such a crisis as the present, to the monotony of an office, which, for the present, is little more than nominal. . . ." [6] In a different vein, the Columbus (Ga.) *Times*, a staunchly Democratic sheet in antebellum days, sharply criticized the retention of legislative seats by Toombs, a former Whig, and the Cobbs as they donned the Confederate gray. When men enter the service, said the *Times*, they should resign their seats in Congress. "This way of a few men monopolizing all the offices smacks too much of Yankeeism, and we trust the Southern people will for once open their eyes and raise their voices against such odious practices." [7]

The entry of Toombs into uniform occasioned some immediate

---

[3]Diary and Reminiscences of Stephen R. Mallory, Pensacola, Fla., Confederate Secretary of the Navy (Typescript in Library of Congress), Entry of August 11, 1861, I, 12; Durkin, *Stephen R. Mallory*, 228.

[4]Pickett Papers, Box 142.

[5]*Daily Richmond Examiner*, August 7, 1861.

[6]Richmond *Dispatch*, July 26, 1861.

[7]Quoted in Sandersville *Central Georgian*, August 21, 1861.

excitement at the Fair Grounds in Richmond. On August 1, Mrs. Mary Boykin Chesnut wrote:

That bold Brigadier, the Georgia General Toombs, charging about too recklessly, got thrown. His horse dragged him up to the wheels of our carriage. For a moment it was frightful. Down there among the horse's hoofs was his face turned up towards us, purple with rage. His foot was still in the stirrup, and he had not let go the bridle. The horse was prancing over him, rearing and plunging, and everybody hemming him in, and they seemed so slow and awkward about it. We felt it an eternity, looking down at him and expecting him to be killed before our very faces. However, he soon got it all straight, and though awfully tousled and tumbled, dusty, rumpled and flushed, with redder face and wilder hair than ever, he rode off gallantly, having to our admiration bravely remounted the recalcitrant charger.[8]

This embarrassing equestrian episode gave Toombs more action than he was to experience with the military for a long time. The army he entered, though flushed with the victory at Manassas, was badly disorganized, as much so as the defeated Federals who had retreated to the outskirts of Washington. The Confederates were within picket sight of the unfinished Capitol dome, but chose to push no farther. General Joseph E. Johnston instead bent his energies toward molding an army out of the thousands of ill-trained recruits in the Manassas area. Almost a year was to pass before Toombs underwent his first real baptism of fire.

The deadly monotony of camp life, though broken occasionally by family visits and trips to Richmond,[9] ran against the Georgian's grain. On September 1, Toombs suggested to Davis that Confederate armies enter Maryland via Leesburg and Martinsburg, thereby cutting off communication between Washington and the North. "Washington would necessarily fall without a blow," he wrote, "or we could compel them to fight us on our own selected battle field

[8]Mary B. Chesnut, *A Diary from Dixie*, ed. Ben Ames Williams (2nd ed.; Boston, 1949), 99.

[9]Mrs. Toombs also was a visitor at the camp site of Tom Cobb's Georgia Legion. What she found here must have pleased her. "Everybody says it is the quietest camp they ever entered. I have not heard an oath or a vulgar word, or a boisterous song since I have been here and last night there was a prayer meeting in every company and the songs of Zion were heard all around me," Cobb to his wife, August 19, 1861, in T. R. R. Cobb Letters, I, 142. Cobb's camp was undoubtedly the most wholesome on either side of the Potomac.

between Balti. & Washington." [10] Lee's invasion of Maryland, however, was a year in the future.

Toombs' letters to Stephens during this period attest to his increasing restlessness and dissatisfaction with the way the Confederate cause was being handled. He regarded Johnston as a "poor devil, small, arbitrary and inefficient," chucking the entire campaign down the drain and "with this mighty army ready and willing to end the war if they had a man of sense and ability to lead them." A short time later Johnston was still under fire. "The army is dying," said Toombs, ". . . and it will not survive the winter. Set this down in your book, and set down opposite to it its epitaph, *'died of West Point.'* " [11]

During the reorganization of the Confederate army in the fall and winter of 1861, Toombs was brigaded first under General E. Kirby Smith and then under General Gustavus W. Smith.[12] His command, the 1st, 2nd, 15th, and 17th Georgia Regiments, plus Blodgett's battery, was essentially a "Middle-Georgia clan freshly called to arms and commanded by its own chief." [13] Sons-in-law, old friends, and neighbors were generously interspersed in the ranks.[14] Although constantly carping at generals of higher rank, Toombs remained loyal and devoted to those serving under him.

[10]Robert Toombs Papers, Duke University.
[11]Toombs to Stephens, September 22, 30 (?), 1861, in Phillips (ed.), *Correspondence*, 575–77.
[12]In a letter to his wife, Kirby Smith observed that Toombs was " 'coarse and unrefined verging upon vulgarity,' yet at heart a man of good sense and considerable natural intelligence. The 'lace and buttons of cavalry' were scarcely able to conceal the 'politician and demagogue' that he was. An amusing talker, in spite of his constant murder of the English language, Toombs was to his associates almost the equal of a daily comedy. A 'square face coarse features and great breadth of jaws' gave him an appearance 'more sensual than intelligent.' " See Joseph Howard Parks, *General Edmund Kirby Smith, C.S.A.* (Baton Rouge, 1954), 147.
[13]Phillips, *Toombs*, 238. Organizational changes in May and June of 1862 saw the loss of the 1st Georgia and the addition of the 20th Georgia. The 2nd, 15th, 17th, and 20th comprised the brigade until Appomattox.
[14]Colonel Dudley M. Dubose and Major William Felix Alexander of the brigade had married Sallie and Louisa Toombs, respectively. Linton Stephens, brother of Alexander Stephens, saw brief service with the Toombs Brigade as lieutenant colonel in the 15th Georgia. For a complete list of officers in the Toombs Brigade, see Hugh O'Neal Richardson, "A History of Toombs' Brigade, 1861–1863" (M.A. thesis, Emory University, 1962), 144–48. For service records of Georgia Confederates, see Lillian Henderson (comp.), *Roster of the Confederate Soldiers of Georgia, 1861–1865* (4 vols.; Hapeville, Ga., 1955–60).

He had retained his seat in the Provisional Congress, and made frequent trips to Richmond to attend to legislative duties. In July, before his resignation as secretary of state, a reporter had seen Congressman Toombs as "looking dreadfully jaded, and speaking ... in those careless and slovenly tones in which, in all his speeches, he precedes the sudden rise and swift and majestic flow of his eloquence."[15] His philosophy of government was basically the same as it had been in pre-war Washington. He was a staunch advocate of economy in government, conservative financing, protection of private property, and close adherence to constitutional procedures. As yet the exigencies of war had not forced the Richmond government into emergency measures that necessarily curtailed individual liberty for the sake of national survival. These Toombs doubtless anticipated, but his prolonged ranting against the tyranny of the central government came primarily after he had departed from the legislative halls.

A sampling of the journal of the Confederate Congress reveals that Toombs favored reducing the pay of army officers, giving specie rather than treasury notes in payment for export duties on cotton, and limiting the ability of the government to confiscate property.[16] In February, 1862, shortly before he left Congress, he joined with nine other strict constructionists in opposing a measure authorizing President Davis to utilize $1,000,000 in carrying out a project linking Danville, Virginia, and Greensboro, North Carolina, by rail. The protesters denied that "military necessity" was involved, only "military convenience." But more important, they argued, the act was unlawful, sapping the "foundations of the Constitution and public liberty."[17] Toombs never changed in his belief that a national crisis was not sufficient grounds for a broad view of the powers of Congress.

The absentee generalship of Toombs apparently did not reduce his command's efficiency, or diminish the ardor of his men for their leader. An army correspondent for the Atlanta *Southern Confederacy* called Toombs' brigade "one of the best, if not the best, in the army" and spoke of his "rare administrative talents."[18] A member of the brigade wrote that Toombs was "courteous, kind

[15]*Daily Richmond Examiner*, July 22, 1861.
[16]"Confederate Journal," 100, 116, 693, 749–50.
[17]*Ibid.*, 781–82.
[18]Atlanta *Southern Confederacy*, December 1, 1861.

and considerate," a "check to tyrants and a private's friend"; and that he was "as accessible to the humblest man in his brigade as a mother is to her offspring, yet no one can approach him without the deepest respect and reverence." [19]

In November of 1861, Toombs was a candidate for a seat in the Confederate Senate which was to be organized under the permanent constitution. The balloting took place at a joint session of the Georgia legislature on the nineteenth. On the first ballot, Benjamin H. Hill received a majority of the votes, and was declared elected for the full term. Not until the sixth ballot did Toombs receive the necessary majority for the short term office.[20] It was apparent that the legislature desired representatives who would cooperate with administration policies, and that Toombs' public posture of recalcitrance had already begun to take shape. A frontrunner all of his life, Toombs refused to serve, petulantly writing Governor Brown in February of 1862 that "the manner in which the legislature thought proper to confer this trust upon me, relieves me from any obligation to sacrifice either my personal wishes or my conviction of public duty in order to accept it." [21] Thereupon Brown appointed Dr. John W. Lewis to the position.

Julia Toombs remained in Richmond until military movements in the early months of 1862 took her husband out of the area. As was their custom in pre-war Washington, they entertained frequently and sometimes lavishly. The Cobb brothers, though not particularly close friends, were often guests. In February, 1862, Tom wrote home of a recent breakfast given by the Toombses for about a dozen people. The menu included stewed oysters, beef hash, beefsteak, cold ham, venison, hominy, omelets, biscuits, light bread, corn bread, and batter cakes, all served amidst a "profusion of silver." [22]

One of Toombs' last acts as a representative of his state in the Provisional Congress was to join with his colleagues in an "Address to the People of Georgia." Bearing the stamp of Tom Cobb, who considered Yankee warfare "worse than that of an Indian or Hottentot," [23] the address was a savage indictment of the enemy and a

[19]Unsigned letter, November 26, 1861 in Atlanta Southern *Confederacy*, December 7, 1861.

[20]*Georgia Senate Journal* (1861), 104–108.

[21]Atlanta *Southern Confederacy*, March 6, 1862.

[22]T. Cobb to his wife, February 8, 1862, in T. R. R. Cobb Letters, II, 59–60.

[23]T. Cobb to his wife, December 17, 1861, in T. R. R. Cobb Letters, I, 338–39.

fervent plea for all-out resistance. If retreat became necessary, the "Vandals" should be met with a scorched earth policy, leaving a "desert more terrible than the Sahara." A "charnel house as a home" was preferable to "the loathsome vassalage to a nation already sunk below the contempt of the civilized world," wrote the legislators. In advice which the authors themselves largely ignored, Georgians as members of a new nation were called upon to be "united, forbearing to one another, frowning upon all factious opposition and censorious criticism, and giving a trustful and generous confidence to those selected as our leaders in the camp and in the council chamber." Lives and fortunes may have to be sacrificed in the holy cause, the Address concluded, "but our honor will be saved untarnished, and our children's children will rise up to call us 'blessed.' " [24]

Three days later, on a very wet February 22, Jefferson Davis was inaugurated President of the permanent Confederate government. The rain-spattered throng, though hearing little he said, cheered the pale, black-suited Mississippian as he became the first and last President of the seceded Southern states. [25]

In March of 1862, the Confederate forces in the Manassas region were pulled back to the line of the Rappahannock River, where it was thought by the Confederate high command a more successful resistance to an expected Federal spring offensive could be made. Toombs, in his customary posture, disagreed with the decision to retreat southward. Writing to his wife in Washington, Georgia, he said that a Federal attack was not imminent. Furthermore, he was bitterly opposed to abandoning Virginians in the northern counties to the mercy of the enemy. "I would have rather fought ten battles than this. . . . We have got to fight somewhere & if I had my way I would fight them as long as I could rally men to defend their own homes." [26]

While Toombs was lamenting the turn of events, the main Federal force under General George B. McClellan began to move from

[24]Athens *Southern Watchman*, February 19, 1862. Signing the address were Toombs, the Cobbs, and Martin J. Crawford.

[25]*Daily Richmond Examiner*, February 24, 1862; Atlanta *Southern Confederacy*, February 25, 1862; [Mrs. Sarah Putnam] *Richmond During the War* (New York, 1867), 106–107; Sallie R. Barksdale to Alexander Brown, March 3, 1862 in Alexander Brown Papers, Duke University.

[26]Toombs to his wife, March 13, 1862, in Robert Toombs Papers, University of Georgia.

Washington to the peninsula between the York and James rivers for a strike at Richmond. As the Union buildup increased, Johnston moved his army from the Rappahannock to join General John B. "Prince John" Magruder, who had for nearly a year been in command of the small Confederate force on the lower peninsula in the vicinity of Yorktown. Most of the troops passed through Richmond on their way south. The city was jammed with cheering people as the gray columns moved through the streets. "General Toombs was quite conspicuous," recalled General G. Moxley Sorrel, Longstreet's chief of staff.

Everyone knows that that luminous intellect embraced no soldier's talent. It might have been so with study, but the Georgian was for once and all a politician, and in the wrong shop with a sword and uniform on.
He marched his troops down Main Street, past the crowds at Spottswood Hotel, with childlike delight. He put himself at the head of one regiment and moved it out of sight amid hurrahs, then galloping back he brought on another, ready himself for cheers, until the brigade was down the street and near the embarkation. It was somewhat amusing, but a harmless entertainment for the brilliant orator and statesman.[27]

Toombs arrived on April 14 before the bulk of Johnston's army, and was given temporary divisional command by Magruder. Howell Cobb, already on the Peninsula, remarked: "We have Georgians enough here to whip the Yankees if we had to do the whole work ourselves." [28]

On the sixteenth, Magruder's thin line of defense from Yorktown to the James River was attacked unsuccessfully at Dam No. 1. Magruder detached part of Toombs' division for front-line action. The remainder of his command was led by Toombs himself "promptly and energetically" into battle at late evening "just before the enemy ceased the vigor of his attack and in time to share its dangers." [29] Toombs' men remained in the trenches around Dam No. 1, "the most exposed part of the line," [30] until the Confederates withdrew from the lower peninsula. It was warfare at its worst—

[27]G. Moxley Sorrel, *Recollections of a Confederate Staff Officer* (New York, 1905), 59.
[28]Cobb to his wife, April 15, 1862, in Phillips (ed.), *Correspondence*, 594.
[29]*Official Records*, Ser. I, Vol. XI, Pt. 1, p. 408.
[30]*Ibid.*, Pt. 3, p. 456.

constant harassment from enemy sharpshooters, fatigue, and physical discomfort from water sometimes a foot deep in the trenches. Toombs told Stephens that he saw no reason for it except the "stupidity and cowardice of our officers." He believed McClellan could have been whipped easily.[31]

In this miserable environment, Toombs' reactions were unfortunate. Tom Cobb, becoming increasingly critical of his fellow Georgian, reported to his wife that during the campaign Toombs drank a lot and preached mutiny because of his violent opposition to the recently passed conscription act. On sobering up, however, the subversive harangues ceased, Cobb noted.[32]

General Johnston was never satisfied with his position at Yorktown. He much preferred "to draw the enemy inland, to concentrate all available forces at Richmond, and to give battle there."[33] Looking forward to the fulfillment of this plan, he ordered a retreat. Near Williamsburg on May 5, a part of Johnston's forces fought a bloody rearguard action against the pursuing Federals. Toombs, moving with Magruder's troops in the vanguard of the retreat, did not participate.

Johnston continued toward Richmond and drew up his defenses around the city. McClellan's 100,000 men came ponderously after him and approached to within sight of the spires of the Confederate capital. The Union commander split his forces; his right flank lay across the Chickahominy River, about 25,000 strong, in anticipation of joining with General Irvin McDowell's army moving south from Washington.[34]

While the two armies waited, the pens of Toombs and Cobb went into action, each disparaging Davis and the high command, and Cobb extending his critical observations to Toombs. On May 13, Toombs wrote his wife that Davis and Lee had been down the day before inspecting the lines, and "that means we shall not fight till frost if they can help it. The truth is Davis has no capacity & his generals but little more than he has & if it be possible to ruin our cause by imbecility they will do it." Toombs felt that if

[31]Toombs to Stephens, May 17, 1862, in Phillips (ed.), *Correspondence*, 594–95.

[32]T. Cobb to his wife, May 1, 1862, in T. R. R. Cobb Letters, II, 139.

[33]Douglas Southall Freeman, *Lee's Lieutenants: A Study in Command* (New York, 1942–44), I, 150.

[34]Jackson's brilliant Valley campaign and its threat to Washington kept McDowell from joining McClellan.

given a chance at the enemy, the Confederates could defeat them and "settle this business in one day." [35] That same day Cobb noted in a letter home that Davis' presence in the lines had evoked no enthusiasm or cheers among the men. He complained that General Johnston was keeping everyone in the dark about proposed military movements. "Oh! how tired I am of this West Point bull frog self sufficiency! But what are we to do? To whom to look? *Toombs?* It is a farce. I have sergeants in my legion in whose military capacity I have more confidence." [36]

Three days later, on May 16, for Cobb it was still open season on Toombs. He wrote his wife: "Toombs is drinking like a fish and making an ass of himself. His disobedience of orders is notorious and his disposition to shirk all positions of danger. His military career is a desperate failure." [37] Toombs' military career may well have been falling apart, but the intimation by Cobb of cowardice was not substantiated by Toombs' action in battle.

On May 17, Toombs was writing to Stephens in his now familiar vein. "This army will not fight," he complained, "until McClellan attacks it. Science will do anything but fight. It will burn, retreat, curse, swear, get drunk, strip soldiers—anything but fight." One bright note was his health, which had improved since he stopped smoking. [38]

Into this arena of polemics stepped a new participant, Adam Leopold Alexander, Toombs' neighbor from Washington, Georgia. On May 23 he wrote his son Edward, an officer in the army, bitterly castigating Toombs for hindering the war effort. The senior Alexander was particularly irritated because Toombs' overt phillipics against authority, both civil and military, had infected another son, William Felix, Toombs' aide and son-in-law. Alexander had heard that the general was going to resign. [39] "I hope in God this is true," said the father, "& that he will come home & stay here, and keep his seditious mouth shut." Another rumor was floating

[35]Toombs to his wife, May 13, 1862, in Robert Toombs Papers, University of Georgia.

[36]T. Cobb to his wife, May 13, 1862, in T. R. R. Cobb Letters, II, 146.

[37]T. Cobb to his wife, May 16, 1862, in T. R. R. Cobb Letters, II, 152.

[38]Phillips (ed.), *Correspondence*, 595.

[39]Tom Cobb had heard the same thing and wrote his wife to this effect on May 25. Cobb said that Toombs had actually written a letter of resignation because of jealousy over the promotion of a fellow officer to major general, but had suppressed the letter at the persuasion of friends. See T. R. R. Cobb Letters, II, 165–66.

around to the effect that Toombs was trying to "subvert" the government, hoping to create a new one, Cromwellian style.

> Now if such a thing is attempted I want Felix to know that *I* shall be found with the Govt, & not with Mr. T. I was sorry that Mr. T. ever entered the Army, for I know he can cooperate with no man or set of men, unless *he* is the ascendant. He yields his opinions to no one, no matter on what subject, & would insanely maintain them against a regiment of Military men, on any movement of army. He is totally unfitted for his present position. He is satisfied with no one, but himself, or those who submit to him.[40]

On May 31, the offensive passed to the Confederates, and Johnston attacked McClellan's forces south of the Chickahominy at Seven Pines. The battle was a fierce, indecisive, two-day engagement which saw the wounding of Johnston and the passing of command to Robert E. Lee. As at Williamsburg, Magruder's command was out of action, being posted on the left northeast of Richmond in reserve. Toombs' brigade, under Magruder, was positioned at Mechanicsville Bridge on the Chickahominy.

Before Lee moved against McClellan in the famous Seven Days Battle, he undertook to shore up the defenses around Richmond. Many of the troops were unhappy about pick and shovel work, "scorning the shelter of fortifications as unworthy of gentlemen in arms." [41] None more so than Toombs. In early June, Lee made an inspection of the lines. On arriving in Toombs' sector he found that the Georgian was having heavy logs thrown together for his defense instead of fashioning the conventional earthworks. Lee chuckled and remarked, "When General Toombs gains a little more experience he will be convinced that *earth* is a better protection against cannon-balls than logs." [42]

In the lull before the Confederate attack, Toombs became involved in an unfortunate episode which reduced his popularity in Georgia. In the spring of 1862, there was a widespread movement in the state to curtail the planting of cotton in favor of foodstuffs, as the grain-producing upper south was being overrun by Federal troops. It became a patriotic endeavor, something the folks at home

[40]Edward Porter Alexander Papers.
[41]Douglas Southall Freeman, *R. E. Lee: A Biography* (New York, 1934–35), II, 86.
[42]Quoted in A. L. Long, *Memoirs of Robert E. Lee* (New York, 1887), 166.

could participate in to help fight the enemy. Committees in various counties spearheaded the movement and most planters cooperated. Toombs did not completely, and became publicly and bitterly embroiled with some of the leaders, for the most part to his discredit.

In May, before the mudslinging began, Toombs explained his feelings in the matter to his wife. "As to what I may choose to plant on my own estate, I shall neither refer it to newspapers nor to public meetings nor to legislatures. I know what sort of people compose all those classes & it is impossible to increase my contempt for them. Let them take up arms & come with me to drive the invader away from our soil & then we will settle what sort of seeds shall be put into it." [43]

Public opinion began to mount against Toombs as somewhat exaggerated reports circulated as to the amount of acreage he had planted in cotton. The Columbus *Sun* stated that such a course of action argued "much selfishness and criminal indifference to the wants of the gallant men fighting for the property, home and family." [44] At a citizens' meeting in Randolph County, where Toombs had a large plantation on the Chattahoochee River, resolutions were adopted harshly condemning Toombs and others who had followed his example. The resolutions called for a withdrawal of Negro labor from cotton cultivation for work on the defense of the river.[45] Toombs was duly advised of the action that had been taken. In response came this telegram:

To Messrs. Geo. Hill, A. T. Newsom, and William Carter, Committee
GENTS: Your telegram has been received. I refuse a single hand. My property, as long as I live, shall never be subject to the orders of those cowardly miscreants, the Committee of Public Safety of Randolph county and Eufala [a committee at Eufala, Alabama, across the river from Randolph County, had adopted the same resolutions]. You may rob me in my absence, but you cannot intimidate me.[46]

Back to the attack came the committee.[47] Toombs was told that

[43]Toombs to his wife, May 19, 1862, in Robert Toombs Papers, University of Georgia.
[44]Quoted in the Milledgeville *Southern Federal Union*, June 3, 1862. This is the same paper as the old *Federal Union*.
[45]Atlanta *Southern Confederacy*, June 17, 1862.
[46]*Ibid*.
[47]These resolutions had actually been adopted at the citizens' meeting and not by the county's Committee of Safety. But they had been published erroneously as the action of the Committee of Safety. Toombs assumed as much and the Committee itself undertook the rebuttal.

his statement reflected "that inflated egotism for which you have acquired some notoriety, and abounds with evidence that if written under *sober* reflection, you have lost all proper appreciation of what is due from a gentleman and a soldier." Those whom Toombs denounced were his equal in all things honorable, and yielded only in the "field of defamation and detraction. You are presuming too much, sir," Toombs was told, "upon the prestige of your past services, and the devotion of your party, when you conclude that either will screen you from merited condemnation, when guilty of infidelity to the interests of the country." [48]

Although Toombs was seemingly contemptuous of public opinion in the matter, Tom Cobb on June 13 wrote his wife that Toombs had been galled excessively by the stand of the Randolph County citizens. He said that his conduct was becoming "daily more insupportable. He is drunk almost every afternoon and makes himself most ridiculous, riding like Jehu driving from camp to camp, and uttering horrible oaths. He will be arrested very soon in my opinion and *I think he wants to be.* . . . His brigade is becoming utterly demoralized and disorganized." Cobb said Toombs had asked him if he approved of his conduct in planting cotton, and that he had replied that he did not. [49]

In the fall, when the furor had subsided somewhat, the press published figures showing that Toombs had actually planted less cotton and more corn than ever before. [50] Had he been less imperious in attitude and more willing to explain what he had done to an easily excitable war-time populace, the whole regrettable affair might have been avoided. But this was not in his nature.

As Lee made ready to smash at the enemy north of the Chickahominy River with the bulk of his forces, he entrusted the immediate defense of Richmond to Generals Benjamin Huger and Magruder, who were south of the river in positions a few miles east of the city. Huger's division of nine thousand troops constituted the right wing of the defensive alignment. Between Huger and the river was Magruder's corps—six brigades in three divisions, totaling about thirteen thousand men. Anchoring Magruder's left,

[48]Milledgeville *Southern Recorder*, July 15, 1862. The reply to Toombs was dated June 17.
[49]T. Cobb to his wife, June 13, 1862, T. R. R. Cobb Letters, II, 179.
[50]Toombs' crop consisted of 560 acres of cotton, 800 acres of corn, and 450 acres of other grain, Milledgeville *Southern Recorder*, September 30, 1862; Milledgeville *Confederate Union*, September 23, 1862. This is another new name for the old *Federal Union*.

a swampy three-quarters of a mile from the Chickahominy, was General David R. Jones' division, consisting of the 1st Brigade under Toombs and Colonel G. T. (Tige) Anderson's 3rd Brigade.

Opposing the Confederates south of the river were some seventy thousand Federals, well-armed and well-entrenched. It was particularly important that the Confederate defenses hold firm, for a break here might prompt the hesitant McClellan into aggressive action against Richmond while Lee was operating north of the river with most of his troops. On June twenty-fourth and later on the twenty-seventh, Lee sent telegrams to Huger urging him to hold his line at all hazards.[51]

Lee's strategy for demolishing McClellan's right wing was imperfectly initiated. On June 26, the impatient Ambrose P. Hill, in violation of Lee's wishes, which called for a simultaneous assault with Jackson, attacked the Union army at Mechanicsville. Confederate losses were heavy and the ground gained insignificant. Undaunted, Lee stifled his disappointment and pushed on, preparing on the twenty-seventh to hurl fifty-five thousand men against the Federal right, then established at Gaines' Mill, a few miles east of Mechanicsville.

The main drama unfolded north of the river on this hot June day, but to the south soldiers were to die no less heroically in the wheat field and woods surrounding the farmhouse of James Garnett. Robert Toombs was the leading actor in this minor engagement. And a disgruntled actor he was. In a letter to Stephens, July 14, he complained that in the weeks leading up to this battle he had been uncomfortably close to the enemy, "doing the hardest kind of the most dangerous and disagreeable service and in the least desirable positions for any purpose whatever and a large portion of the time without the least conveniences of any kind, most of [the] official work having to be done with a pencil as I could get often neither pen or ink and was debarred the use of lights at night for military reasons arising from close proximity to the enemy." [52]

The events of the day were not to lessen the Georgian's discontent. Toombs' brigade was established around the Garnett farmhouse less than a mile from the Chickahominy. The main Union entrenchments were about three-quarters of a mile to the east, near

[51]Douglas Southall Freeman (ed.), *Lee's Dispatches* (New York, 1915), 13, 18.
[52]Phillips (ed.), *Correspondence,* 599.

the Golding farmhouse. During the night of the twenty-sixth and the morning of the twenty-seventh, however, a large enemy force moved threateningly close to the Confederates at Garnett's. Toombs' pickets, two hundred yards east of the house, were within one hundred yards of the Federal vanguard, each post occupying a belt of timber separated "by a field of wheat that promised a good yield." [53] In command of the Union forces directly opposite Toombs was future Democratic presidential candidate, General Winfield S. Hancock, commander of the 1st Brigade of the 2nd Division of General William B. Franklin's 6th Corps. "Both sides were strong for defense, but an advance from either was hazardous in the extreme," reported General Jones, Toombs' division commander. [54]

On the morning of the twenty-seventh, an artillery duel of short duration ended in favor of the Union guns. The Confederate batteries which had been ordered to the front near the Garnett house were forced to retire. The sun climbed high in the sky but there was still no massive action on either side of the river. Then, early in the afternoon, Lee hit McClellan north of the Chickahominy at Gaines' Mill.

South of the river, Magruder notified Jones "of his intention to feel the enemy along his entire front" and directed his left wing division commander to carry out the order in his sector. [55] The order from Jones to "feel the enemy in their front with strong pickets, and to follow up to the utmost any advantage which may offer or success which may ensue" was communicated to Toombs in writing, lest a "serious engagement with his brigade . . . be the result of the movement." A feint, not a general fight, then, was the word that was sent out. [56]

---

[53]E. R. Jones, *Four Years in the Army of the Potomac* (London, n.d.), 62, 63. Jones speaks of the close fraternization between Federals and Confederate pickets at this point in the line—how they met sometimes in the wheatfield "to compare notes and have a chat."

[54]*Official Records*, Ser. I. Vol. XI, Pt. 2, p. 689.

[55]*Ibid.* Similar orders were sent to General Lafayette McLaws, commanding the troops on Magruder's right wing, who moved two regiments out about 4 P.M. Finding the enemy in force, they retired back to camp about ten.

[56]*Ibid.*, 689. Toombs gave a slightly different version of the situation. "I objected to the order [because of the heavy Federal force in his front]," he said, "and required it in writing and peremptory." Toombs to Stephens, July 14, 1862, in Phillips (ed.), *Correspondence*, 599–600. Jones by his order implied that Toombs had to be controlled lest he precipitate a general engagement; Toombs said he did not want to advance at all.

Shortly before sunset, Confederate batteries behind Toombs' position opened up on the Union lines, "the most rapid and incessant fire of shell that I had ever witnessed," wrote Colonel Amasa Cobb of the 5th Wisconsin of Hancock's brigade.[57] As the cannonading ceased and the shadows lengthened, the Southerners moved out, Anderson on the right and Toombs on the left, to carry out the order of "that old ass Magruder," Toombs' appraisal.[58] Toombs ultimately threw his entire brigade into this bloody and inconclusive contest that lasted until twilight blackened into night.[59] Much of the advance was made through the wheat field into the face of a withering Union fire. The high-water mark of the attack was a crest in the field, about forty yards from Hancock's line, which Toombs' men reached around 7:30 P.M., and beyond which they could move no farther. A strange and confusing engagement it was, being fought "principally in the dark and the little space separating . . . [the soldiers] so dense with smoke that nothing could be seen but the flash of musketry." [60] When the firing ceased, both lines were pulled in under cover of darkness to await the developments of a new day. North of the Chickahominy Lee rested in victory. South of the river an unhappy Toombs pondered his brigade's brave but futile assault.

The next day, June 28, a restless Lee held his troops in position as he awaited substantiation of the Union army's next move. Still somewhat apprehensive lest a provoked McClellan pierce his slim defenses in front of Richmond, he ordered Magruder not to make an attack unless success was absolutely certain, and further, except in cooperation with movements north of the river. Confusion in Magruder's chain of command, however, led Toombs to order an assault by part of Anderson's brigade on Golding's farm, an attack which ended ingloriously. Toombs emerged from the fiasco as the

[57]*Official Records*, Ser. I, Vol. XI, Pt. 2, p. 476.

[58]Toombs to Stephens, July 14, 1862, in Phillips (ed.), *Correspondence*, 600.

[59]See *Official Records*, Ser. I, Vol. XI, Pt. 2, pp. 688–705 for the Confederate reports of the battle and *ibid.*, 462–79 for Union reports. Bearing the brunt of the Confederate assault were the 2nd and 15th, which suffered heavily in frontal positions near the Union lines. The 2nd lost 120 out of 271, and the 15th lost 71 out of 300. The 17th and 20th, posted on the left and right flanks, had only minor losses. Union losses were 118 killed, wounded, captured, or missing. Anderson's two regiments, the 1st and 9th, became sharply engaged but withdrew when they ran into direct enemy fire and found themselves beyond support of the troops on their right.

[60]Hancock's comment, *ibid.*, 468.

scapegoat, but the shortcomings exhibited in this minor engagement were numerous enough to be shared by all the participants.[61]

Early on June 29, Lee learned that McClellan was in full retreat, and rapidly set his commanders in pursuit. Jackson was directed to cross the Chickahominy River at Grapevine Bridge several miles downstream from Gaines' Mill, and remain on McClellan's right flank. Longstreet and A. P. Hill were ordered to cross at New Bridge (behind Magruder), move southward, and press McClellan's left. Magruder and Huger were put in immediate pursuit, with Magruder ordered to "press him vigorously in front." [62] Lee was impatient, now sensing a fine opportunity for McClellan's complete destruction.

In spite of the urgency and specific nature of his orders, Magruder moved cautiously along the line of Federal retreat, constantly fearing attack. Not until late afternoon did he assault the Union rearguard at Savage Station, on the Richmond and York River Railroad, about five miles southeast of his position that morning. Toombs was north of the railroad on Magruder's left during the battle. All day his brigade had marched in echelon behind Anderson's brigade on the left flank, making only brush contact with the enemy. Outside of sustaining some shell fire which did little damage, Magruder's force above the railroad did not take an active part in the clash at Savage Station. Toward evening, Jones' division was ordered to fall back to support Magruder's right, which was bitterly engaged. But darkness and a soaking rain ended the battle and troop movement.[63]

The day had been displeasing to Lee. McClellan was neither caught nor destroyed, and time was now on the Union side. Particularly vexing to the Confederate commander was Magruder's

---

[61]*Ibid.*, 473–74, 481, 661, 690, 706, 710–11; Freeman, *Lee's Lieutenants*, I, 544–46. In the author's opinion, the largest share of the responsibility for the blunder should fall on General Jones who created conditions which almost precluded Toombs from acting in any other manner. Two definite errors occur in Freeman's account of Golding's Farm. In his *R. E. Lee*, II, 158, he places the battle on the twenty-seventh which is incorrect. *Lee's Lieutenants*, I, 544–46, places it in proper chronological context. Also, in *R. E. Lee*, II, 158, he says that "some 400 men" were lost by the Confederates in the clash. Official reports placed casualties at 159. See *Official Records*, Ser. I, Vol. XI, Pt. 2, pp. 710–11.

[62]*Official Records*, Ser. I, Vol. XI, Pt. 2, p. 662.

[63]*Ibid.*, 691; Toombs to Stephens, July 14, 1862, in Phillips (ed.), *Correspondence*, 600.

faltering pursuit of the Union rear, which Lee had hoped that morning to catch before it crossed the White Oak Swamp. To accelerate the Confederate movement, Jackson's command, which reached Savage Station early on the thirtieth, was ordered in close pursuit of McClellan. Magruder was removed from the front, and sent to the rear and southward down the Darbytown Road in support of Longstreet on McClellan's left flank.[64]

On Monday morning, June 30, Magruder moved out. All day and into the night, for eighteen hours, his men marched, reaching Longstreet's command around 2 A.M. on July 1 in the vicinity of Frayser's Farm. There, "amid the dead and dying and wounded" from the previous afternoon's clash, they rested until daylight. "It was a scene never to be forgotten," Toombs told Stephens.[65]

By noon of July 1 the Union army was strongly entrenched on Malvern Hill near the James River. It was a discouraging picture, but Lee was determined to have one more chance at McClellan. While assault plans were being pondered, Magruder was groping his way toward the rest of the Confederate army. He had taken the wrong road, "due to poor guides and poorer maps," and was moving in a westerly direction away from the enemy. It was past mid-afternoon before his command finally arrived at Malvern Hill.[66]

Lee's plan of attack was predicated upon a successful denting of the Federal line by his artillery. A very heavy Union bombardment, however, emasculated the Confederate guns which had been moved forward, and by 2:30 P.M. Lee's "long arm" was paralyzed. Although with little chance of success, shortly after 4:30 P.M. an uneven, ill-coordinated, and ill-omened general infantry assault was launched. As Toombs moved out, a very disheartening scene began to unfold in front of him—"dense woods, intersected by ravines, [and] occasionally thick brier patches" and beyond the woods an open field sloping gently upward to the "red flashes of the [Union] guns and the crimson-looking Federal colors floating above the dark line of men plainly visible." [67] Toombs' brigade was situated on the left of the assaulting Confederate right in a supporting

---

[64]*Official Records*, Ser. I, Vol. XI, Pt. 2, p. 666.

[65]Toombs to Stephens, July 14, 1862, in Phillips (ed.), *Correspondence*, 600.

[66]Freeman, *R. E. Lee*, II, 205; *Official Records*, Ser. I, Vol. XI, Pt. 2, pp. 667–68, 691; Freeman, *Lee's Lieutenants*, I, 591–92.

[67]*Official Records*, Ser. I, Vol. XI, Pt. 2, 696; *Southern Historical Society Papers*, XVIII, 61.

position. Order soon melted into chaos on the death-strewn northern slope of Malvern Hill. Confusion mounted in Toombs' sector as "Magruder . . . lost his grip on his troops." [68] Regiments became mixed and separated. "The demoralization was great and the evidences of it palpable everywhere," wrote a Confederate artillery officer.[69] Toombs' own brigade became hopelessly disorganized in the course of the attack, and many of his men veered to the left and back into the woods skirting the open field. Here Toombs attempted to put his command back together, but was unsuccessful.

Up rode General Daniel H. Hill whose troops attacking from the Confederate center were suffering heavily. Hill was embittered, because he felt that much of the carnage in his division was the result of a lack of support on the right from Magruder, who had not thrown his full force into the initial assault. Angry words were exchanged between the two hot-tempered officers as Hill ordered Toombs' brigade forward in support of a brigade of his own command, and personally accompanied it. According to Hill, "the brigade advanced handsomely to the brow of the hill, but soon retreated in disorder." [70]

Although the fighting at Malvern Hill continued into summer's late darkness, Lee had failed. McClellan was still intact and in good order. The personal war between Hill and Toombs went on for about two weeks after the battle officially closed. Toombs, in an angry correspondence, accused Hill of having derided the fighting qualities of his brigade. Hill replied that the remarks made during the battle were directed at him personally and not at his brigade. "It is notorious," he said, "that you have a thousand times expressed your disgust that the commanding general did not permit you to fight. It is equally notorious that you retired from the field." Finding this unsatisfactory, Toombs challenged Hill to a duel. This Hill refused on the ground that "we have a country to defend and enemies to fight," and such an encounter "would be abhorrent to my principles and character." Thus the correspondence ended.[71]

---

[68]Freeman, *Lee's Lieutenants*, I, 602.
[69]Robert Stiles, *Four Years Under Marse Robert* (New York, 1910), 105.
[70]*Official Records*, Ser. I, Vol. XI, Pt. 2, p. 628. General Jubal Early, in his official report, stated that on a road leading to the battlefield he found a "large number of men retreating in confusion, being mostly from General Toombs' Georgia Brigade." He tried to rally them, "but found it very difficult to do so." *Ibid.*, 612. Toombs' own account makes no mention of the encounter with General Hill, *ibid.*, 696–98.
[71]The exchange of letters is found in Stovall, *Toombs*, 254–58.

Tom Cobb, in a letter to his wife on July 16, uncharacteristically defended Toombs: "Hill did most wantonly charge Toombs with cowardice to his face. He now makes many excuses for not fighting him. Toombs is denouncing Hill as a poltroon. I don't know how it will end, but I think you will hear that Toombs is under arrest in less than a week." [72] A week later, Cobb reported that rumors of Toombs' resignation were going around. He added that he "was sorry to hear he was still making a beast of himself from liquor. It is pitable [sic] to see a great intellect debased by so contemptible a temptation." [73]

A less sympathetic version of the Hill-Toombs wrangle was given by Thomas Jordan, Beauregard's chief of staff, as he explained the incident to his superior: "D. H. Hill told Toombs on the field either to move up or resign his brigade into hands that had the nerve to lead it. Toombs challenged Hill; he declined on religious grounds. Toombs has a divided judgment as to his course, and halts, as an ass between two bundles of hay, whether to resign and cowhide Hill, or resign, make some facile Georgia member of Congress resign, take his place and overturn the Government from the floor of Congress." [74]

During the night after the battle of Malvern Hill, the Union army continued its retreat, and the next day reached Harrison's Landing on the James River, a position strongly protected by Union gunboats. The Peninsula campaign was over. The immediate threat to Richmond had been relieved, but Lee was disappointed that he had not destroyed the Union army.

Robert Toombs shared Lee's unhappiness, but unlike the Virginian bubbled over with some sharp criticism of the Confederate effort. Writing to Stephens in July while encamped near Richmond, he described the campaign as a great success with McClellan's army "utterly defeated and broken up and demoralized." Success came, however, as the result of "dead hard fighting" and not because of great leadership, since the soldiers "were fought without skill or judgment." In the campaign, Toombs continued,

Stonewall Jackson and his troops did little or nothing . . . and Lee was far below the occasion. If we had had a general in command we could

[72]*Southern Historical Society Papers*, XXVIII, 294.
[73]T. Cobb to his wife, July 23, 1862, in T. R. R. Cobb Letters, II, 239–40.
[74]*Official Records*, Ser. I, Vol. XVII, Pt. 2, p. 770.

easily have taken McClellan's whole command and baggage. . . . I shall leave the army the instant I can do so without dishonor. Davis and his Janissaries (the regular army) conspire for the destruction of all who will not bend to them, and avail themselves of the public danger to aid them in their selfish and infamous schemes.[75]

A reorganization of the Confederate army took place after Malvern Hill. Magruder, a nagging thorn in Lee's flesh, was sent west. D. R. Jones' division of Magruder's command, consisting of Toombs' and Anderson's brigades, was soon placed under General James Longstreet.[76]

All was quiet for several weeks in the works around Richmond where the Confederates lay watching the still powerful McClellan down on the James River. Apparently Toombs fell prey to a lack of vigilance. One day, according to Henry Kyd Douglas, Stonewall Jackson was inspecting defenses and found that Toombs' picket lines "were not connected on the right or left but were swinging in the air, contrary to Jackson's explicit orders and to his surprise." Jackson rode immediately to Toombs' headquarters, and "found this gallant but not very military officer lying under the shade of a small fly-tent at full length—for it was a very warm day." The routed-out Georgian explained how he had passed the responsibility of the picket line to a staff officer, and he in turn to a subordinate. Toombs was of the opinion that "it must be all right, while General Jackson was of the decided opinion it was all wrong." Toombs was told "with some sharpness to go at once, in person, and make the necessary connection and then [Jackson] turned and rode away." [77]

Meanwhile, news from above Richmond brought fresh problems to Lee. In June a new Union army, the Army of Virginia, was created under the command of General John Pope. After the failure of McClellan's offensive on the Peninsula, Pope had marched southward across the Rappahannock River. Lee now sent part of his army under Jackson to meet the advancing Federals, remaining with the bulk of his forces between Richmond and McClellan. Before McClellan's army was removed from the James River, it made a feint toward Richmond that caused a stir among the de-

---

[75]Toombs to Stephens, July 14, 1862, in Phillips (ed.), *Correspondence*, 601.

[76]*Official Records*, Ser. I, Vol. XI, Pt. 3, p. 650; Freeman, *Lee's Lieutenants*, I, 605–11.

[77]Henry Kyd Douglas, *I Rode With Stonewall* (Chapel Hill, 1940), 114.

fending Confederates. On August 5, Malvern Hill was reoccupied by Union troops. Lee immediately dispatched a strong force of four divisions to cope with the threat. After a brisk encounter, the Federals withdrew. Toombs, on the Confederate left, did not make contact with the enemy, but his brigade was one of three which occupied the heights after the battle.[78]

A few days after this, Toombs paid Tom Cobb a visit and, among other things, expounded on the subject of engineers and fortifications. Declared the offensive-minded Toombs: "One engineer could find work for all the men that had been sent to hell since Adam sinned, 'and according to scripture, Tom, . . . that is a big pile.' " [79]

The scene of conflict now shifted from the Peninsula to northeastern Virginia. Lee, moving rapidly away from Richmond, hoped to engage Pope before reinforcements from McClellan's army, vacating the Peninsula, could reach him. On August 13, Longstreet's command, which included Toombs' brigade, was ordered to proceed immediately by railroad car to Gordonsville, on the Orange and Alexandria Railroad forty-seven miles west of Fredericksburg, in support of Jackson.[80] Lee arrived soon after Longstreet, and on the fifteenth sat down with "Old Pete" and Jackson to plot Pope's downfall. An excellent chance lay within the Confederate commander's grasp, for if Pope's army, massed between the Rappahannock and Rapidan Rivers, could be attacked successfully it might be destroyed.

Between campaigns Toombs had a penchant for becoming entangled in regrettable incidents. The one that now followed was particularly damaging, and clearly reflected his disinclination to cooperate with the army as a whole except on his own terms. On August 17, Longstreet ordered two regiments of Toombs' brigade posted as a guard on the road leading north to Racoon Ford on the Rapidan River, about thirteen miles east of Lee's headquarters, until the approaching cavalry of Fitzhugh Lee could relieve them. Toombs was not present when the order was given, having galloped off that morning to visit and break bread with a former congressional friend. Colonel Henry L. Benning, next in rank to Toombs, complied with Longstreet's command. When Toombs returned, ac-

---

[78]*Official Records*, Ser. I, Vol. XI, Pt. 2, pp. 956, 963–64.
[79]T. Cobb to his wife, August 10, 1862, *Southern Historical Society Papers*, XXVIII, 296.
[80]*Official Records*, Ser. I, Vol. XI, Pt. 3, p. 675.

cording to Longstreet's account, he came upon his pickets, "claimed that his troops should not have been moved except by orders through himself, and ordered the detail back to their camps." [81]

Down the unguarded road early on the morning of the eighteenth came some Federal cavalry on a scouting detail. They almost caught the unsuspecting Jeb Stuart, who had spent the night at Verdiersville, eight miles south of Racoon Ford, awaiting the arrival of Fitzhugh Lee. Captured was Major Norman Fitzhugh and with him a copy of an order from Lee to Stuart, showing the disposition of Lee's troops and his determination to crush Pope before he could be reinforced by McClellan.[82]

When Longstreet heard of what had transpired, he placed Toombs under arrest. The next day (the nineteenth) during a troop movement, Toombs, riding in the rear of his brigade, wore his sword in violation of regulations and, from the report of Longstreet's chief of staff, "upon his men going into camp had made them a violent speech." This time Longstreet ordered Toombs back to Gordonsville and told him to stay there. Two charges were prepared against the Georgian: ". . . withdrawing the regiment from picket duty and breaking his arrest." [83]

Toombs' own account put events in a different light. In a letter to Stephens from Gordonsville, dated August 22, he explained that he had been ordered to have rations cooked and prepared for immediate troop movement. He discovered that A. P. Hill's division was between his pickets and the ford, and felt that there was no need for his men to remain on duty any longer, particularly since they had to cook and make ready. When Longstreet could not be found, on his own authority he ordered his men back in. Then, failing to mention the Stuart incident, he told Stephens that Longstreet had put him under arrest for "usurpation of authority." The next day, continued Toombs, he rode forward to ask Longstreet to suspend his arrest so he could fight in the impending action. But unfortunately for him, as he approached his brigade "it raised a loud cheer, which so incensed the magnates Lee and Longstreet, etc., who were near by, that I got no reply to my request but was

[81]James Longstreet, *From Manassas to Appomattox* (Philadelphia, 1896), 161.
[82]Freeman, *Lee's Lieutenants*, II, 58–60; *ibid.*; Freeman, *R. E. Lee*, II, 285–87; *Official Records*, Ser. I, Vol. XII, Pt. 2, p. 29; J. B. Mitchell, *Decisive Battles of the Civil War* (New York, 1955), 84.
[83]Sorrel, *Recollections*, 100–101.

ordered peremptorily to this place [Gordonsville] and two charges put in against me for breaking my arrest and disobeying orders in not immediately coming here." In conclusion, Toombs stated: "My zeal for the public service and desire to prepare my starving regiment for battle is my sole and only fault." [84] Notwithstanding Toombs' elaborate defense to Stephens, he was clearly guilty of violating orders and endangering Confederate security.

While Toombs remained at Gordonsville under arrest, Pope escaped across the Rappahannock. The two armies collided near Manassas Junction on August 29 and 30. Jackson brought Pope to battle on the twenty-ninth, and on the thirtieth the reinforced Confederates swept the field in "one of the great counterstrokes of military history." [85] Meanwhile, Toombs had been released from arrest. Riding hard on his mare, Gray Alice, he reached his cheering command near dark at the conclusion of hostilities. Dramatically he told them: "Boys, I am proud of the report given me of you by General Jones. I could not be with you to-day, but this was owing to no fault of mine. To-morrow I lead you." [86] The generally accepted account of Toombs' return to his brigade has him arriving in time to lead a charge, but the reports of the regimental officers give solid support to the contention that it was practically all over when Toombs got there. [87]

After his great victory, Lee sent Jackson to press Pope's flank. Longstreet was to follow, after caring for the dead and wounded. On September 1, Jackson engaged Pope at Chantilly, northeast of Manassas on the Little River Turnpike. Toombs' and Anderson's brigades were sent to aid Jackson, but darkness ended the fighting before Longstreet's men became engaged. The Union army con-

[84]Phillips (ed.), *Correspondence*, 603–604. The dating of events in Toombs' letter is inaccurate. Phillips, *Toombs*, 244–45, sympathetically states that Toombs was arrested for a "trivial disobedience of orders."

[85]Kenneth P. Williams, *Lincoln Finds a General* (New York, 1949–59), I, 336.

[86]*Official Records*, Ser. I, Vol. XII, Pt. 2, p. 591.

[87]Stovall, *Toombs*, 259–62, makes Toombs something of a hero in this second engagement at Manassas. Stovall relied in part on Longstreet's account in Robert U. Johnson and Clarence C. Buel (eds.), *Battles and Leaders of the Civil War* (New ed.; New York, 1956), II, 526. The report of the battle by General Jones (*Official Records*, Ser. I, Vol. XII, Pt. 2, p. 580) supports Stovall. It seems, however, to the author that statements of the regimental officers, including that of Captain H. L. French of the 17th Georgia who recorded Toombs' declaration given above in the text, indicate that Toombs had little or no participation in the engagement. See *ibid.*, 585, 587–88.

tinued its retreat through heavy mud toward Washington, and Lee declined further pursuit.

A few days later, Lee's victorious army splashed across the Potomac River into Maryland in quest of military and political goals. To maintain a supply route for his army through the Shenandoah Valley, it was necessary to capture Harpers Ferry. Boldly, Lee split his army into four segments, three to invest Harpers Ferry while Longstreet and D. H. Hill were to move from Frederick to Boonsboro. If all went well, the Confederate forces were to unite at Boonsboro or at Hagerstown, prior to a movement into Pennsylvania.

A copy of Lee's orders for the disposition of his troops, however, fell into McClellan's hands as he moved cautiously into western Maryland after the invaders, and the picture quickly changed. McClellan, emboldened by this incredible piece of good fortune, moved out against Lee, now with Longstreet at Hagerstown, hoping to crush him before he could be reinforced from the south.

When Lee became aware that the superior Union force was advancing against him, he decided to concentrate Longstreet and Hill at South Mountain east of Boonsboro, praying for a successful containment of McClellan until his scattered forces could join him. Toombs had previously moved with Longstreet toward Hagerstown, and was temporarily commanding three brigades. A few miles outside of town, Toombs' own brigade was sent forward to occupy the town and hold it awaiting further orders. On the morning of the fourteenth, the rest of Longstreet's command was sent back to South Mountain to support Hill against the approaching Federals. Toombs and his men remained in Hagerstown, guarding the wagon trains and supplies, and took no part in the battle which ensued to the east.[88]

The Union army was stopped on the fourteenth at the mountain passes, and Lee had gained one day in his desperate race against time. The Confederates then moved west toward Sharpsburg to await support from Harpers Ferry. About 10 P.M., after the battle of South Mountain, Toombs received orders to proceed to Sharpsburg. He started at once and reached the town before daylight the next morning.[89]

[88]*Official Records*, Ser. I, Vol. XII, Pt. 2, pp. 566, 580; Vol. XIX, Pt. 1, pp. 140, 188.
[89]*Ibid.*, XIX, Pt. 1, pp. 140, 188.

Lee's line of defense was established between Antietam Creek and the Potomac River in the hills just east of Sharpsburg. His thinly manned lines extended about three miles north and south, with D. R. Jones' division on the right flank south and east of the town near the sluggish little creek. The key to the Confederate right was a bridge over the knee-deep Antietam which would support at most a narrow column of eight men abreast. The Confederate bank of the creek rose steeply for about fifty yards below and above the bridge, and was thinly covered with trees. A rail fence ran along the top of the slope.[90]

Toombs' orders were to hold the bridge as long as possible, and when dislodged to move to high ground which commanded the fords below the bridge. When this position became untenable, he was to join the rest of the division posted about one-half mile to the rear on the heights near town. On the morning of the battle, Wednesday, September 17, Toombs found himself with a depleted brigade. Two of his regiments, the 15th and 17th, had been detailed to protect a Confederate wagon train from Union cavalry, and had not returned. In compensation he had been given General Thomas F. Drayton's 50th Georgia, reduced in strength, and a company of South Carolinians from General Micah Jenkins' brigade.[91]

Toombs' position lent itself favorably to defense. The road leading to the bridge from the Union side paralleled the creek for about a hundred yards. This afforded the Confederates a devastating flanking fire of pistol range before the bridge could be reached. Two regiments, the 2nd and 20th Georgia, some four hundred strong, were placed behind trees and fence rail barricades at the top of the slope looking down on the bridge. The other troops under Toombs' command were extended thinly downstream to the lower ford, while artillery support was readied in the rear.[92]

The sixteenth had seen the return of most of Lee's scattered forces as McClellan withheld attack. On the morning of the seventeenth, Lee awaited the Union assault with an army reduced by straggling to less than forty thousand. McClellan had eighty thou-

[90]*Ibid.*, LI, Pt. 1, pp. 161–62; *Battles and Leaders*, II, 650.
[91]*Official Records*, Ser. I, Vol. XIX, Pt. 1, pp. 888–89; Longstreet, *Manassas*, 258.
[92]*Official Records*, Ser. I, Vol. XIX, Pt. 1, pp. 889–90; LI, Pt. 1, pp. 161–62, 165.

sand at his disposal. From dawn to darkness the battle of Antietam was fought. Each general Union attack—on the Confederate left, center, and right—came close to spelling destruction for Lee's veterans. Particularly on the Confederate right was survival snatched from the jaws of defeat at the last possible moment.

Around 9 A.M., the first attempt was made to carry the bridge by Union forces under General Ambrose E. Burnside. It was repulsed. By one o'clock, the intrepid four hundred had turned back four additional assaults, fighting "until their gun barrels were too hot for the naked hands." [93] But the situation was worsening. Ammunition was running low and artillery support had been withdrawn. On the other side of the creek, the Federals were massing for an all-out attack on the bridge and the fords.

At one o'clock, with artillery fire playing heavily on the Confederates across the creek, fresh Union troops with bayonets fixed rushed the bridge, and this time effected a crossing. The Stars and Stripes were planted on the Confederate bank, "amid the most enthusiastic cheering from every part of the field from where they could be seen." [94] Toombs' weary men now fell back all along the line, as the Federals flooded the bridge in large numbers and began wading across the Antietam at the fords. [95]

Toombs moved to a new position, a hillside cornfield, about a half-mile southwest of the bridge. Before the deployment was completed, his absent brigades, the 15th and 17th, plus five companies of the 11th Georgia, arrived and relieved the front-line defenders, who were sent to the rear for rest and ammunition. [96]

For two hours the Union buildup on the Confederate side of the Antietam continued. By three o'clock, Burnside's troops were ready for the advance on Sharpsburg. As the blue masses moved up the

[93]*Southern Historical Society Papers*, XXXI, 40.
[94]*Official Records*, Ser. I, Vol. XIX, Pt. 1, p. 444.
[95]It is a little puzzling why the Union troops did not earlier wade the shallow creek *en masse* instead of concentrating on the bridge. Williams, *Lincoln Finds a General*, II, 453, speaks of the Antietam as being deep in this area, but most of the evidence points to its lack of depth. Colonel Benning of the 17th Georgia found it wide but shallow, See *Southern Historical Society Papers*, XVI, 393. Henry Kyd Douglas wrote that Burnside's Bridge was no Thermopylae and that the Union troops "might have waded it that day without getting their waist belts wet in any place." Some years later, a Union officer told Douglas that the puzzling thing was how "Burnside . . . [kept] his troops from breaking over." Douglas, *Stonewall*, 172.
[96]*Official Records*, Ser. I, XIX, Pt 1, pp. 890–91.

hill, "the earth seemed to tremble beneath their tread." For the out-numbered Confederates of Jones' division holding the heights south and east of town, "it was a splendid and fearful sight. . . ." [97] The Union attack crunched forward successfully, smashing the Confederates in front of Sharpsburg and reaching the outskirts of town. The day was almost lost. At this moment Lee received the thrilling news that A. P. Hill was coming up with the last of the Confederate forces from Harpers Ferry, his "battle flags gleaming redly against the dark background." [98]

Toombs meanwhile had been ordered from his position, which had escaped the main Federal assault, to the heights occupied by the remnants of Jones' division. Advancing swiftly with a reduced brigade, he found as he neared the town that Union troops had pierced the Confederate defenses, were occupying his designated place on the battle line, and were threatening to cut Lee's line of retreat to the Potomac. After rallying a portion of General James L. Kemper's broken brigade, Toombs threw his men into battle. A member of Kemper's 1st Virginia wrote that Toombs galloped "up and down the line like one frantic, telling the men to stand firm. . . ." [99]

Toombs' men and the footsore troops of A. P. Hill struck the Federals simultaneously. The Union assault faltered, ground to a halt, and then receded downhill to the protection of the high banks along the creek. An exultant Toombs wanted to push the enemy across the Antietam, but he was ordered back to the heights near town. "Night came at last," recorded a Southern soldier, "stopping the carnage of the dreadful day, and the tender, pitiful stars shone in the vast dome above and looked down upon the scene of desolation and death." [100]

On the following evening, Toombs and some of his staff were riding to the headquarters of Colonel Benning when they stumbled upon a troop of Federal cavalry. A short engagement followed in

[97]*Battles and Leaders*, II, 629.
[98]*Southern Historical Society Papers*, XXXI, 42.
[99]Joseph T. Durkin (ed.), *John Dooley Confederate Soldier: His War Journal* (Georgetown, 1945), 47.
[100]*Southern Historical Society Papers*, XI, 21. Opinions vary as to whether Toombs or Hill was the hero of the hour. The preponderance of thought is on Hill's side, Freeman, *Lee's Lieutenants*, II, 275–76. For a strong statement supporting Toombs, see article by Colonel Benning in *Southern Historical Society Papers*, XVI, 393–95.

which Toombs was shot through the hand.[101] The Georgian went home to recuperate, and did not return to his command until the end of the year. It was not a happy convalescence. His action at Burnside's Bridge had drawn praise, but no promotion was forthcoming for Toombs. His wound healed slowly, and in his eyes that "scoundrel Jeff Davis" seemed bent on ruining not only him but the entire Confederacy as well.[102]

Within a short time after his return to duty, Toombs decided to resign his commission. Although burning antipathy to Davis was at the root of his action, he did not elaborate on causes in his farewell message to his troops, dated March 5. "Under existing circumstances," he stated simply, "I [can] no longer hold my commission under President Davis with advantage to my country, or to you, or with honor to myself."[103]

Toombs' resignation became a conversation piece throughout the Confederacy. J. B. Jones wrote in his diary that the move created "some sensation" in Richmond. In Jones' opinion, Toombs' departure stemmed from the "failure of the President to promote him to higher position, which he may have deemed himself entitled to, from his genius, antecedents, wealth, etc. But it is probable he will cause some disturbances."[104] The Richmond *Enquirer* said that "there will be a general feeling of regret that this distinguished statesman and soldier has resigned his command."[105] Robert E. Lee's laconic comment read: "Dispatch Received—I make no objection to the resignation of Genl Toombs."[106]

Some months after Toombs had left the army, President Davis explained his role in the affair. Writing to an interested Georgian, he stated that he was sorry that Toombs had become angry over the matter of a lack of promotion, but it was not possible for him at the time to gratify the general's wish. "I observed with regret that while General Toombs' superiors were urgent in pressing for

[101]Stovall, *Toombs*, 268. In *Official Records*, Ser. I, Vol. XIX, Pt. 1, p. 841, is the statement that Toombs was "severely wounded at the close of the engagement."

[102]Lee's report of the battle of Antietam stated that Toombs' command had conducted itself "with distinguished gallantry." *Official Records*, Ser. I, Vol. XIX, Pt. 1, p. 150.

[103]Phillips (ed.), *Correspondence*, 612.

[104]Jones, *War Clerk's Diary*, I, 273.

[105]Richmond *Enquirer*, March 7, 1863.

[106]Lee to General Samuel Cooper, March 3, 1863, in Robert Toombs Staff File.

promotion other officers whom they reported for distinguished conduct and ability in the field, they never presented his name for promotion to a vacancy." Davis pointed out that he was "almost exclusively dependent on official reports for a knowledge of the claims of officers to promotion." Having already appointed Toombs to the position of brigadier general "before his capacity to command had been tested," he felt he could go no further without the recommendations of his superiors. "It may be fairly expected," the Confederate President concluded, "that, when time shall have soothed the irritation now felt by General Toombs, he will do me justice and no longer attribute to unworthy motives my having selected others for the promotion to which he judged himself entitled." [107]

The record of Robert Toombs as a Confederate soldier was hardly exemplary, and it is clear that the Southern high command felt no great loss at his departure. He was headstrong, at times insubordinate, and given on occasion to commanding his brigade "as a sovereign and independent body." [108] Although possessed of spirit, gallantry, and a deep devotion to those who served under him, Toombs had too many shortcomings to endear himself to Richmond authorities. He could have better served the cause had he been willing to bridle his actions and tongue. But then that would not have been Robert Toombs.

[107]Dunbar Rowland (ed.), *Jefferson Davis, Constitutionalist: His Letters, Papers and Speeches* (Jackson, 1923), VI, 43.
[108]Stovall, *Toombs*, 272.

CHAPTER X

At Home and Abroad

IN April of 1863, Toombs, in Washington, Georgia, now far removed from the war and convalescing from a recent illness, wrote Stephens that for the next year he would probably have nothing to do. He planned to pass his time "in pursuit of . . . neglected political studies" and in visiting his plantation in Stewart County.[1] It was impossible, however, for a man of Toombs' temperament to be idle. Within a short time he was back as a vigorous player in the game of polemics against the Davis administration, he had taken up arms with the state troops, and had thrown his somewhat battered hat in the ring for political office.

Toombs did not stand alone in his bitter opposition to the Richmond government and its wartime policies. He was ardently supported by Governor Brown and the Stephens brothers. These "anarchists" failed or refused to see the necessity of subordinating the principle of states rights to the general goal of winning the war. So recalcitrant did they become that "toward the end of the war the political front in Georgia was almost as dangerous to the Confed-

---

[1] Toombs to Stephens, April 21, 1863, in Phillips (ed.), *Correspondence*, 615–16. Toombs' illness which dated from the middle of March had been quite severe. His daughter Sallie called the malady "Cramp Colic." See Sallie T. DuBose to Stephens, March 20, 1863, in Alexander H. Stephens Papers, Emory University.

eracy as was the military front around Richmond." [2] Toombs' animosity was particularly vehement, being motivated by his personal dislike of Davis.

Soon after Toombs returned home from Virginia there was considerable speculation over the possibility of his entrance into the gubernatorial race in November. If Governor Brown, the incumbent, declined to run for a fourth term, then Toombs, Brown's friend and political supporter, loomed as a likely successor. Such a contingency was not received with widespread enthusiasm. The Columbus *Enquirer* said the time was not ripe for the partisan strife that this would engender. Nothing could be worse at the moment than a political contest involving the war policy of the Confederate administration. Until the war was over all controversies over domestic policy should be laid aside. [3]

In spite of misgivings on the part of the press and some of his advisors, Brown did offer to step aside and support Toombs if the general would consent to run. [4] Toombs declined, as he later told a friend, because of the diminishing power of the governor's position. He preferred trying to "preserve rights and check abuses" as a member of the Confederate Congress, and was determined to stand election for that body. [5] In May, Brown announced that he would seek reelection, and subsequently won his fourth term of office in November, with the support of Toombs and other Georgia obstructionists.

On June 17, Toombs spoke before a large audience at the Sparta Baptist Church on the subject, "The State of the Country." [6] He stated that he had come at the call of his countrymen. In his hour and a half address, he endorsed Governor Brown's candidacy, and put into clear focus, though in a surprisingly restrained manner, his thoughts on many of the controversial issues of the time involving the program of the Davis administration. He condemned conscription, a policy he had opposed from its inception in 1862 along with Brown and Alexander H. Stephens. Toombs' well-known record of opposition in the United States Congress to anything that smacked of military despotism and regular, as opposed to volunteer,

[2]E. Merton Coulter, *Georgia: A Short History* (Chapel Hill, 1947), 328.
[3]Quoted in the Milledgeville *Southern Recorder*, March 17, 1863.
[4]Toombs to W. W. Burwell, June 10, 1863, in Phillips (ed.), *Correspondence*, 619.
[5]*Ibid.*
[6]Athens *Southern Watchman*, July 8, 1863.

armies made his stand on this matter inevitable. Particularly did he censure at this time those features of the Confederate conscription system which threw much of the power of officer appointment into Confederate rather than into state hands. Toombs labeled the policy of impressment of supplies by the central government, at prices under market value, unjust, and called the recently established "tax in kind," a tithe of the farmer's crops, unfortunate. The latter would lead, he said, to the "accumulation of government stores which would rot for the lack of transportation. . . ." Toombs stood opposed to the plan of Secretary of the Treasury Memminger which called for state endorsement of Confederate bonds to appreciate their value and give them a larger market at home and abroad. He felt that this would have the effect of depreciating the credit of Georgia, which was fairly sound, instead of raising the credit of the Confederacy, generally below that of the states. Lastly, Toombs said he was utterly opposed to martial law and the suspension of the writ of habeas corpus under the military authority of Richmond. The constitution conferred sufficient powers upon the government for the prosecution of the war without resort to this deprivation of civil rights. "Maintain your personal liberty," he told the crowd, "while you are achieving your independence." Toombs' speech was well-received, although the "prolonged applause" was doubtless as much for his calm, invective-free delivery, as for what he said.

Throughout 1863, "the slow paralysis of inflation crept deeper into the vitals of the Confederacy," [7] worrying public officials and causing Toombs on August 12 to write a long letter on finance to the editor of the Augusta *Constitutionalist*.[8] He scored the decline of public credit through excessive issue of paper money, and called for a return to sound financing. Through the classical pattern of "simple, rigid and equal" taxation to support a sound currency and "new bonds with principal and interest payable in gold and silver," Toombs asserted that the fiscal structure of the Confederacy could be repaired. Time was running out, he said. "Patriotism demands that all good men should unite to correct the evils." Various innovations and a new secretary of the treasury in 1864 failed to check the financial confusion of the Confederate government, which continued to worsen to the end of the war.

[7]Coulter, *Confederate States*, 157.
[8]Phillips (ed.), *Correspondence*, 622–27.

Toombs' published letter attracted some attention in the camp of the enemy. Gideon Welles, Lincoln's secretary of the navy and a prewar acquaintance of Toombs, remarked in his diary:

> The Rebels are demoralized and discouraged, yet have not the manly reluctance to confess it. . . . Toombs of Georgia published a letter in which he speaks with freedom and boldness of the wretched condition of affairs among the Rebels, and of the ruin that is before them. This is audacity rather than courage. Toombs is a malcontent. Scarcely a man has contributed more than Toombs to the calamities that are upon us, and I am glad to see that he is aware of the misery which he and his associates have inflicted on the country. I have ever considered him a reckless and audacious partisan, an unfit leader in public affairs, and my mind has not changed in regard to him. Toombs, however, was never a sycophant.[9]

In the summer of 1863 a restless Toombs wrote Alexander Stephens that he wanted to return to military life with the Georgia militia "in the prospective defense of our homes." He said he would try to raise a volunteer regiment in the area.[10] Toombs echoed the same sentiments to Linton Stephens a few days later. He said he felt he could not serve his country to advantage in the "public counsels," and was inclined to "challenge the army." He was glad that Lee was back from Gettysburg, as the Virginian had "not sufficient genius to command an invading army. An army in a defensive position needs but little talent in its commander & Lee has scarcely enough even for that." Davis had not improved in Toombs' estimation and was termed a "malignant wretch."[11]

On August 8, 1863, Toombs was commissioned a colonel in the State Guard, commanding a regiment of cavalry for local defense.[12] In a letter to Howell Cobb, soon to be assigned by Davis to the command of the Georgia state troops brought into Confederate service, Toombs described his force as "only a body guard to

[9]Entry of August 28, 1863, *Diary of Gideon Welles, Secretary of the Navy Under Lincoln and Johnson* (Boston, 1911), I, 428.

[10]Toombs to Stephens, July 14, 1863, in Phillips (ed.), *Correspondence*, 621.

[11]Toombs to Stephens, July 19, 1863, in Alexander H. Stephens Papers, Emory University.

[12]Adjutant General's Letter Book (MS and typescript in Georgia Archives), XIX, 82, 345; XX, 42. Toombs' regiment, "six months troops," consisted of companies from Clarke, Elbert, Madison, and Franklin counties.

protect us when we have all to flee to the mountains. Davis will soon bring us to that point," he added.[13] In a second letter on this same day to W. W. Burwell, Toombs lamented the increasing power of the central government. He thought that the people should hold every governmental department "to the strictest account. I am fully persuaded," he said, "that the road to liberty for the white man does not lie through slavery." [14]

In the early fall Toombs' regiment bivouacked in Athens and Atlanta. In November he left his military duties long enough to run again for the Confederate Senate. He was not optimistic about his chances of election by the state legislature, but told Stephens that he was "inclined to run even if I find myself in a minority, with a view to rally and embody those who agree with me in principle, in order to offer whatever resistance I can to the ruin of the revolution and the destruction of public liberty." [15] In a preelection speech before the legislature, Toombs hewed to his familiar anti-government line, and called on the people to guard their rights jealously.[16]

Although supported by Brown, who won the governorship at this time, Toombs lost his election to Herschel V. Johnson. On the third ballot, Johnson got the necessary majority, as Toombs trailed a distant and unhappy second.[17]

His rejection by the Georgia legislature left Toombs in a sullen and uncompromising mood. As he and his regiment boarded a train in Augusta in bitterly cold weather for service in the Savannah area, his men started fires on the floors of the cars. An agent of the railroad company remonstrated with them and told them that the train would not leave until the fires were extinguished. Up came Toombs in the middle of the altercation. "Cursing and using much bitter language. . . ," he put the agent under guard, threatened to have him cut in pieces for engine fuel, and ordered the train

[13]Toombs to Cobb, August 29, 1863, in Howell Cobb Papers, Duke University.

[14]Phillips (ed.), *Correspondence*, 629.

[15]Toombs to Stephens, November 2, 1863, in Phillips (ed.), *Correspondence*, 630.

[16]Atlanta *Daily Intelligencer*, November 13, 1863.

[17]*Georgia Senate Journal* (1863), 110. The votes for Johnson and Toombs over the three ballots tabulated 79 to 43, 92 to 47, and 115 to 51, respectively.

on its way. The harassed agent duly reported the incident to the company.[18]

Several weeks later, on January 23, 1864, Toombs made an incendiary speech before a large number of the Georgia militia at a camp near Savannah. Throwing restraint to the wind, Toombs rehashed in intemperate language all of his old grievances against the Confederate government—the tax-in-kind, military impressment, conscription, and the sometime suspension of the writ of habeas corpus. He hinted ominously at open resistance for the preservation of individual liberty.[19]

Shortly after his speech, Toombs was put under arrest, a situation not unknown to him as a military man. He was summoned to attend a general court martial called by General Beauregard, commanding the Department of South Carolina and Georgia, to answer charges preferred against him by the Central Railroad and Banking Company.[20] The Confederacy was rocked by wild rumors attending this involvement of one of its foremost citizens. There was considerable speculation, although groundless, that Toombs had been charged with treason for his harangue to the troops in Savannah.[21] He made one appearance before the court, in early February. At that time he asserted that the court was improperly constituted, and lacked jurisdiction over him since his term of service had expired on January 31. He also pointed out that one of its members, Colonel George A. Gordon, was a nephew of the company president, and hence was unqualified to take part in the proceedings.[22] Beauregard, around the middle of February, for reasons not disclosed, ordered the proceedings dropped, and thus ended this unfortunate chapter in Toombs' career.[23]

When his regiment disbanded at the expiration of six months'

[18]Savannah *Republican* article quoted in Richmond *Daily Dispatch*, February 13, 1864.

[19]Athens *Southern Watchman*, March 2, 1864; Henry W. Cleveland, "Robert Toombs," *The Southern Bivouac* (January, 1886), 455–57.

[20]Toombs to Beauregard, February 13, 1864, in Robert Toombs Staff File.

[21]Richmond *Daily Dispatch*, February 13, 1864; *Daily Richmond Examiner*, February 3, 1864; Athens *Southern Watchman*, February 17, 1864.

[22]Toombs to Beauregard, February 13, 1864, in Robert Toombs Staff File.

[23]Toombs to Thomas Jordan, February 26, 1864, in Robert Toombs Staff File. Apparently Beauregard's cessation order reached the court martial tardily, for the trial was conducted for a while with Toombs *en absentia*. See also Richmond *Daily Dispatch*, February 13, 1864.

service, Toombs went back home. There he stayed the spring, looking after personal affairs and writing occasionally to friends on public issues. He supported the state legislature's condemnation of the suspension of habeas corpus by the Confederate government, a movement spearheaded by Governor Brown and the Stephens brothers. On April 1, he wrote the elder Stephens that he was "greatly delighted at the vote." [24]

In May of 1864, an ominous shadow began to lengthen slowly across the state of Georgia from northwest to southeast—Sherman. "To arms, and to the front," proclaimed Governor Brown to the people, "and the vandal hordes will soon be driven back." [25] Toombs donned his uniform again and went to Atlanta. There he entered military service as chief of staff and inspector-general under General Gustavus W. Smith. On June 1, Smith took command of the Georgia militia which Governor Brown had assigned during the emergency to General Joseph E. Johnston, Confederate commander opposing Sherman.[26]

During May and June, Sherman's large army rolled inexorably and destructively toward Atlanta, in spite of the dogged and skillful opposition of peppery Joe Johnston. Late June found the Confederates several miles west of the Chattahoochee River, blocking the Union advance. Smith's militia was positioned in support of Johnston's vulnerable left flank.[27] Much of Toombs' time was spent trying to make an effective fighting force out of raw troops. He wrote his wife on July 1 that sometimes he had been riding twenty to thirty miles a day in the process.[28] It was a cat and mouse game for the militia, retreating when pressed, but remaining always between the Federals and the river. Toombs commented that "this

[24]Phillips (ed.), *Correspondence*, 638. On March 10, Linton Stephens, who had introduced the resolutions of condemnation in the legislature, wrote his brother that he wished Toombs were in Milledgeville. "*Perhaps* his presence would prejudice the cause from the idea which has been so industriously disseminated, that his opposition to the course of the government is founded on personal animosity and a desire for a second revolution; but still I believe his *ideas* and his *view*, would more than counterbalance this prejudice." Letter in Alexander H. Stephens Papers, Duke University.
[25]Candler, *Georgia Confederate Records*, III, 568–69.
[26]*Battles and Leaders*, IV, 332–33; J. E. Johnston to J. E. Brown, June 4, 1864, in Candler, *Confederate Records*, III, 574–75; Linton to Alexander H. Stephens, June 10, 1864, Alexander H. Stephens Papers, Emory University.
[27]*Battles and Leaders*, IV, 332.
[28]Toombs to his wife, July 1, 1864, in Robert Toombs Papers, University of Georgia.

army can not tell for half a day where they will be." [29] The Confederates on the night of July 9 finally fell back across the river and into entrenchments directly around Atlanta. On July 17, Johnston was relieved of his command by Davis, who now entrusted the defense of Atlanta to the more pugnacious and aggressive General John B. Hood.

On July 20, Hood attacked Sherman at Peachtree Creek, but was repulsed with heavy casualties. Two days later, with Smith's militia participating, Hood hit Sherman east of the city in the battle of Atlanta, but without success. Hood wrote Brown on July 23 that the state troops "fought with great gallantry" [30] in the contest. Toombs told his wife that the militia had far exceeded his expectations. "God give them the spirit of men & all will be well," he concluded. [31]

After this engagement Hood went primarily on the defensive, as Sherman pushed his lines closer to the city on the north and west. The Confederates sallied forth on July 28 at Ezra Church to harry the encircling Sherman, but were beaten back.

For some forty days, Atlanta withstood Sherman and the Union bombardment. An interesting vignette of Toombs during the siege was recorded by Confederate captain, Thomas J. Key, who wrote on August 4:

Yesterday I saw an aged man [Toombs was only fifty-four] of corpulent dimensions riding behind the lines and telling the Georgia troops to 'stand by the artillerists and you will whip the Yankees like the devil.' His remarks 'took' so promptly that an involuntary cheer was raised, and I walked near the individual to get a close view of him. It proved to be Hon. Robert Toombs, of Georgia, who in better times had figured largely on the political stage in the capital at Washington, and who had a wide reputation as a debater and statesman. He is no longer known as a Senator but now goes by the title of General of Militia. It was to the Georgia militia that he was addressing himself. [32]

Toombs wrote his wife on August 22 that the Union commander "shells the town furiously every day doing not much harm, kills

29*Ibid.*, July 6, 1864.
30*Battles and Leaders*, IV, 335.
31Toombs to his wife, July 25, 1864, in Robert Toombs Papers, University of Georgia.
32Wirt A. Cate (ed.), *Two Soldiers: The Campaign Diaries of Thomas J. Key and Robert J. Campbell* (Chapel Hill, 1938), 108.

a few every day. We lose from three to twelve of our poor milish every day from shells & minnie balls." But the outlook was still good, he stated.[33] A week later Toombs' composure had begun to fray a bit under the monotony of siege and cannonading. He told his wife that were it not for Atlanta's importance to the Confederacy, "I would like to see it burned up, for there is not a single musket in this division held by a resident of Atlanta. I never dreamed that as many cowards & villains could be found in one lot this side of the place of final punishment." He said he was worn out by the "toils & vexations" of maintaining efficiency among the militia. Half were "brave honest fellows" but the rest spent all of their time using "every imaginable pretext to get out of the army." [34]

By the end of the month Toombs was convinced that the fall of Atlanta was imminent. He wrote Stephens that Sherman was moving to cut off the city from the south. This would compel the Confederates to "fight him in his works or evacuate the place as soon as our rations are out." Toombs called Sherman's actions "the Vicksburg movement acted over again, except we can get out when we want to and Pemberton [Confederate commander] could not." [35] When Sherman gained control of the Macon railroad, Hood felt compelled to evacuate the city. On September 1 the Confederate exodus began, and on September 3 Union troops moved in.[36]

A few days after the fall of Atlanta, Governor Brown withdrew the state militia from Hood's command to permit them, as he informed Hood, "to return to their homes, and look for a time after important interests." [37] Sherman, more to the point, told General H. W. Halleck that the militia was disbanded "to gather the corn and sorghum of the State." [38] At this juncture, Sherman the general became Sherman the diplomat, as he tried to capitalize upon a

[33]Toombs to his wife, August 22, 1864, in Robert Toombs Papers, University of Georgia.

[34]Toombs to his wife, August 29, 1864, in Robert Toombs Papers, University of Georgia.

[35]Toombs to Stephens, August 30, 1864, in Phillips (ed.), *Correspondence*, 651. On July 4, 1863, General John C. Pemberton had surrendered encircled Vicksburg to Grant after a long siege.

[36]*Battles and Leaders*, IV, 335, 343–44; *Memoirs of General William T. Sherman* (Bloomington, Ind., 1957), 104–109.

[37]Brown to Hood, September 10, 1864 in *Sherman Memoirs*, 139; Bryan, *Confederate Georgia*, 163, says Brown's real reason was to circumvent the enrollment of the Georgia militia in the Confederate service.

[38]*Sherman Memoirs*, 138.

"peace conspiracy" which had been initiated in Georgia by Brown and the Stephenses.[39] Through Georgia Unionists acting as intermediaries, Sherman tried to induce Brown to withdraw Georgia from the war, in return for which he would keep his troops to the main roads and pay for supplies which his army consumed. He wanted a meeting with Brown and the Confederate Vice-President in Atlanta to effect such an arrangement.[40]

Toombs, at home in Washington, advised Stephens in strong language to avoid entanglement. "Do not by any means go to see Sherman," he counseled, "whatever may be the form of his invitation. It will place you in a wrong, *very wrong* position." He told Stephens that the issue of peace was committed by fundamental law to Davis' hands, and "nothing could be of more evil tendency than for other officers of the Confederacy, or state governments, to meet any person, and much less a general of an army, to discuss the question." [41] Neither Stephens nor Brown met with Sherman, although their disruptive tactics, weakening the total Confederate war effort, continued to the end of the conflict.

After Atlanta was evacuated, Hood marched his army northwestward toward Tennessee, hoping to draw Sherman after him. Sherman gave chase into Alabama but then returned to Atlanta, after giving Southern-born General George H. Thomas, one of the North's best officers, the task of pursuing the Confederates.

On November 15, Sherman began his famous March to the Sea, after destroying much of Atlanta. "Wrecked engines, bent and twisted iron rails, blackened ruins and lonesome chimneys saddened the hearts of the few peaceful citizens who remained there," wrote a Union general.[42]

Sherman's first objective was Milledgeville, the state capital. His sixty thousand man army moved out in two divisions, the right wing toward Jonesboro and the left toward Decatur and Covington. Opposing Sherman were a few thousand troops under General Smith and Joe Wheeler's cavalry. The militia had been assembled in mid-October at Lovejoy's Station, a few miles south of Atlanta, to assist a small body of cavalry in observing Federal movements.

[39]Coulter, *Confederate States*, 540–42; Bryan, *Confederate Georgia*, 96–99, 163–64.
[40]*Ibid., Sherman Memoirs*, 139–40.
[41]Toombs to Stephens, September 23, 1864, in Phillips (ed.), *Correspondence*, 652–53.
[42]*Battles and Leaders*, IV, 663.

As Sherman's right wing commenced its march, Smith fell back toward Macon, via Griffin and Forsythe, reaching that city on November 17. At Forsythe, the militia clashed successfully with Union cavalry, saving a large supply depot.[43]

On November 17, Toombs wrote Brown from Macon that things were bad there and that the city would have to be abandoned unless immediately reinforced.[44] Brown, however, had problems of his own in Milledgeville, which lay directly in the path of the left wing of the Union army, and could be of no assistance. Macon was by-passed by the main body of Union troops with only "demonstrations" being made in the city's direction. Contrary to General Smith's instructions, the militia on the twenty-second attacked the Union rear guard near Griswoldville, just east of Macon. The Federals, partially armed with Spencer repeating rifles, repulsed the Confederates with heavy losses.[45]

The Union envelopment of Milledgeville sent Governor Brown scurrying to Macon and into conference with Smith, Toombs, Howell Cobb, and General Richard Taylor, who had recently arrived at the command of Lee for a tour of inspection. On Taylor's advice, the decision was made to move the state troops by a circuitous route south and east to Savannah. Then Taylor departed from Macon ahead of the troop movement.[46]

Shortly afterwards, the Georgia militia moved by car from Macon to Albany, and then marched overland to make rail connections again at Thomasville. Toombs, riding ahead of his troops, found a stalled General Taylor in Thomasville. Taylor had had very little success in obtaining transportation either for himself or for the approaching state militia. Exploding, Toombs browbeat local officials into getting an engine ready for Taylor, and then by telegraph "threatened dire vengeance on superintendents and road masters" in Savannah if they did not have the necessary transportation ready for his own men in time. Success was forthcoming. "A man of extraordinary energy, this same Toombs," observed Taylor.[47]

The first contingent of Georgia militia arrived in Savannah at 2 A.M. on the thirtieth of November. Before the train was un-

[43]*Ibid.*, 667.
[44]Candler, *Georgia Confederate Records*, III, 673.
[45]*Sherman Memoirs*, 187–88; *Battles and Leaders*, IV, 664–667.
[46]Richard Taylor, *Destruction and Reconstruction: Personal Experiences of the Late War*, ed. Richard B. Harwell (New York, 1955), 259–60.
[47]*Ibid.*, 261.

loaded General Smith was ordered by General William J. Hardee, in command of the Savannah area, to move his men immediately by car to a position across the Savannah River in South Carolina where Federal raiding parties were active. Smith at first balked, claiming he could not legally move Georgia militia out of the state, but finally agreed because of the emergency. At eight in the morning, the first train arrived at Grahamville Station on the Charleston and Savannah Railroad, and a second within half an hour. A short distance from the station, the militia repulsed repeated Federal attacks throughout the day and saved the railroad. The Union troops withdrew to coastal fortifications and the militia went back to Savannah.[48]

Sherman had resumed his march from Milledgeville on November 24, and on December 9 reached the Savannah area. General Hardee's defending Confederates numbered only about ten thousand and were at best a token resistance force. During the brief siege of the city, Smith's militia, about two thousand strong, occupied a position about three miles above the city from the Savannah River to the Ogeechee Canal.[49] On the seventeenth of December, Sherman demanded surrender of the city but Hardee refused. As the Union army made plans for a general assault, the Confederates, on the night of the twentieth, evacuated Savannah, and crossed over into South Carolina on pontoon bridges.[50] On December 21, Federal occupation of the city began. The "one big picnick" as a Union officer described the march from Atlanta, was now concluded, and Lincoln's Christmas present had been secured.[51]

Smith's militia moved from Savannah to Augusta, where winter encampment was set up. Toombs fell ill and went home on sick leave. He was sufficiently well to return to Augusta on February 16 and make a public address in the city hall on the progress of the war. The former senator was still having difficulty even at this late stage of the war in determining whether Richmond or

[48]*Battles and Leaders*, IV, 167–68; Taylor, *Destruction*, 262–63, has Toombs playing a major role in getting the Georgia troops into South Carolina, but Smith's account (*Battles and Leaders*, IV, 167–68) does not mention him.

[49]*Battles and Leaders*, IV, 669; *Official Records*, Ser. I, Vol. LIII, p. 35; Charles C. Jones, *The Siege of Savannah* . . . (Albany, Ga., 1874), 55.

[50]*Battles and Leaders*, IV, 669; *Sherman Memoirs*, 210–12, 216–17.

[51]George C. Osborn (ed.), "Sherman's March Through Georgia: Letters from Charles Ewing to His Father Thomas Ewing," *Georgia Historical Quarterly*, XLII (September, 1958), 326.

Washington was enemy headquarters. He saw as great dangers facing the South "bad management and bad legislation" from the Davis administration in Virginia. He felt that if the citizens of the Confederacy could be made to feel secure in their property, they would fight on unfailingly. Toombs thought that the South was too big for the enemy to control even if they overran and despoiled it. He wanted no peace on Northern terms and strongly urged the continuation of the war.[52] An observer commented that in his speech Toombs, though wanting the war for the next twenty years if necessary, "did not see any good in what anybody did." [53]

Toombs, except for a mid-March message of encouragement to the state legislature, remained out of the public eye for the remainder of the war. He attended to his law practice, corresponded with Stephens, and entertained guests in Washington. His health improved, but not his opinion of Davis. On March 23, 1865, he commented to Stephens that there was but one remedy for the evils that beset the South. It was "begone Davis." [54]

According to Stovall Toombs was dining with Governor Brown when he first heard of Lee's surrender. "The two men looked at each other intently, when they realized that all was over," records Stovall.[55]

On May 3, 1865, the remaining vestiges of Confederate civil authority in the persons of Jefferson Davis and his entourage rode into Washington, Georgia. With Davis were cabinet members Stephen R. Mallory and John H. Reagan, a few officers, men, and baggage. The wagons carrying the Confederate treasury lumbered some six miles behind under the supervision of John C. Breckinridge, Davis' last secretary of war. After an overnight rest, the party was to continue in its "flight into oblivion." [56]

Robert Toombs was in the same village that spring night. A man who seldom forgave and never forgot, he evidently still nurtured his dislike of the now harassed Davis. As he was to say years later of the President's sojourn in his community, "I did not even invite

[52]Athens *Southern Watchman*, February 22, 1865.
[53]Ruffin Thomson to William H. Thomson, February 18, 1865, in Ruffin Thomson Papers, Southern Historical Collection, University of North Carolina.
[54]Toombs to Stephens, March 23, 1865 in Phillips (ed.), *Correspondence*, 661.
[55]Stovall, *Toombs*, 281.
[56]A. J. Hanna, *Flight Into Oblivion* (Richmond, 1938).

Mr. Davis to my house—never spoke to him after I left the service. . . . I offered to send my carriage for his use, and do any other courtesy I could, but I could not receive him at my house." [57] Reagan, who was the house guest of Toombs' at this time, seemed much impressed by Toombs' efforts in Davis' behalf.[58] If the words of an old man are to be trusted, however, the unlovely blight of his hostility for Davis that had infected Toombs during his Confederate service lingered on at this moment as the very pillars of his government were crumbling around him.

The next morning, after a last "cabinet" meeting, the Confederate hierarchy left Washington, moving southward. Toombs remained at home, as apprehensive no doubt of oncoming Federal bayonets as were those with Davis, but preferring to await his unsettled future with his wife. A brief glimpse of Toombs at this time was given by Colonel Burton N. Harrison, Davis' private secretary, who was accompanying Mrs. Davis' party as it left Washington just a few hours before the President's small group arrived. Toombs, watching Harrison ride away, "was dressed in an illcut black Websterian Coat, the worse for wear, and had on a broad brimmed shabby hat." He stood beside an old buggy drawn by old horses, waiting to ride over to Crawfordville to see Stephens. Harrison wrote that the "atmosphere was murky with blasphemies, and denunciations of the Yankees." [59]

On May 5, Eliza Andrews wrote in her journal: "It has come at last—what we have been dreading and expecting so long— . . . the Yankees are actually in Washington." [60] The presence of some Negro troops doubtless increased the apprehensions of the citizens. For several days, the town's leading citizen, Robert Toombs, was not molested. As he moved about Washington freely, he probably saw the handbills posted in public places offering rewards for the arrest of Jefferson Davis, Clement C. Clay, former Alabama senator, and Beverly Tucker, onetime Confederate agent in Canada, as

[57] Atlanta *Constitution*, July 1, 1881.
[58] John H. Reagan, *Memoirs* . . . (New York and Washington, 1906), 215.
[59] Rowland (ed.), *Davis*, VII, 8. Shortly after President Davis and his party had left Washington, a curious incident involving Toombs took place. He found on his property a bag containing $6,000 in specie, apparently money from the mobile Confederate treasury fleeing from the pursuing Federals. Toombs turned the money over to Federal authorities. See Phillips, *Toombs*, 253–54; Andrews, *Journal*, 245; *Official Records*, Ser. I, Vol. IL, Pt. 2, p. 955.
[60] Andrews, *Journal*, 212.

accomplices in Lincoln's assassination, and may have wondered about his own safety.[61]

On May 11 the answer came. Around noon, fresh troops under the command of a Captain Saint of the 4th Iowa Cavalry arrived in town, and headed for Toombs' home to arrest him. As they entered his front gate, he went out the back door. After a fruitless search of the premises, Julia Toombs was told that unless her husband were given up, the house would be burned. She replied, "Burn it then," and with her pregnant daughter, Sallie, moved out with family valuables, which were distributed among friends in town. On the following day Captain Abraham Lott, provost-marshal in command of the area, returned from Augusta and ended the threat to the house. According to Miss Andrews, he apologized to Mrs. Toombs for her ordeal, saying that the orders for the raid had been issued over his head and without his knowledge.[62]

In 1877 Toombs told the story of his escape in a light vein: "The federal troops came to my house about half-past one o'clock one day. Mrs. Toombs was taking an account of what had been left us, when they called. . . . I didn't like the idea of staying in Boston harbor and Fort Warren, even in company with Mr. Stephens. I preferred Paris, so I took my horse and scooted." [63]

Earlier that morning, Stephens had been arrested in Crawfordville by Captain Saint. The party had then proceeded by rail to a point four miles outside Washington where Stephens and a guard were deposited, while the bulk of the troops went on into town. After dark the train returned with the soldiers but without Toombs. On being asked by Stephens if he had his friend in custody, the captain said, " 'No, . . . Mr. Toombs flanked us . . . ,' in a rather disappointed and irate tone." [64]

From this precarious hour until Toombs boarded a ship at New Orleans on November 4 bound for Havana, he was an outlaw in the land of his birth.[65] It was a new and unaccustomed role for the

---

[61]*Ibid.*, 237–38.

[62]*Ibid.*, 241, 243–44.

[63]Atlanta *Constitution*, August 29, 1877; Stovall, *Toombs*, 286–87; Phillips, *Toombs*, 254. It is highly improbable that Toombs knew of the arrest of Stephens at this time as he implies in his brief account.

[64]Avary (ed.), *Stephens' Recollections*, 100–104.

[65]The following account of Toombs, the fugitive, is based on Stovall, *Toombs*, 286–307, and an article in the Washington (Ga.) *Gazette*, n.d., which was published in the Atlanta *Constitution*, July 31, 1887.

lordly Toombs, traveling at night along the byways, using an assumed name, and wearing a "common checked suit, sack coat and slouch hat." [66] His companion in his wanderings was a young friend from Washington, Georgia, Charles E. Irvin, who had seen service in the war as a lieutenant in the artillery. Irvin served as a volunteer bodyguard, guide, and courier for the distinguished fugitive.

After a brief stay at a secluded island in the Savannah River, the two men headed for the wild and picturesque country around Tallulah Falls in the northeastern corner of the state. Here they remained until late June. When Irvin was unsuccessful in making arrangements for Toombs to leave the country from Savannah, they came down from the mountains into central Georgia, intent, as Irvin said later, on reaching the Florida coast. Although they passed within a few miles of his home, Toombs dared not chance a brief reunion with his wife.

Had Toombs been fully aware of what his wife was undergoing at the time, he may well have ridden into town in broad daylight and taken his place at her side. Writing to a friend in early July, she said, "What I have suffered I leave you to imagine—it beggars description." She remarked how wonderful the people in town had been to her. Her friends were as "numerous as the sands on the sea shore." But, she said, "I stay at home to keep out of sight of the Yankees, who are perfectly despisable to me." [67] On July 30, Mrs. Toombs and Sallie were summarily evicted from their home by the military. A Negro school was to be set up in the basement, with the other floors serving as officer's quarters. Mrs. Toombs was told that the house and lot were considered abandoned property, subject to confiscation.[68]

Toombs and Irvin, meanwhile, had found the Ocmulgee River heavily guarded, and so concluded to go back to the mountains until the Federal vigilance was relaxed. In August Julia Toombs, again restored to her home, inquired of Federal authorities if her husband could be paroled if he surrendered himself. Through Secre-

[66]Atlanta *Constitution*, July 31, 1887.

[67]Julia Toombs to Virginia Caroline Clay, July 5, 1865, in Clement Claiborne Clay Papers, Duke University.

[68]Andrews, *Journal*, 354–55; Marion Alexander to Mrs. George G. Hull, July 31, 1865, Edward Porter Alexander Papers. By order of General J. B. Steedman, Mrs. Toombs was soon restored to her house. See Andrews, *Journal*, 360; Avary (ed.), *Stephens' Recollections*, 466.

tary of War Edwin M. Stanton came the terse answer from President Andrew Johnson: "If Mr. Toombs comes within reach of the U. S. forces, he [is to] be immediately arrested and sent in close custody to Fort Warren." [69]

The fugitives remained in the mountains until October, when they followed their previous route back into the middle part of the state. Turning west, they then crossed the Ocmulgee and state line Chattahoochee River, and proceeded to Evergreen, Alabama, southwest of Montgomery. At Evergreen they boarded a train which carried them to Tensas Station, and from here they went by river steamer to Mobile.

In Alabama's bay city, Toombs stayed at the home of the father of Miss Augusta J. Evans, popular novelist. "These were among the most agreeable moments of General Toombs' long exile," said Stovall. Here in a quiet, restful atmosphere he "would walk to and fro along the shaded walks and pour forth, in his matchless way, the secret history of the ruin of Confederate hopes." [70] While Toombs remained in Mobile, Irvin went to New Orleans and obtained from the Spanish consul a pass to Cuba for Toombs under the name of Major Luther Martin. Both men then went by boat to the Crescent City. On November 4, Toombs boarded the steamship *Alabama* and left the country whose wounds he had once helped bind in 1850 and whose life he had attempted to destroy in war. Toombs' wife joined him in Havana in December. [71]

On December 15 Toombs wrote old friend Stephens from Cuba. [72] Stephens had been released two months before from his confinement at Fort Warren, and the cold and dampness of a prison cell had impaired his already weak and emaciated body. Toombs said that he was glad he escaped, for he was convinced that had he been apprehended he would have been "imprisoned and treated with indignity by . . . [his] beloved brethren of the North. . . ." He was vigorous in condemning President Johnson and his mild reconstruction policy, of which most Georgians approved. Still and forever the unreconstructed, whatever the method to restore the

[69]*Official Records*, Ser. II, Vol. VIII, pp. 714, 716.
[70]Stovall, *Toombs*, 302.
[71]Julia Toombs to Alexander H. Stephens, December 4, 1865 and May 16, 1866, in Alexander H. Stephens Papers, Emory University.
[72]Toombs to Stephens, December 15, 1865, in Phillips (ed.), *Correspondence*, 673–76.

Union, he saw "nothing in the conduct of President Johnson to approve, not a single act." Of some of the Georgia leaders[73] who were cooperating in rebuilding their state, Toombs said he had a "contempt that no language can measure. They seem to glory in their shame, and revel in the ruin and degradation of those whom they pretend to serve." He wanted nothing of the new regime, although his own people were acquiescing. His idols broken, the old order gone, he would have retired to a vantage point and hoped for the conquerors' entanglement in their own victorious dictates. Toombs considered the true policy of the South that of standing still and doing nothing.

While in Havana, Julia Toombs received a discomforting letter from Sallie. Writing on the evening of March 4, the day on which her sister had died eleven years before, and obviously depressed by its memories, she poured forth a tale of grief and despondency to her mother. Afraid for her four children, the youngest less than six months old, and afraid for her parents, she confirmed an earlier conjecture that she did not have long to live, but asked her mother not to mention this in her letters home as no one was aware of her condition.[74]

In May of 1866 Toombs left Havana and went to Paris, while his wife returned home for a visit before joining him in Liverpool on August 4. [75] Julia Toombs brought with her to Georgia a message to the young men of the South from her husband. It was printed in the local newspaper. Toombs, surprisingly moderate in contrast to his private statements, charged young Southerners to stay where they were and work toward rebuilding their section. Though "they may sow in tears, they will reap in joy," he thought.[76]

In his wife's absence, Toombs spent some time at Enghien, a "dull watering place" near Paris, taking sulphur baths for the relief

---

[73]Toombs mentioned the "Johnsons, Browns, etc." The Johnsons in Georgia were James and Herschel V. The former had been appointed provisional governor by President Johnson and the latter presided over the constitutional convention which met in October, 1865. Joseph E. Brown had early declared for reconciliation but fell from favor later when he urged acceptance of carpetbag rule.

[74]Sallie Toombs Dubose to Julia Toombs, March 4, 1866, in Robert Toombs Papers, University of Georgia.

[75]Julia Toombs to Stephens, May 16, 1866, in Alexander H. Stephens Papers, Emory University; Toombs to Stephens, September 28, 1866, in Alexander H. Stephens Papers, Library of Congress.

[76]Washington (Ga.) *Gazette*, July 27, 1866.

of a throat ailment.[77] The Toombses lived in first-class style abroad, staying at the best places and traveling extensively. He was still a man of great wealth, although during his stay in Europe he found it necessary to sell some of his Texas land to defray expenses.[78]

After their reunion in Liverpool, the Toombses visited in Germany and Switzerland for a few weeks, and then returned to Paris near the end of September. A glimpse of the Georgian in Parisian social life was recorded by Burton N. Harrison, who had last seen him shabbily dressed in Washington, Georgia, in the waning days of the Confederacy. Toombs was attending a musical performance at the Theatre du Chatelet, which was dazzling the sophisticated Parisians with its beauty. When Harrison viewed him, "fashionably dressed, [he] sat in an Orchestra Chair, regarding it all with the stolid composure of an Indian; and with an expression of countenance suggesting he had seen spectacles more brilliant than that, in Washington, Georgia, a thousand times!" [79]

On September 28, Toombs wrote Stephens a letter as long as it was bitter, reflecting a classic example of extremists who always seem to despise moderates more than those at the other end of the pole.[80] His stern criticism of events at home remained unabated. Toombs had no sympathy with Andrew Johnson in his fight against the Radicals. He thought the only difference between the two factions was that the Radicals proposed to compel the Southern states to enfranchise the Negro by threatening to reduce their representation in Congress, and Johnson desired to put the government "in the hands of traitors and let them manage the negro suffrage question as they please."

For the disqualification clauses in Johnson's reconstruction program and subsequent amnesty proclamations, Toombs had only ridicule. He said he was not surprised that the Radicals could not accept the President's pardonings. These Toombs labeled a "new political sacrament of transsubstantiation [sic]." He called them "both puerile and ridiculous. . . , unsupported by law, principle or precedent even in the capricious annals of despotic clemency." Said Toombs: "If my vote could decide tomorrow the Presidency of the U. States between Thad Stevens [Pennsylvania congressman

[77]Toombs to Dudley M. DuBose, July 11, 1866, in Robert Toombs Papers, University of Georgia.
[78]Phillips, *Toombs*, 256.
[79]Quoted in Rowland (ed.), *Davis*, VII, 8.
[80]Toombs to Stephens, September 28, 1866, in Alexander H. Stephens Papers, Library of Congress.

and Radical leader] & A. Johnson, I would give it to Stevens. He stood by his State & section in the fight & Johnson betrayed his, & still continues to harass, betray & degrade them. The Lord reward him according to his works."

He declared that the "Jim Johnsons, & Herschel Johnsons, and Jenkinses" [81] [current state leaders] were not real Georgians. The poor people of the state were in despair "and could offer no effective resistance to the old traitors who . . . were leading them back to the leeks & onions & slavery of Egypt." Toombs hoped that if ever again the people reassumed the power to act that they would "take full vengeance for their former misplaced generosity."

He refrained long enough from his assaults, which were quite out of harmony with prevailing opinions in Georgia, to remark that it had come to his attention that Andrew Johnson did not "measure his whiskey with sufficient care." [82] Toombs asked if this were so, and added that he never had supposed Johnson would fall on "this stumbling block," an obstacle not unknown to Toombs himself.

In closing this letter of frustration and undue harshness, Toombs expressed his desire to come home again. Although he had the previous December stated that he and his family would never live in a conquered country, exile seemed to be wearing thin for him now.

A message of sorrow came from Georgia just before the end of the year, and buried itself deep in the hearts of the expatriate and his wife in France. Their third and last surviving child, Sallie, had died on October 27, leaving behind four children. [83] Toombs wrote Stephens on December 9: "This blow is insupportable, it has crushed my heart and buried my hopes in the grave. . . ." But not wishing to burden Stephens with his personal misfortunes, he digressed to comment on the general political scene. Against the Radicals Johnson had only one mode of successful resistance, and that was through the courts. He thought that if the President would restore their vigor and arouse the people to combat unconstitutional acts through the state and Federal judiciary, then his success would be certain. Toombs seemed to have softened somewhat in his de-

81Charles J. Jenkins was elected governor of Georgia in November, 1865. He had labored tirelessly for his state and vigorously opposed military reconstruction.

82An unsubstantiated charge which Johnson's enemies constantly played up.

83Gabriel Toombs to Stephens, October 29, 1866, in Alexander H. Stephens Papers, Emory University.

nunciation of his former fellow senator. He told Stephens that both he and Julia were returning to Havana by the next steamer, he to remain there while his wife hastened on home. His own departure for Georgia would depend on certain letters he hoped to receive in Havana.[84]

Julia Toombs, evidently fearing for her husband's safety, persuaded him to remain a while longer in Europe. She sailed by herself to America around the first of January, 1867, finding a "sad and desolate home, without husband or child."[85] Toombs could not bear being alone in a strange land, and made up his mind to return to the United States. Writing his wife, he said, "The worst that can happen to me is a prison, and I don't see much to choose between my present condition and any decent fort."[86]

Toombs left France around the middle of January. He reached Havana on February 7, but did not proceed immediately to his own country.[87] Apparently it was not safe for him to come within Federal jurisdiction as yet. His travels until he finally reached Georgia cannot be definitely accounted for. Stovall writes that from Cuba Toombs went to Canada and then on to Washington, where he had an interview with President Johnson. From the capital city, he returned to his native state in the spring and was never troubled again by Federal authorities.[88]

Toombs remained "unreconstructed" through the remainder of his life. He refused to apply for pardon or take any oath of allegiance, saying as late as 1881, "I am not loyal to the existing government of the United States & do not wish to be suspected of loyalty."[89] Not until 1898 did Congress pass a universal amnesty bill which removed all disabilities imposed in the Reconstruction era on ex-Confederates and restored full United States citizenship. Under this bill, Toombs would have been "reconstructed" whether he desired it or not. But by this time he was dead.[90]

[84]Toombs to Stephens, December 9, 1866, in Alexander H. Stephens Papers, Emory University.

[85]Julia Toombs to Stephens, January 15, 1867, in Alexander H. Stephens Papers, Emory University.

[86]Stovall, *Toombs*, 313.

[87]Gabriel Toombs to Stephens, February 18, 19, 1867, in Alexander H. Stephens Papers, Emory University.

[88]Stovall, *Toombs*, 313; Atlanta *Constitution*, July 6, 1879.

[89]Toombs to B. R. Charles, February 14, 1881, in U. R. Brooks Papers, Duke University.

[90]Jonathan T. Dorris, *Pardon and Amnesty Under Lincoln and Johnson* . . . (Chapel Hill, 1953), 175–76, 391.

CHAPTER XI

The Post-War Years

IN the spring of 1867 Georgia, like most of the other Southern states, was bowing to the yoke of military reconstruction and alien political control. The Federal government had temporarily lost its constitutional structure of three separate, co-equal branches, as the Radical-dominated Congress, backed at the moment by Northern opinion, had emasculated the power of President Johnson and the Supreme Court. The South now lay prostrate at the feet of the victors.

Unhappy though he was over Georgia's future, Toombs' immediate concern after ending his exile centered around the mending of his personal fortune which had been strained somewhat by the war and his stay abroad. He estimated that he had lost a million dollars and between three and four hundred slaves because of the war.[1] This was clearly an exaggeration, as state and Federal records place the value of his real and personal estate in 1860 at $450,000, no small sum, and his slave holding in an undetermined year between 1850 and 1860 at only ten.[2] Nonetheless he was not as financially secure as he once had been, a situation he proposed to change.

[1]Atlanta *Constitution*, October 4, 1877.
[2]United States Census Report, 1860, Wilkes County, Georgia; Wilkes County Tax Digest [1850-1860]. Tax digest records in this decade are incomplete and those available cannot be absolutely verified as to year.

Toombs was involved almost constantly in the post-war period with the management of his large land holdings in Texas.[3] He carried on a lengthy correspondence with his agents and his partners, securing his claims, seeing to the payment of back taxes, and selling certain tracts.[4] In the 1870's his original partner in the enterprise, George W. Crawford, gave his half interest to his son and to his son-in-law, Captain S. W. Mays, whom Toombs bought out for $27,500. Over the years the value of his holdings increased, and when Toombs made his final sale in 1884, it was estimated that his investment had been worth over $200,000 to him.[5]

After he arrived home, Toombs resumed his law practice in partnership with his son-in-law, Dudley DuBose.[6] He took his place as of old as a prominent member of the Georgia bar, and made sometimes as much as $40,000 a year. By 1870, Toombs' estate, real and personal, was appraised at $200,000. [7]

Toombs, although disfranchised, could no more stay out of politics than he could have stayed permanently out of Georgia. But as a political figure, he never recovered the balance he had exhibited during most of his congressional career. The frustrations and disappointments of secession, war, defeat, and exile had apparently blurred beyond recall the Southern moderate who had once condemned as imprudent the advocacy of Federal protection of slavery in the territories. He remained devoted with all of his being to a shattered image of his state and section. Other Southerners, less inflexible and more opportunistic than he, were able to regroup and move successfully with the changing times. The post-war Toombs was unwilling, and perhaps unable, to do so.

With the fortunes of his people at a low ebb, Toombs entered the fight against Radical Republican domination. On July 4, 1868, the Democratic convention meeting in New York nominated Ho-

[3]See p. 93.
[4]There are sixty-five letters (1857–79) in the Robert Toombs Papers, University of Georgia, which deal with this subject.
[5]Atlanta *Constitution*, December 16, 1885.
[6]This ad ran for several weeks in the Washington *Gazette* in the late fall of 1867: "Toombs & DuBose, Attorneys at Law, Washington, Ga. Will practice in counties of Taliaferro, Elbert, Hart, Wilkes, Warren, Hancock, Oglethorpe, and Lincoln of the Northern, and Columbia, of the Middle Circuit, the Supreme Court of Georgia, the United States District and Circuit Courts. Special attention will be given to all cases in Bankruptcy."
[7]Atlanta *Constitution*, December 16, 1885; United States Census Report, 1870, Wilkes County.

ratio Seymour and Francis P. Blair to head the ticket in the November election. Their platform denounced the Radical program of reconstruction and demanded restoration of home rule in the South. Later in the month, some fifteen to twenty thousand persons gathered near the railroad terminal in Atlanta, the famous Bush Arbor meeting, to hear an impressive roster of favorite sons speak in behalf of the Democratic party, prior to a giant torchlight procession as the night closed in.[8] It was a sweltering day. "A pall of stifling dust hung over the massed throng and the swarming city. But for five mortal hours of unspeakable discomfort, the solid mass of people, with fully one-third of it ladies, sat unmindful of the discomfort, hanging eagerly upon the torrid utterances of the speakers." [9]

The featured orators for the rally were Toombs, Howell Cobb, and Benjamin Hill.[10] "The rising of Mr. Toombs," wrote a reporter, "was the signal for a deafening shout that carried us far back to the times when Georgia *was* Georgia." [11] Toombs condemned Radical reconstruction and the adventurers and conspirators who were enforcing it. He praised the people for having "not despaired of the republic. Though despoiled, plundered and manacled, your spirits are unbroken; you have heart and hope to make new sacrifices—aye, to make all sacrifices to regain your lost liberties and to redeem your country from bondage." His peroration brought the crowd to its feet as he shouted: "Your country says come, honor says come—duty says come—liberty says come—the country is in danger—let every freeman hasten to the rescue." [12]

Following the speechmaking the exuberant crowd paraded in the streets, hoisting posters which condemned in vigorous language those considered enemies to Georgia. In the shadowed torchlight, such inscriptions as the following could be read: "The B's are hived: Perjured Blodgett, Traitor Brown, Convict Bradley, and

[8]Atlanta *Constitution*, July 24, 1868.

[9]I. W. Avery, *The History of the State of Georgia from 1850 to 1881* (New York, 1881), 392.

[10]Hill later defected to the Radicals. His action, coupled with that of Joseph E. Brown, led Georgians to remark ruefully, "Joseph is not, and now they have taken my son Benjamin," Coulter, *Georgia*, 376.

[11]Atlanta *Constitution*, July 24, 1868.

[12]Lucian Lamar Knight, *Reminiscences of Famous Georgians* (Atlanta, 1907), 609, 612.

Thief Butler. Joe Brown—a traitor to his section, and an outcast from society—Judas Escobedo Brown." [13]

Great satisfaction was felt in Georgia when wartime governor, and now Radical collaborator, Joseph E. Brown, was defeated for the office of United States senator by Joshua Hill, onetime Georgia Unionist, in a contest involving the newly-elected legislature. Remarked Toombs: "There was political justice in making the earliest traitor defeat the worst one and break down his party. . . . His [Brown's] special knowledge, especially, of all the rogues in the State, is prodigious, and I think it was about worth the State to best him. Hill is a poor devil. . . . I did my utmost to elect him, and ask of him no other favour than not to join us or speak to me." [14]

Two days after the Atlanta rally, Toombs returned home to Washington. That night a torchlight procession of local citizens, white and colored, marched up to his home. Although painfully hoarse, Toombs spoke briefly, expressing optimism over the November presidential election.[15]

On August 24, Toombs and Ben Hill went to Augusta where, following an impromptu demonstration in their honor, Toombs addressed a crowd at the Central Hotel. In strong language he dealt "unsparing blows upon the Browns, Bullocks, Blodgetts." [16] The following day, together with General John B. Gordon, Confederate war hero, and Alfred Colquitt, another ex-Confederate warrior, he spoke to a political rally at Cedartown. He told the people that the Northern policy of reconstruction under which they suffered was concocted for the sole purpose of defeating the popular will. Toombs called the Republican platform, which endorsed carpetbag reconstruction, "a model of audacity, of falsehood and of a shameless contempt for popular intelligence." Not forgetting his pet hate of the reconstruction era, Joe Brown, he said: "He is false

---

[13]Atlanta *Constitution*, July 25, 1868. Foster Blodgett was a leader of the Radical-dominated constitutional convention, December, 1867–March, 1868, and a henchman of Radical-supported Governor Rufus Bullock. Aaron Alpeoria Bradley, Negro, was a one time convict and delegate to the constitutional convention. The Butler mentioned here was presumably Ben Butler of New Orleans fame.

[14]Toombs to Stephens, August 9, 1868, in Phillips (ed.), *Correspondence*, 703.

[15]Washington *Gazette*, July 17, 1868.

[16]Atlanta *Constitution*, August 25, 1868.

to nature. He went to Chicago [to the Republican convention]. What more can I say to commend this wretch to your detestation; he has fatigued public indignation, it is no longer equal to his crime. Ignoble villain, buoyant solely from corruption, he only rises where he rots." [17]

Through the strenuous efforts of Toombs and other leaders, the Democrats were able to carry Georgia in the November presidential election won nationally by the Republicans, something almost unique among Southern states at that time.

On January 24, 1870, Toombs wrote Stephens of a recent visit he had made to Atlanta to see if he "could be of any service in the present *coup d'etat* of [Radical-supported Governor Rufus B.] Bullock and his conspirators." It was a difficult job, Toombs said, since Bullock was "perfectly reckless, fully supported by the military, stakes all upon success, and offers all the offices, places, money and the plunder of the people for help to aid him to obtain the dictatorship of the state." [18]

Federal troops had returned to Georgia in December, 1869, at the request of Governor Bullock. Under his supervision, they purged the legislature of recalcitrant conservatives who were blocking the implementation of the Radical program. The familiar story of reconstruction extravagances followed, with particular emphasis in Georgia on venality in government printing and in the endorsement of railroad bonds. It was an unhappy year for native Georgians. Toombs' correspondence with Stephens bristled with denunciations of the Bullock regime. "If I can do nothing else I will teach as far as I can the next generation to hate the vile scoundrils [*sic*]," he said.[19] And again, "It is worth thirty years of war to get rid of negro suffrage in the South. . . . God grant that I may be able in some way before I die to contribute something to hasten their possession of their eternal heritage. It is a political cancer that is rapidly eating out our vitals. . . ." [20]

The "prostrate state" era was of briefer duration in Georgia, however, than in some of her sister Southern states. In December,

[17]*Ibid.*, August 27, 1868.
[18]Toombs to Stephens, January 24, 1870, in Phillips (ed.), *Correspondence*, 707.
[19]Toombs to Stephens, February 14, 1870, in Alexander H. Stephens Papers, Library of Congress.
[20]Toombs to Stephens, September 4, 1870, in Alexander H. Stephens Papers, Library of Congress.

1870, the Democrats secured control of the legislature. Governor Bullock, facing certain prosecution for mismanaging state funds and the state-owned Western and Atlantic Railroad, resigned secretly in October, 1871, and fled the state. Soon after, the Democrats in a special election won the governorship in the person of James M. Smith, whom the Radicals did not oppose.

Robert Toombs was, perhaps, as popular among his fellow Georgians during reconstruction as he was at any time in his life. Although often impolitic in word and action, he was respected as a proud, unbridled, and staunch opponent of the Radical regime. His influence in state politics, however, began to wane in the 1870's, as he adamantly refused to become a part of a new movement sweeping the old Confederacy which called for the erection of a New South out of the ashes of the old. Although observing appropriate homage to the glories of the lost cause and white supremacy, the oligarchical leadership of the "New Departure" was primarily interested in burying the past and fashioning an industrial South in the Northern pattern.[21] Not so Toombs. At an agricultural fair speech in Selma, Alabama, in November, 1872, he said the South should continue to look primarily to cotton for its wealth. He extolled the virtues of agrarian pursuits while decrying the "helter skelter scramble for wealth" of the post-war materialistic era.[22] In 1872 the New Departurists in Georgia urged Democratic support for anti-Grant Republicans. Toombs remained the unreconstructed rebel, desiring to keep his state and section free from any kind of amalgamation. So vociferous was he in his denunciations that a roving correspondent for the Atlanta *Constitution* wrote back from New York saying: "One rebellious bugle-blast of a fiery secessionist out volumes the peaceful note of the entire Northern Democracy. The Northern conservative Republicans—the missionary ground for Democratic proselyting—laugh to scorn the sincerity of the Departure in the echo of Davis' 'I accept nothing' utterance, or the shrill sound of Toombs' war-cry."[23]

Wrote an editorialist for a Chicago newspaper: "Toombs is a ponderous, inappeasable old blatherskite, as malignant as Jeff Davis,

[21]Judson Clements Ward, Jr., "The New Departure Democrats of Georgia: An Interpretation," *Georgia Historical Quarterly*, XLI (September, 1957), 227–36; C. Vann Woodward, *Origins of the New South, 1877–1913* (Baton Rouge, 1951), 14–18.

[22]Rome (Ga.) *Tri-Weekly Courier*, November 19, 1872.

[23]Atlanta *Constitution*, August 1, 1871.

but lacking discretion sufficient to go under shelter from a rain-storm. The South needs more than anything else at this time about a hundred first class funerals, and her own sensible people would gladly give nuisances like Toombs and Davis the precedence in ordering their coffins." [24]

To fill the gap in the ranks of leadership that was to be left by Toombs came Joseph E. Brown, the villain of reconstruction. In their minds, but perhaps not in their hearts, Georgians accepted the change. The beginning of this strange story dated back to 1870, when Brown evidently saw the handwriting on the wall and began to loosen his ties with the Bullock regime. The former governor was even found on the same side of the political fence as Toombs, working to elect a Democrat as speaker of the house. Of this Toombs said: "My rule is to use the devil if I can do better to save the country." [25] Two weeks later he wrote again to Stephens saying that "Brown seems really in earnest in his endeavors to defeat Bullock and his schemes. I don't [know] whether or not he sees where his present course will land him, but I suppose he does." [26] The governor always did. Completing his break with the Radicals, Brown reentered the Democratic fold. At the inauguration of Smith in January, 1872, he was among the dignitaries who participated in the ceremonies.[27] A very neat trick indeed had been accomplished by the shrewd man whom Georgians had cast from their ranks a few years before.

If others accepted Brown's redemption through Democratic saving grace, Toombs emphatically did not. In a private letter which was published in the Griffin *Daily News*, June 27, 1872, [28] he accused Brown and others of misconduct in connection with certain litigation known as the "Mitchell heirs" case. He charged that they had lobbied a bill through the legislature by which state interests in some real estate had been defrauded.[29]

Brown, in an open letter to the Atlanta *Constitution*, stated that

[24]Columbus *Daily Sun*, June 21, 1871, and attributed to an unnamed Chicago newspaper.

[25]Toombs to Stephens, January 24, 1870, in Phillips (ed.), *Correspondence*, 707.

[26]Toombs to Stephens, February 8, 1870, *ibid.*, 708.

[27]Louise B. Hill, *Joseph E. Brown and the Confederacy* (Chapel Hill, 1939), 290.

[28]Avery, *History of Georgia*, 477–78.

[29]*Ibid.*, 479–83; Hill, *Joseph E. Brown*, 300–301; Atlanta *Constitution*, August 5, 1872.

if by his language Toombs intended to imply that he was guilty of bribery, then "his statement [was] an infamous falsehood and its author an unscrupulous liar." The public now witnessed through the newspapers a parry and thrust, but apparently incomplete, correspondence between the two men.[30] It appeared that Toombs, through a Colonel J. C. Nicholls, asked Brown if he held himself bound by the "code." Brown asserted that he told Toombs he was ready at any time to receive any communication. Whether Brown's "acceptance" ever reached Toombs remains a matter of conjecture. It is certain, however, that the ex-governor was determined to go through with the duel if Toombs had pressed what he started.

Henry W. Grady, famous voice of the *Constitution*, recounted some years later what did happen at the time and what might have happened had the antagonists met on the field of honor.

In the first place, General Toombs made no preparation for the duel. He went along in his careless and kingly way, trusting, presumably, to luck and a quick shot. Governor Brown, on the contrary, made the most careful and deliberate preparation. He made his will, put his estate in order, withdrew from the church, and clipped all the trees in his orchard practicing with the pistol. Had the duel come off—which fortunately it did not—General Toombs would have fired with his usual magnificence and his usual disregard of rule. I do not mean to imply that he would not have hit Governor Brown; on the contrary, he might have perforated him in a dozen places at once. But one thing is sure—Governor Brown would have clasped his long white fingers around the pistol butt, adjusted it to his gray eye, and sent his bullet within the eighth of an inch of the place he had selected. I should not be surprised if he drew a diagram of General Toombs, and marked off with square and compass the exact spot he wanted to hit.[31]

Early Toombs biographers state that this incident helped restore Brown to public favor because of his firm resolve to defend his honor, which he believed damaged by Toombs. Conversely, it lessened the prestige of the man who evidently had embarked on a dangerous venture, and had not followed through according to the custom of the day.[32]

Two years after the Brown affair, Toombs was involved in a minor altercation in Washington, D.C., which again found him

[30]Atlanta *Constitution*, July 3, 17–20, 1872.
[31]*Ibid.*, August 29, 1880.
[32]Phillips, *Toombs*, 267; Stovall, *Toombs*, 335–36.

emerging second best according to a creditable witness. After visiting with President Grant, he attended a dinner given by John B. Gordon, then United States senator from Georgia. Other distinguished guests included Congressman L. Q. C. Lamar of Mississippi and Henry Watterson, editor of the Louisville *Courier-Journal*. Lamar had the previous month delivered in the House of Representatives an eloquent tribute to the late Charles Sumner, a man generally detested in the South. The speech was hailed as a magnanimous effort at sectional reconciliation. According to Watterson, the old rebel Toombs began to goad Lamar, who bridled restlessly under his banter. Sensing trouble, the ladies left the table. Then the Mississippian turned on Toombs in great wrath. "I have never heard such a scoring from one man to another," declared Watterson. "It was magisterial in its dignity, deadly in its diction. Nothing short of a duel could have settled it in the olden time." Toombs, however, took it all "without a ruffle" and when Lamar, "white with rage," had finished he said only, "Lamar, you surprise me." It was over quickly, Watterson noted, and according to Lamar's biographer, did no lasting damage to the long-standing friendship of the two men.[33]

In June, 1872, Toombs was a member of the state Democratic convention which met in Atlanta to elect delegates to the national convention scheduled for assembly at Baltimore. By now the threatened breach in the Republican party had materialized, with the reforming bolters, the Liberal Republicans, rallying in support of Horace Greeley for the presidency against Grant. Most Democrats rejoiced at this political rupture, and hastened to join hands with the new third party.

Toombs and Stephens remained apart from the proposed merger, considering it an unwise political marriage. Toombs labeled the Greeley group "Know nothing villains & thievish democrats who are united solely 'by the cohesive power of the public plunder.' " [34] In 1871 Stephens had purchased the Atlanta *Sun* through whose columns he and Toombs fought a losing battle against coalition.[35]

[33]Henry Watterson, *Marse Henry: An Autobiography* (New York, 1919), I, 65–66; Wirt A. Cate, *Lucius Q. C. Lamar* (Chapel Hill, 1935), 360; William H. Hidell to Alexander H. Stephens, May 17, 1874, Alexander H. Stephens Papers, Emory University.

[34]Toombs to Stephens, August 26, 1872, Alexander H. Stephens Papers, Library of Congress.

[35]Johnston and Browne, *Stephens*, 505–506; Avary (ed.), *Stephens' Recollections*, 549.

At the convention in Atlanta, Toombs was able to prevent the delegates chosen from being sent as pledged for Greeley. Uninstructed as they were, however, it was obvious that they were of Greeley sentiment. When Toombs heard the names of the delegates called out, "he rose to his full height, and exclaimed in a voice of thunder: 'Packed by God!'" [36]

Toombs never did get in step with Georgia politics again. The New Departure or Bourbon Era, with Henry W. Grady its voice, John B. Gordon, Joseph E. Brown, and Alfred H. Colquitt its leaders, and industrialism its theme, rolled on largely without him. His decline on the political scene was mirrored in the Atlanta *Constitution* in December of 1872. Toombs, said the writer, was "much admired by Georgians for his eloquence and genius, yet not very influential by reason of his extreme views. Georgia's favorite son to-day, seems to be Gen. John B. Gordon, and since the death of her wisest statesman, the Hon. Howell Cobb, he has been the most decidedly representative man of this great and energetic commonwealth." [37]

Although considered as unreasonable in his views, Toombs could never have been criticized for inconsistency. In 1876, prior to the disputed Tilden-Hayes election, he wrote to Stephens, saying he was glad he had committed himself not to support Tilden, the Democratic nominee. "I never hoped for anything good from an old Van Buren freesoiler trained in Tammany Hall and Wall Street . . . ," he said. "The mongrel crew who call themselves Democrats have the control of the 'organized democracy' [and] would as [lief have] Be [el] zebub as God, and [prefer] Mammon to either if thereby they could perchance reach the treasury. . . . They want Tilden elected for the same reason that Falstaff rejoiced at Prince Hal's reconciliation with the old King— 'Hal, rob me the exchequer.'" [38]

Toombs was often bitter and pessimistic in his judgment. At times his political sterility seemed to weigh heavily upon him, although he would have been the last to admit it, glorying as he did in his ostracism. In 1879 he said, "I have never believed the constitution of the United States was a good one, and as an original

[36] Atlanta *Constitution*, December 16, 1885.
[37] *Ibid.*, December 17, 1872. Howell Cobb died in New York in October, 1868.
[38] Toombs to Stephens, October 30, 1876, in Phillips (ed.), *Correspondence*, 722. Editor's brackets.

question I would have never voted for it. . . . ." The Constitution, he went on,

has no power within itself to enforce itself. It depends solely on the good faith of the people, and that guarantee alone cannot continue to bind together a great country of diverse interests. . . . I have no faith in the Puritan New Englander—the fellows that Macaulay said were opposed to bear-baiting, not because it hurt the bear, but because it pleased the people. As to the talk about the northern people forgiving me, I have nothing to say. As I haven't forgiven them, and don't expect to, I am indifferent as to the state of their feelings.[39]

In 1879, on the eve of the third presidential election since the end of reconstruction in Georgia, Toombs had not changed the political tune of his 1872 song one note. Writing to Stephens, he stated that there was a strong feeling over the South to "begin to reassert principles and cut loose from the Northern Democracy. We have been the servile tools of knaves and fools, mostly the former, long enough. And many thoughtful men would tremble to see the Democratic party as now constituted in power, even to beat Grant or the devil. I think the true policy of the South is to cut loose from them and run candidates of their own." [40] The general still represented himself as speaking for others, but for the most part he spoke only for himself.

Although Robert Toombs' political leadership waned considerably after reconstruction days, as a member of the Georgia bar he was always prominent. His special interest lay in cases in which he considered railroad interests unfairly opposed to those of private parties or the state itself. It was his belief that railroads were servants of the people and should be regulated accordingly in strict fashion. Toombs' views on the control of railroads seemed to reflect an early-day Populism. Actually the Georgian's antipathy toward corporations was of long standing. As a young Whig congressman, he had gone along dutifully but not enthusiastically with Clay's program of protection for American industry. But he gradually abandoned this posture for one of free trade and in his Tremont Temple address, his Utopian South was distinctly pastoral. Toombs' own great wealth was primarily agrarian-based although he engaged

[39]Atlanta *Constitution*, July 6, 1879.
[40]Toombs to Stephens, March 10, 1879, in Phillips (ed.), *Correspondence*, 737.

in considerable moneylending. He did not invest in corporation stocks and only infrequently represented corporations in court.

Toombs' forthcoming career as state's counsel in railroad litigation and as constitution framer paralleled similar efforts at corporate control, particularly in the mid-West. The patrician Toombs was no Granger from Illinois with personal grievances against the railroads. But he shared the belief that the public interest was served by government control of corporations. In this he was ahead of most of his fellow Georgians and most of his countrymen.

Before 1877 and the constitutional convention, the regulation of railroads had not provoked any serious public controversy. The prevailing spirit toward them in an era of expansion was one of charitable aid, rather than control. Such restrictions as did exist were incomplete in scope and weak in effectiveness.[41] Georgians, however, had a real taste of corruption in railroad circles during the days of the Bullock administration. After the war the former policies of state aid to railroads—exemption from taxation except on income and state subscription to railroad stock—were not feasible. The finances of the state were in an unsettled condition and not suited to either plan. State aid of some kind, however, was needed, as the Civil War had been disruptive to transportation in Georgia. Endorsement by the state of railroad bonds was resorted to, as this would work no immediate hardship on state finances and would help bolster the hard-pressed roads. Bonds were extravagantly and corruptly endorsed during the Radical administration, and soon state aid had turned into financial disaster.[42]

The state-owned road, the Western and Atlantic, instead of making the customary profit, piled up an indebtedness of $750,000 within two years of Radical thieving, plundering, and mismanagement.[43] In 1870 the Radical-dominated legislature, somewhat chastened, enacted a law which required that the state road be leased for twenty years for not less than $25,000 a month. Ex-

[41]Maxwell Ferguson, *State Regulation of Railroads in the South* (New York, 1916), 228, 13–20, hereinafter cited as Ferguson, *Railroad Regulation*; Peter S. McGuire, "The Railroads of Georgia," *Georgia Historical Quarterly*, XVI (September, 1932), 192–93, hereinafter cited as McGuire, "Georgia Railroads"; Coulter, *Georgia*, 258–64; Henry W. Thomas, *Digest of the Railroad Laws of Georgia* (Atlanta, 1895), 7–10.
[42]McGuire, "Georgia Railroads," 193–94; C. Mildred Thompson, *Reconstruction in Georgia, Economic, Social, Political, 1865–1872* (New York, 1915), 229–38.
[43]Coulter, *Georgia*, 375.

governor Brown, heading a company which included among others H. I. Kimball, Northern adventurer and Bullock's financial advisor, Benjamin H. Hill, who had recently "surrendered" to the Radicals, and, strangely enough, Alexander H. Stephens, secured the lease under questionable circumstances.

Toombs, along with most Georgians, was chagrined to see his friend in such company. He wrote Stephens: "I must candidly say while I look upon your conduct as perfectly honourable and free from reproach I did regret seeing your name among the lessees." [44] Stephens apparently regretted his action also, for a few days later he withdrew from the company and turned his one-fourth share of stock over to the state.[45]

The legal handling of this part share led to the only serious personal rift in the long friendship of Toombs and Stephens. Bullock refused to accept the part share in the state's name, and turned it over to one of his henchmen shortly before he left the state. In 1874 Democratic Governor Smith informed Toombs that the title to the stock was not legally in the state's name, as Stephens had intended it to be. Toombs, thinking he was authorized by previous conversations with Stephens to do so, then brought suit in Stephens' name to recover the share for subsequent tender to the state for the second time. Stephens reacted violently to this, saying Toombs acted without authorization and that the suit in his name to recover the tainted stock reflected adversely on him. An airing of the affair in the press did not diminish Stephens' strong feelings. Toombs' patient explanation of events and the passage of time, however, healed the breach between the two men.[46]

With the Democrats in control of the legislature in December, 1870, investigations of the Radical administration were begun. The lease of the state road to Brown and Company was declared "unfairly obtained" by an investigating committee in 1872. Despite this, the legislature by vote upheld the lease. A large number of Bullock-endorsed railroad bonds were repudiated by legislative enactment in the same year.[47] Toombs was appointed counsel for the bond

[44]Toombs to Stephens, December 30, 1870, in Phillips (ed.), *Correspondence*, 712.

[45]Phillips, *Toombs*, 266; Johnston and Browne, *Stephens*, 501–502.

[46]Phillips, *Toombs*, 266; Stephens to Toombs, March 8, 1874, in Alexander H. Stephens Papers, Emory University; Toombs to Stephens, March 14, 1874, in Phillips (ed.), *Correspondence*, 718–20.

[47]Thompson, *Reconstruction*, 251–54; Amanda Johnson, *Georgia As Colony and State* (Atlanta, 1938), 545.

committee which carried out this phase of house cleaning for the state.[48]

The reconstruction state aid fiasco added to Toombs' belief that such aid should be abolished forever and that a stricter control over railroads should be exercised by the state. From reconstruction days until 1883, two years before his death, he used the medium of the courts to bring to fruition these principles.

The litigation in which Toombs was employed as an opponent of railroads involved primarily the issues of monopoly, rate regulation, and taxation. In 1869 he was one of the attorneys prosecuting the case of *Collins v. Central Railroad Company*, in which a controlling amount of stock in the Atlantic and Gulf Railroad was about to pass into the possession of the Central company. The court upheld Toombs' contention that such an act was an effort toward monopoly, with the following opinion: "It is a part of the public policy of the State as indicated by the charter of several Railroads from the seaboard to the interior to secure a reasonable competition between said roads for public patronage, and it is contrary to that policy for one of the said roads to attempt to secure a controlling interest in another, and any contract made with that view . . . is illegal, beyond the objects of the charter, and contrary to public policy." [49]

In 1873 Toombs' services were engaged by interests who were bringing suit against the Georgia Railroad and Banking Company to recover an excessive freight charge. Although it was established during the case that overcharging had been committed by the company, the court did not sustain Toombs' suit. It held that the payment was made in full view of all the facts, and that there was no misplaced confidence. Therefore no action lay to recover the excessive rate.[50]

In 1871 the railroads paid only $9,624.87 in taxes to the state, a small sum in proportion to their valuable properties.[51] The figure was computed on the basis of one-half of one percent of

[48]Atlanta *Constitution*, February 15, 1873. The official life and conduct of Bullock was the subject of another investigation for which committee Toombs acted as attorney. Although declared guilty of indictable offenses by the committee, Bullock was acquitted when he stood trial in 1876, Coulter, *Georgia*, 376; Thompson, *Reconstruction*, 226.

[49]*Georgia Cases*, XL, 582 (1869).

[50]*Georgia Cases*, L, 304 (1873).

[51]Judson Clements Ward, Jr., "Georgia Under the Bourbon Democrats, 1872–1890" (Ph.D. dissertation, University of North Carolina, 1947), 324, hereinafter cited as Ward, "Bourbon Democrats."

their net earnings. In 1873 the taxation was increased to one percent. Finally in 1874, the Georgia legislature required the presi-
dents of all the companies in the state to return on oath to the
comptroller-general the value of the property of their respective
companies to be taxed as other property in the state. As the new
law increased the amount of taxes above that stipulated in most
of their charters, the railroads fought the law in the courts. Toombs
was retained by Governor Smith as counsel for the state.[52]

In 1875 the state brought three railroads to the supreme court
for refusal to recognize the new law and pay the increased taxes.[53]
They were the Augusta and Savannah, the Southwestern, and the
Central Railroad and Banking Companies. Representing the state
were the attorney general and Toombs. The decision hinged on
the general law of January 1, 1863, which in part read: "In all
cases of *private* charters hereafter granted the state reserves the
right to withdraw the franchise unless such right is expressly
negatived." [54] Over the protests of the railroads who stood on their
chartered rights, the court held that consolidation had taken place
within the Southwestern and Central Companies since 1863, and
that new privileges had been granted them by the state, resulting
therefore in virtual new charters. Hence, the chartered tax rate
could be withdrawn from these two roads according to the law
of 1863, and the new tax imposed. In the case of the Augusta and
Savannah, the court upheld the road's refusal to pay the taxes, since
no privileges had been accorded it since 1863 and therefore no
new charter granted. The case was hailed as a great victory for
the state, both in principle and financial enrichment. It was no
less a triumph for Toombs, who saw railroad interests subordinated
to the public welfare, a situation he so strongly desired.

Other litigation handled for the state by Toombs saw the court
rule the Atlantic and Gulf Railroad subject to the tax increase.[55]
Brown's group, which controlled the Western and Atlantic, won its
case, however, when the court declared that the faith of the state
had been pledged to the lessees that the tax privileges in the lease
would not be disturbed during the tenure of the lease. An increase
in taxation would be in violation of the state's honor.[56]

[52]Atlanta *Constitution*, April 26, 1881.
[53]*Georgia Cases*, LIV, 401 (1875).
[54]*Ibid.*, 404.
[55]*Ibid.*, 312.
[56]*Ibid.*, 429–39.

In May, 1876, in the case of *Central Railroad and Banking Company v. State of Georgia,* the United States Supreme Court nullified the tax increases which had been sanctioned by the Georgia tribunal, saying that the "gift of new powers to a corporation does not destroy its identity nor change it into a new being." [57] Hence, the Georgia railroads had not been given new charters, and there could be no tax increase. After this decision, the state railroads enjoyed a tax holiday for several years.

Toombs' efforts at railroad regulation, although temporarily checked in the matter of increased taxation, reached a successful conclusion in the constitution of 1877. The story of that document might be said to date back to the Radical constitution framed in 1868. Though the latter was basically sound and contained many admirable features,[58] it was associated in the minds of Georgians with carpetbag rule. Consequently, when the Democrats assumed full power in the state in 1872,[59] the Radical constitution appeared doomed. From that time until the convention was called, there was constant agitation over the state for a new document.[60] Toombs was a leading exponent for change, and his denunciations of the Radical handiwork were loud, long, and often impolitic.

Among those openly opposing a convention were the Atlanta *Constitution* and the Republicans in the state. The *Constitution* seemingly wanted to leave well enough alone, although, perhaps, its main objection was the fear that the capital might be moved from Atlanta, where it had been established in 1868 by the Radical convention. In 1876, when the calling of a convention seemed highly probable, the paper shifted its stand, and gradually entered the ranks of the convention supporters. The Republicans in the state opposed a convention primarily because of the ties of loyalty to their members who had constructed the 1868 constitution. Although some of the New Departurists, or Bourbons, joined in the

[57]*Cases Argued and Decided in the Supreme Court of the United States* (New York, 1901–47), XC–XCIII, 757–62, hereinafter cited as *U. S. Cases.*

[58]Ward, "Bourbon Democrats," 204–11; Avery, *History of Georgia,* 528; William P. Brandon, "Calling the Georgia Constitutional Convention of 1877," *Georgia Historical Quarterly,* XVII (September, 1933), 188, hereinafter cited as Brandon, "Convention of 1877"; Ethel K. Ware, *A Constitutional History of Georgia* (New York, 1947), 144.

[59]Although the legislature was in the hands of the Democrats in December, 1870, it was not until January, 1872, that the office of governor became Democratic also.

[60]Ward, "Bourbon Democrats," 211–15; Brandon, *"Convention of 1877,"* 189–203.

movement to call a convention, they were probably not enthusiastic advocates of change. Joseph E. Brown and John B. Gordon were involved in the expanding industrialism of the 1870's, and doubtless looked with disfavor upon an assembly which could curb the profitable enterprises in which they were participating. In many respects, then, the new constitution was a defeat for the New Departurists. Others in the opposition camp included those who feared the liberal homestead provision of 1868 might be abolished, the free public schools hampered, and the Negro disfranchised.[61]

At first, those favoring a convention advocated that the legislature issue the call. But finding the lawmaking body disinclined to act, they changed their tactics and began to demand that the issue be submitted to the people.[62] Toombs spoke and wrote often on the convention issue. In addition to his desire not to live under a Radical constitution, there were other changes he wished to bring about by a convention. The subject of the regulation of railroads and other corporations lay close to his heart. He advocated reducing the four year senatorial term and changing the inequality of representation in that body. He considered the judiciary inadequate for a speedy and impartial trial of either criminal or civil cases, and wanted it more efficient. The four-year tenure of office of the governor he regarded as too long and the patronage powers of the chief executive too broad.[63]

In January, 1876, agitation for the convention was at a high peak. The legislature was considering bills which would authorize the calling of one if the people so decided by popular referendum. At this time Toombs made an address in Atlanta in which he repeated his customarily violent attacks on the constitution of 1868, calling it a "nigger constitution constructed by knaves and carpetbaggers." He told the crowd that if "you have a convention I can make you a constitution by which the people will rule and the nigger will never be heard of!" Toombs called the opponents of a convention "imposters, trying to betray the people." [64]

His harangue helped kill the convention movement for 1876. Apart from the general resentment produced, it stirred up the fear of Negro disfranchisement and gave political ammunition to Re-

[61]Ward, "Bourbon Democrats," 201, 212, 227.
[62]*Ibid.*, 214–15.
[63]Toombs to L. N. Trammel, April 26, 1877, in Phillips (ed.), *Correspondence*, 727–30.
[64]Atlanta *Constitution*, January 27, 1876.

publicans in the North. What Toombs said was particularly unfortunate from his party's point of view, for 1876 appeared to be the time for the return of a Democrat to the White House. Such wild philippics obviously could do the national Democratic cause little good. The legislature of Georgia hastened to declare that it had no intention of depriving the Negro of the suffrage, and postponed the matter of a convention.[65] Despite this defeat, the convention forces continued their agitation throughout the year.

In February, 1877, the legislature finally passed a convention bill and set a referendum for June. In the early summer voting, the people responded favorably by a fairly close vote, 48,181 to 39,057, and elected 194 delegates to the convention. Although there was a great deal of prestige attached to the assembly which gathered at the state capital in Atlanta on Wednesday morning, July 11, 1877, there were many important Georgians who were absent. Notables not participating were Joseph E. Brown, John B. Gordon, Ben Hill, Alexander H. Stephens, and Herschel V. Johnson. For the moment it seemed that Georgians had fallen out of step with these leaders.[66]

After listening to an opening address by Charles J. Jenkins, who was chosen president of the convention, the delegates settled down to the work at hand. Toombs was made chairman of both the committee on the legislative department and the committee of final revision.[67] So from the outset he had a firm grasp on the control reins, which he never relaxed throughout the proceedings.

There was a prevailing sentiment to curb the freedom of future legislatures and embody the convention's desire for economy in the constitution. Although Toombs desired to prohibit state aid and keep the state's treasury locked from investments in corporations, he did not feel that it was the convention's place to operate beyond the sphere of organic law. "All this convention has to do," he said, "is to establish a few fundamental principles and leave these other matters to the legislature. . . ."[68]

[65]Brandon, "Convention of 1877," 193.

[66]Ward, "Bourbon Democrats," 221–22, 229–30; Avery, *History of Georgia,* 528–29.

[67]Samuel W. Small (reporter), *Georgia Constitutional convention, 1877. A stenographic report of the proceedings of the Constitutional convention held in Atlanta, Georgia, 1877* . . . (Atlanta, 1877), 22, 29, hereinafter cited as Small, *Convention Report.*

[68]*Ibid.,* 87.

The discussions on proposed changes in the judiciary were of vital importance to Toombs. He desired to increase the number of judges on the supreme court bench from three to five and have them elected by the general assembly. The current practice was the appointment of judges by the governor, but there seemed to be no support for the continuation of this policy. The struggle at the convention lay between those favoring their election by the legislature or by popular vote. Toombs' main contention was that the state legislature was less affected by popular passions and was better qualified than the average citizen in the selection of judges. He explained: "I may shoe my own horse, but I get a nigger blacksmith near my house who knows better how to do it." [69] Of the popular vote method, he said: "Five hundred thousand savages have been thrown in among these people as voters, and we must protect ourselves against them." [70] The convention refused to enlarge the court, but did provide for its election by the legislature as Toombs wished. The Wilkes County delegate received some severe condemnation for his comments on the Negro as a voter before the debate on this issue closed.[71]

The proposal, supported by Toombs, to base representation in the state senate on population was defeated by the bloc voting of rural delegates, but the convention did approve the reduction of senatorial tenure from four to two years. Toombs felt that the provision in the constitution of 1868 dealing with homestead rights was too liberal. A more rigid provision was drawn up by the convention, but it was decided to refer the matter to a vote of the people in separate balloting from that on the constitution as a whole.[72]

Toombs' principal speeches from the floor were connected with the subject of corporations. On this issue he stood out as the leader of the anti-New Departure agrarians, who saw no particular benefit to be derived from the South patterning itself after the industrial North. State aid to railroads was one aspect of the general discussion on corporations. On this question Toombs said:

It was one of the main objects of my coming here, and of my

[69]*Ibid.*, 224.
[70]*Ibid.*, 215.
[71]*Ibid.*, 487, 228.
[72]*Ibid.*, 313, 343, 483; Phillips, *Toombs*, 271; Ware, *Constitutional History*, 163–64.

urging the people to vote for the call of this convention that it [state aid] should be buried and buried forever. . . . There has never been a single railroad aided by the state of Georgia which has ever paid a dividend. They wreck and ruin themselves and then plunder the public treasury. . . . It is unsound and it is incompetent [for the state] to take this money except for the public defense and to administer justice between man and man.[73]

Toombs was of the opinion that all corporations should be required by law to pay their full share of taxes and not be favored by exemptions and privileges, as had been the policy of the state. He proposed that any law which made an irrevocable grant of special privileges or immunities be prohibited.[74] "You have got to the point where we exempt corporations and individuals from the payment of taxes to the state. . . . You have virtually taken away so much of the life of the state and given it to these corporations for their support. . . . When this power of taxation is gone and when you say that the legislature can give this power to them, you then and there put yourself in the power of these corporations. The truth is that this power resides in the sovereign state."[75]

Toombs further desired that the charters of railroads be taken from them and replaced by new ones, so that they would not be exempt from taxation under the state tax law of 1874.[76]

His exertions to place checks on corporations drew strong opposition. President Jenkins left his chair and took the floor to battle against some of his proposals. On the subject of prohibiting grants and privileges he said: "I tell you this is a deadly blow aimed at the prosperity of the state. It is calculated, and will have the effect, to some extent, to put a quietus and an end to all industrial enterprises proposed in the state of Georgia. . . . No prudent man will invest in any chartered enterprise when he knows that in one or two years it may be abrogated."[77]

Another of Toombs' opponents stated: "While we ought to guard

[73]Small, *Convention Report*, 299.

[74]It will be remembered that the United States Supreme Court in 1876 had reversed the state court's ruling which upheld the increase in the railroad tax on the grounds that new privileges granted meant a new charter. Toombs desired this chartered privilege done away with entirely, beginning with the date of the constitution of 1877. At this time the state was also applying for a new ruling of the Supreme Court on its right to increase the rate of taxation of railroads whose charters had been heretofore granted.

[75]Small, *Convention Report*, 385.

[76]Ware, *Constitutional History*, 164.

[77]Small, *Convention Report*, 106.

them [corporations] so that they may not infringe upon the rights of other people, we should surround them with guarantees that their property invested therein shall not be subject to either legislative caprice or the envy and malice of other corporations. . . . They are composed of citizens of our state, and are as much entitled to our care as any other." [78]

As on the state aid and taxation issues, Toombs took the lead in advocating state regulation of railroad rates. Here the battle was fiercest, and here the veteran warrior fought one of the best fights of his long and stormy career. In a lengthy speech to the convention he stated in terms "unusual in that generation but common in the next," [79] that corporations were creatures of the law and legislation, and that they had no powers except what the law gave them. "Keep the hand of the law on corporations," he said, "and you keep up competition; keep up competition, and you preserve liberty." He demanded that railroad tolls, like taxes, be put under the power of the state.[80]

The railroad interests supplied vigorous opposition to Toombs and the anti-corporation forces. One of their spokesmen, reflecting the currently popular laissez-faire economics, replied that "trade cannot be legislated against. So far as trade is concerned it must be regulated by the law of supply and demand. It must be free." Another asserted: "Without them [the railroads] the state of Georgia would be today almost a primeval wilderness." It was wrong to attempt "to cripple these institutions which once were so eagerly sought and which have been blessings to the states. . . ." [81]

To the argument that railroads, unrestricted by rate regulation, had brought prosperity wherever their tracks had been laid, Toombs replied in the words of the American colonists who said to the English government, "We have grown in spite of your oppressions." In closing his remarks, he said: "I stand upon the principle that these railroads shall be subject to the state . . . , a principle, which I trust that for the benefit of yourselves and posterity you will put upon your seal of patriotic favor, and that it will last . . . till time itself shall end." [82] Stovall gives a graphic picture of Toombs as he stood in the Hall of Representatives and waged his

[78]*Ibid.*, 104–105.
[79]Phillips, *Toombs*, 271.
[80]Small, *Convention Report*, 405.
[81]*Ibid.*, 402–404.
[82]*Ibid.*, 406, 410.

battle for the state of Georgia. "From the galleries hundreds of interested Georgians looked down upon the last public service of Robert Toombs. He never appeared to finer advantage. His voice lacked its old time ring, his beard was gray and his frame was bent, but he was fearless, aggressive, alert, eloquent. He was master of the whole subject." [83] Toombs lost a few battles but won the war against the corporations. The constitution of 1877 embodied his main aims regarding state aid to railroads, state regulation of railroad tariffs, taxation of corporations, and monopoly. [84]

The convention adjourned on August 25. Toombs emerged as the popular hero, and was lauded for having advanced out of his own pocket money to defray the remaining convention expenses when the $25,000 appropriated had been exhausted. For this benevolent gesture he was tendered a vote of thanks by the convention and by the people of Georgia. [85]

From the convention hall Toombs went out among the people and stumped the state for the adoption of the constitution in the coming referendum. As he had led the convention, so he led the people. In February, 1878, the vote was 110,442 to 40,947 in favor of acceptance, an overwhelming majority. In a separate vote, the homestead provision of the new constitution was adopted. [86]

Toombs continued his efforts in championing the state against the railroads in the courts for several years after his constitutional work was finished. In 1879 the United States Supreme Court reversed

[83]Stovall, *Toombs*, 348.

[84]For example, Article VII, Section V, Paragraph V: "The credit of the State shall not be pledged or loaned to any individual, company, corporation or association, and the State shall not become a joint owner or stockholder in any company, association, or corporation"; Article IV, Section II, Paragraph I: "The power and authority of regulating railroad freight and passenger tariffs, preventing unjust discriminations, and requiring reasonable and just rates of freight and passenger tariffs, are hereby conferred upon the General Assembly . . . ; Article IV, Section I, Paragraph I: "The right of taxation is a sovereign right—inalienable, indestructible—is the life of the State, . . . and neither the General Assembly, nor any, nor all other departments of the Government established by this Constitution, shall ever have the authority to irrevocably give, grant, limit, or restrain this right. . . ." See Small, *Convention Report*, 479–93, for the constitution of 1877.

[85]Small, *Convention Report*, 422. Governor Colquitt later repaid Toombs the money he had loaned the convention. Avery, *History of Georgia*, 530–31, points out that Toombs had performed a similar act when Governor Smith was elected soon after Bullock resigned. "Money was needed to run the State. Bullock left us stranded and without credit. Gen. Toombs raised $300,000 on his own account to bridge over the emergency, until money could come in by taxes."

[86]Avery, *History of Georgia*, 530.

its ruling of 1876 and declared in *Atlantic and Gulf Railroad Company v. State of Georgia* that by consolidation a new corporation had been created and the original companies dissolved.[87] As a result, the new corporation was subject to the tax law of 1874, since the general law of 1863 gave the legislature the right to withdraw, change, modify, or destroy a charter of a corporation granted after 1863 unless expressly stated otherwise. The state now reopened its tax cases against the railroads, with Toombs again being retained as counsel. The prosecutions of Toombs and the attorney general were generally successful, although the Western and Atlantic succeeded once more in escaping the tax increase. Toombs continued his legal work for the state as late as 1883, just two years before his death. In that year, after forcing the Southwestern Railroad to come under the law and pay back taxes from 1874, he retired to his home in Washington, Georgia.[88]

[87]*U. S. Cases*, XCVIII, 185 (1879).
[88]*Georgia Cases*, LXIII, 483 (1879); LXVI, 563 (1880); LXVIII, 311 (1881); LXX, 11 (1883).

CHAPTER XII

The Toombs Legend

TOOMBS' robust vitality began to fade soon after the days of his constitution making. The hot and strenuous summer of 1877 sapped a great deal of strength from his sturdy physique as he toiled tirelessly for a new framework for his state. In January, 1878, he wrote Stephens that he was threatened with a general break-down and that troublesome cataracts were progressing slowly on his eyes. "And yet," he said, "I have outlived the Constitution of the U. States." [1]

Around this indomitable old warrior there developed a legendary atmosphere which grew with the passage of time. It was Toombs in whom Georgians could see a flashback to the times when "Georgia was Georgia." And so he became a symbol. And so he has remained.

Toombs was constantly sought by the press. His remarks were sure to be flavorful, for he was completely uninhibited in con-versation. He spoke rapidly, "his tongue . . . [running] like a bell clapper." [2] A reporter stated that it was an impossible task to hear Toombs talk and get down correctly all he said. "It would be comparatively an easier task to gather up a handful of gold-dust

[1] Toombs to Stephens, January 25, 1878, in Phillips (ed.), *Correspondence*, 732.
[2] Atlanta *Constitution*, March 2, 1873.

fired from a shotgun." [3] Toombs spoke boldly and openly of his enemies, and made his verbal attacks with complete disregard and disdain of consequences. He could roar with laughter or swear profusely. A typical scene found him in Atlanta "swearing at his enemies and being jolly with his friends by turns." [4] He took great delight in shocking Northern newspapermen with wild and imaginary tales.

When Toombs went to Atlanta it was his custom to stay at the Kimball House, in which he had a ninth interest.[5] It was a fine establishment, and with its construction after the war "Atlanta moved into the limelight of Southern hospitality and conviviality." [6] The hotel burned in August, 1883, and Toombs was a member of the syndicate that financed the building of a second Kimball House that was completed in the spring of 1885.[7]

At this, his favorite hotel, Toombs was always the center of attraction. "Every night a stout, thick, heavy man would appear in the rotunda . . . ; long, uncombed locks, borne down by his slouch hat to his very eyes, big mouth, a small patch of long, thin chin whiskers, hair well sprinkled with gray, and a face that lit up with a wealth of intelligence whenever animated in conversation." The moment he left his room he was surrounded by a crowd, "all eager to be in his presence and hear every word that . . . [fell] from his lips." [8] This was Toombs at his best. This was Toombs, the newspaperman's delight. Georgians enjoyed reading what the general had to say, and the press kept them supplied with his opinions.

[3]*Ibid.*, August 20, 1878.
[4]*Ibid.*, March 2, 1873.
[5]*Ibid.*, December 16, 1885.
[6]Willard Range, "Hannibal I. Kimball," *Georgia Historical Quarterly*, XXIX (June, 1945), 53.
[7]There were charges of mismanagement of funds levied against Hannibal I. Kimball, who was in charge of rebuilding the hotel. But as he explained in a lengthy article in the Atlanta *Constitution*, December 5, 1885, the syndicate over which he had no control purchased far more expensive equipment than was necessary to meet the original requirements, resulting in a greater cost for the hotel than was earlier anticipated. It was rumored that Toombs had lost a great deal of money, but Kimball stated that Toombs told him that "he invested his money in the enterprise willingly, and was greatly pleased with it." See also Rome *Daily Courier*, December 29, 1885, and Savannah *Evening News*, December 20, 1885, for comments on Toombs' connection with the Kimball House.
[8]Atlanta *Constitution*, November 5, 1871.

Toombs never softened his severe appraisal of Jefferson Davis. In 1881 he was asked if he had read Davis' recently published book, *The Rise and Fall of the Confederate Government.* "No, sir," he replied, "I never intend to. . . . The trouble with Davis was and is, that he has an exalted idea of his own importance." Toombs said that Davis had asked him for permission to use his picture in the work, but that he had refused. "I didn't want my picture to go down to posterity in such company." [9] Of the Georgian's caustic remarks, Davis shortly afterwards said only this: "He is an erratic man, and not always accurate in what he says." [10]

As might be expected from one so unreconstructed, Toombs thought little of the Negro in the role of citizen. "You might as well expect a ball to maintain itself in the air without support and against the laws of physics, than that this people should become an element in our social system," he once said.[11] And again, "They are of the human race, but they are not of my race. They are a lower order of human beings." [12] On one of his last visits to Atlanta, a reporter confronted him again with the problem of the Negro in Southern society. Toombs replied: "I have placed my opinion of the negro on record . . . and I stand by every word of it. I have always maintained, and still hold, that so long as the African and Caucasian races co-exist in the same society, the subordination of the African is the necessary, proper, and normal condition, and that such subordination is the condition best calculated to promote the highest interest and greatest happiness of both races and consequently of society at large." [13]

An editorial in the Atlanta *Constitution* based on information from a "very close friend of Toombs" stated that during the Georgia constitutional convention of 1877, a secret resolution was prepared to be used to petition Congress for the removal of the former statesman's political disability. It appears that the resolution was to be the initial step in eventually running Toombs against Gordon for the United States Senate.[14] When Toombs heard about this, he declared he would kill the resolution if it were presented. "I would not go if I were elected," he said. "If I have any political

9*Ibid.,* July 1, 1881.
10*Ibid.,* July 10, 1881.
11*Ibid.,* November 21, 1877.
12*Ibid.,* August 29, 1877.
13*Ibid.,* December 16, 1885.
14*Ibid.,* February 21, 1878.

ambition at all, it is to be the first governor under the rules of the new constitution." [15] Nothing ever came of this faint inference that his hat was in the gubernatorial ring.

Although barred by his own wish from entering the political arena, Toombs constantly talked politics and history. His was generally the jaundiced appraisal of a person out of step with reality. It was a frustrated man who wrote Stephens on April 15, 1880, that he preferred the election of Grant to anyone in his party because "if a crisis should come he would be more apt to destroy the Union, which I so earnestly desire." [16]

The reminiscences of Toombs as he surveyed American history, although frequently biased and sometimes inaccurate, were colorful. He had served in Congress for fifteen years and had known most of the leading politicos of the day intimately. The two most eloquent men he ever heard were Rufus Choate, Massachusetts senator, and Seargent Prentiss, congressman from Mississippi. "They were incomparable," he said. "Prentiss was the most eloquent, probably, but Choate was the best debater. I saw Choate and Webster pitted once and to Webster's discomfiture." [17] George McDuffie, prominent South Carolina political leader, Toombs named as the greatest Southerner of his acquaintance and probably the greatest man produced by the South. He termed Daniel Webster the greatest man he had ever known.

Toombs said he had known every President personally except Washington, John Adams, and Thomas Jefferson.[18]

I saw Jackson inaugurated and sat by Quincy Adams when he died [in the House of Representatives in February, 1848]. I was not intimate, perhaps, with Pierce, the best gentleman of them all. He did not have any especial force, but was clever and correct. Mr. Fillmore was a fine scholar, and an honest man. . . . Taylor was the most ignorant [p]resident of them all. It was amazing how little he knew. He was a soldier and nothing else. Van Buren was probably the most accomplished statesman—but he was not a broad man. He was shrewd, rather than sagacious or wise. Tyler was great at a female seminary commencement or a cow show. When he was selected to go and deliver the address

15 *Ibid.*
16 Toombs to Stephens, April 15, 1880, in Phillips (ed.), *Correspondence,* 742.
17 Atlanta *Constitution,* July 6, 1879.
18 It is possible that he met Monroe and Madison when he was a law student at the University of Virginia.

of welcome to Lafayette, Webster said to me that he never knew a man who could make a pretty speech that was fit for much else, and this truth, I think, goes without exception. . . . Old Buch [Buchanan] was a good president, a fine statesman in a small way, and unequalled leader of small bodies of men.[19]

Toombs was a long-time trustee of the University of Georgia. Though dismissed from its campus when a student, he was an ardent champion of its interests and of higher education in the state. His correspondence in the post-war era is liberally sprinkled with references to the university in Athens, and shows his concern for its growth. On March 30, 1872, he wrote Charles C. Jones, Jr., Georgian historian, saying: "We must place our university in the front rank of the educational institutions of the country . . . and my most ardent [?] efforts will be directed to its speedy accomplishment." [20]

Toombs was instrumental in the creation of a State College of Agriculture and Mechanic Arts at the University of Georgia under the terms of the Morrill Land Grant Act of 1862, whereby each state received thirty thousand acres of the public domain for each of its senators and representatives. There were differences of opinion as to how the funds derived from the sale of the land were to be used. Toombs was appointed a member of a three-man committee from the Board of Trustees of the university, which argued for the creation of an agricultural and mechanical college as an integral part of the university, rather than the establishment of a separate institution or the widespread dispersal of the funds over the state. The committee's stand was endorsed by Governor Smith, who in March, 1872, turned the $243,000 land grant fund over to the university. A recent historian of the institution has written that "it would be no exaggeration to say that the land-script fund saved the life of the University of Georgia." [21]

Shortly before his death Toombs became involved in a fight over university business with a fellow trustee and old enemy, United States Senator Joseph E. Brown, that led to his tendered resignation. Brown desired to create a loan fund for needy university students in memory of his son, Charles McDonald Brown. In the summer

[19]Atlanta *Constitution*, July 6, 1879.
[20]Toombs to Charles C. Jones, Jr., March 30, 1872, in Charles C. Jones Papers, Duke University.
[21]Brooks, *University of Georgia*, 53; Trustee Minutes, IV, Pt. 2, 316-20; Toombs to Colonel William B. Mitchell, January 19, 1872, February 19, 1872, March 23, 1872, in Toombs Letters, Coulter Collection.

of 1882 he proposed that the state accept $50,000 from him to be applied on the state debt, and in turn issue a bond of that amount at 7 percent interest to the board as a basis for the fund. The board accepted the proposition, but the legislature took no action on it. In November at a meeting of the trustees, Toombs moved that the board reconsider its favorable action on the donation by Brown. The motion failed to carry.

In March, 1883, Brown made a second offer, under the terms of which $50,000 in Georgia bonds was to be given to the trustees. On maturity the bonds were to be redeemed by the state not in cash but in the form of a single $50,000 bond at 7 percent interest for fifty years, thus guaranteeing an income for the university. The vote by the board was eleven to one in favor of acceptance, with Toombs casting the negative ballot. Toombs requested and was given permission to file a formal protest. In the July meeting his protest was received and ordered filed. Toombs claimed that Brown's proposition would entail unconstitutional procedure, as the state legislature under the constitution of 1877 could not borrow money to donate to the university. Brown asked Toombs if this were not a reversal of a stand he had previously taken. Toombs replied that it was not. After Brown had again asked the question and received Toombs' negative response for the second time, undoubtedly with great pleasure he took from his pocket a letter written by Toombs in which he had specifically endorsed such a course of action as now proposed by Brown. Toombs was humiliated, particularly so since Joe Brown had been the author of his discomfort. The next day he offered his resignation as a trustee, and although the board never took action on it, the records do not show that Toombs ever attended another meeting.[22]

In 1883 two events occurred which destroyed Toombs' hold on life. In March he lost his friend Alexander H. Stephens. Their lives had been almost inseparably entwined, both publicly and privately. Except for the split over the Democratic nominees in 1860 and the issue of secession, there had been no serious cleavage in their political association. The rift over Stephens' possession of stock in the state

[22]Trustee Minutes [August 2, 1878–1886], 335–47, 366–67, 398–99, 401; Thomas Walter Reed, "History of the University of Georgia" (Typescript at University of Georgia), V, 1170–73; Herbert Fielder, *A Sketch of the Life and Times and Speeches of Joseph E. Brown* (Springfield, Mass., 1883), 586–88; Brooks, *University of Georgia*, 73; Washington (Ga.) *Gazette*, April 6, 1883.

railroad seemed the only incident, and it but shortly, to mar the cordial personal relationship between the two. Toombs came to Atlanta to speak at Stephens' funeral, but "stood sobbing for fully five minutes before he could proceed. For almost twenty minutes his emotions were so great that he was almost unintelligible." [23] The remarks he finally made abounded in affection and praise for his departed companion.

Just before his second great tragedy, his wife's death, Toombs was pictured in his infirmities by his friend John C. Reed: "One eye quenched by cataract and the other failing fast; his contemporaries of the bar and political arena dead; the wife whom he loved better than he did himself sinking under a disease gradually destroying her mind; ever harrowed with the thought that his country was no more, and that he was a foreignor and exile in the spot which he had always called home." [24]

On August 31, Julia Toombs was stricken with paralysis at her summer home in Clarkesville in Habersham County, Georgia. There, in the mountains where Toombs had spent some time as a fugitive after the war, she died on September 4. Funeral services were conducted two days later by an old family friend, Bishop George F. Pierce, at the Methodist Church in Washington. "General Toombs," reported the local paper, "looked as if the bereavement were greater than he could bear—the light of his life was shut out forever from this world." [25]

Toombs' devotion to his wife and family, all of whom he had now outlived, had been unfailing, and the domestic scene in Washington was one of happiness and love. Their home was once a center of brilliance and culture. Now it was an empty place where an old man lived alone. In October he wrote movingly of his wife to a friend: "We lived and loved together over the continents of the earth & the islands of the sea for nearly fifty three years, and she never gave me a moments pain from the bridal alter [sic] to the morning when I kissed away her last breath, when her quiet, gentle loving & noble spirit, took its flight to the regions of bliss except for her sufferings & the fear of loosing [sic] her." [26]

[23] Atlanta *Constitution*, March 9, 1883.
[24] John C. Reed, *The Brothers' War* (Boston, 1905), 279.
[25] Washington (Ga.) *Gazette*, September 7, 1883.
[26] Toombs to James A. Alexander, October 19, 1883, in Adam Leopold Alexander Papers, Duke University.

Toombs' drinking increased as he neared the end. With ravaging cataracts blurring his vision, "he deliberately chose to drain full cups of purpose to sweeten bitter memories. . . . During all this time he was dying by inches." [27]

Tradition has it that one day in the latter part of his life Toombs met Bishop Pierce and asked that he be baptized. "When I am dead," said Toombs, "I do not want these young men who drift so naturally into infidelity to claim me as an unbeliever." The subsequent baptism caused a sensation throughout the state. "Once more there was a tender feeling for Toombs, such as had not been felt since the days when he was the pride of Georgia manhood." [28]

After his wife's death, Toombs seldom left his home. But his lifelong custom of making his mansion a hotel for visitors in Washington never changed. In October, 1884, he entertained J. L. M. Curry, noted Alabama educator, who told his son that he fared well as the General's house guest. He described Toombs as "an incessant talker" with interesting reminiscences of the past. Curry commented that Toombs had joined the church after his wife's death and was "trying to live a better life," struggling "to master or undo habits of profanity & intemperance." But the habits, he said, "have become a second nature." Curry wrote of the "sluggishness & poverty" of the area. "The poor South," he lamented, "it makes my heart bleed." [29]

The election of Grover Cleveland to the presidency in November was the occasion for Toombs' last public speech. A crowd with banners and lanterns marched from the public square to his home where the cry went up as of old: "Toombs, Toombs, Toombs." The general came out of the front door to the head of the steps leading up to the porch, and in a voice trembling with emotion commented on the great victory just won. He said he was glad that he had lived long enough to see the return of honesty in the national government, and thanked the people for having always stood by him. After other speeches, the crowd was invited in for wine from Toombs' hospitable board.[30]

[27]Reed, *Brothers' War*, 280.
[28]Atlanta *Constitution*, July 3, 1884.
[29]J. L. M. Curry to M. B. Curry, October 11, 1884, in J. L. M. Curry Papers, Duke University.
[30]Washington (Ga.) *Gazette*, November 15, 1884.

In September, 1885, he was confined to his home by his last illness. Although his mind wandered, there were lucid intervals when the spirit of the Toombs of old would reassert itself. At one time he was told that the Georgia legislature, for which he had no love, had not adjourned. "Lord, send for Cromwell," Toombs implored.[31] When informed that the prohibitionists were assembling in Washington, the old Georgian observed, "Prohibitionists are men of small pints." [32] Toombs lapsed into unconsciousness on December 10, and died on Monday, December 15, at six o'clock in the evening.

The day of Toombs' funeral, December 17, was "calm and bright, in strange contrast with [his] . . . stormy life." [33] A large crowd including many dignitaries attended services at the Methodist church. One of the participating clergymen was the Reverend S. G. Hillyer, whose brawl with Toombs many years before at the university had contributed to his dismissal. Following graveside rites, Toombs was interred beside his wife in the city cemetery.[34]

The close of the controversial and almost legendary life of Robert Toombs not unexpectedly evoked considerable comment. The New York *World* called him "one of the last of the implacable school of Southern statesmen" who proudly bore the title of fire-eater. The Washington *Post* said that "he would have made, if not more brilliant, at least a much more substantial record . . . [in politics and in the army] had he been less dogmatic and more disposed to pay due attention to the opinions of others."

From the Philadelphia *Press:*

The death of Robert Toombs, of Georgia, the man and the private citizen, will be regretted by those who know the rugged integrity of his character, but the death of Robert Toombs, the politician and comfortless mourner of a cause irrevocably crushed and destroyed, because it deserved to be, will be deplored by no one. He long ago outlived his usefulness to his country, just as the memories of his brilliant attainments as orator and lawyer will outlive the shadows of his bitter bigotry and musty prejudices against the principles and ideas which crowded him into the background of American statesmanship.[35]

[31]Quoted in Stovall, *Toombs*, 374.
[32]*Ibid.*
[33]Atlanta *Constitution*, December 18, 1885.
[34]Augusta *Chronicle*, December 18, 1885; Atlanta *Constitution*, December 18, 1885.
[35]The quotations are printed in the Augusta *Chronicle*, December 18, 1885. No dates are given.

By his own people, Toombs was generally eulogized. Wrote Henry Grady in Toombs' last years:

He is the most remarkable man in many respects that the south ever produced, and it is doubtful if the records of a lordlier life than his can be found in the history of our republic. He has never moved as other men move, nor walked by ordinary methods. He has been lavish in his opinions, kingly in all his ways, disdaining all expedients, or deliberations, and moving to his ambitions with a princely assumption that has never been gain-said by the people, and seldom by circumstance.[36]

Remarkable, Toombs doubtless was. But a more penetrating analysis came from another Georgian, Charles C. Jones, Jr., who suggested that the fruit of Toombs' life was not proportionate to his superior talents; that he missed the stature of greatness.[37]

Where did Toombs fail? Was it in the secession crisis that saw his statesmanlike image completely unravel in the eleventh hour? Probably not. Although undoubtedly affected to some extent by the excitement of the hour and the growing popularity of the cause of Southern independence, he seemed genuinely convinced that the dismemberment of the Union was the only answer to Republican victory. Additionally, Toombs never seemed to weigh his decisions by what the grass roots response to them might be. He did not court favor.

Was it during the Civil War? To some extent. Restless under the authority of Davis and despised West Point generals whom he considered unequal to their tasks, he rendered little constructive service to the Confederate government.

Was it in the post-war period? Primarily. A petulant and irresponsible Toombs became so bitter in his denunciations of economic and political developments in the New South that he lost most of his influence, and became a sort of ghost wandering around

[36]Atlanta *Constitution*, July 6, 1879.
[37]Charles C. Jones, Jr., *Brigadier General Robert Toombs. An Address Delivered Before the Confederate Survivors Association in Augusta, Georgia, At Its Eighth Annual Meeting, On Memorial Day, April 26th, 1886* (Augusta, 1886), 10; Augusta *Chronicle*, December 16, 1885. On February 20, 1886, Toombs' real and personal estate was appraised at $34,507.77. Notes and accounts payable to him amounted to $62,065.85, bringing his total wealth to $96,573.62. See Wilkes County Inventories & Appraisements & Sales, 1869–1925 (Microfilm MS in Georgia Department of Archives and History), 522–27.

pathetically in the wings of the public stage. His great energies and abilities would have benefited his state and section in a trying period, but Toombs failed to respond. Only as a constitution framer and legal counsel for the state did he make any significant contributions. He could have done much more. Robert Toombs, unfortunately for himself and his country, will live mainly as a legend.

Critical Essay on Authorities

The correspondence and papers of Robert Toombs are not conveniently located in any large single collection. The largest manuscript collection is at the University of Georgia. Two smaller collections are at Duke University and in the private possession of Dr. E. Merton Coulter of Athens, Georgia. Scattered Toombs letters in varying numbers are found in the Alexander H. Stephens Papers at Emory University, Duke University, the Library of Congress, and the University of North Carolina. Others are found in the Adam Leopold Alexander Papers, U. R. Brooks Papers, Armistead Burt Papers, Clement Claiborne Clay Papers, Charles C. Jones, Jr. Papers, and Francis W. Pickens Papers, at Duke University; Edward Porter Alexander Papers, Alexander-Hillhouse Papers, and John MacPherson Berrien Papers, at the University of North Carolina; Howell Cobb Papers and Telamon Cuyler Papers, University of Georgia; William C. Rives Papers, Library of Congress; James Madison Spullock Papers, Georgia Department of Archives and History, Atlanta; and the Archives of Union College, Schenectady, New York.

The Georgia Department of Archives and History contains a good deal of manuscript material (much of it on microfilm) on Toombs, his father, and grandfather. County court records, military records,

261

tax digests, wills, inventories, and census reports are invaluable. Records in the Archives Division of the Virginia State Library, Richmond, are disappointingly meager on Toombs' forebears, but parish registers and will books allow brief glimpses of the seventeenth and eighteenth century Toombs clan. The Robert Toombs Staff File at the National Archives, Washington, D. C., sheds some light on Toombs' military career.

At the University of Georgia, in addition to the Toombs manuscripts, are the faculty minutes and transactions plus the minutes of the Board of Trustees for the Toombs era. The manuscript collection at Union College in Schenectady is scant for this early period. That of the University of Virginia is larger, but Toombs' behavior there was more conventional and his tenure briefer than at Georgia and hence he was less marked for notice.

Other manuscripts which are very useful are the Thomas Reade Rootes Cobb Letters (typescript), 2 vols., University of Georgia; the Stephen R. Mallory Diary (typescript), Library of Congress; and the Confederate States of America Archives, Pickett Papers, Library of Congress.

PRINTED DOCUMENTS, OFFICIAL AND PRIVATE

Brief mention is made of Major Robert Toombs, (the senator's father) in the following: Francis B. Heitman, *Historical Register of Officers of the Continental Army During the War of the Revolution, April 1775, to December, 1783* (Washington, 1914); *Historical Collections of the Joseph Habersham Chapter, Daughters American Revolution*, III (Atlanta, 1910); Catherine L. Knorr, compiler, *Marriages of Culpepper County, Virginia, 1781–1815* (Pine Bluff, 1954); Grace G. Davidson, compiler, *Early Records of Georgia. Volume One. Wilkes County* (Macon, 1932).

Reports of Cases in Law and Equity Argued and Determined in the Supreme Court of Georgia, at Atlanta, 202 vols. and *Cases Argued and Decided in the Supreme Court of the United States*, 332 vols. are helpful for Toombs' legal career. Also useful is Henry W. Thomas, *Digest of the Railroad Laws of Georgia* (Atlanta, 1895).

The state legislative career of Toombs can be followed in the *Journals of the House of Representatives of the State of Georgia,* the *Journals of the Senate of the State of Georgia*, and the *Acts of the* [Georgia] *General Assembly*. Since, however, the journals print for the most part only the bills, amendments, resolutions, and voting records, they must be supplemented by contemporary newspaper accounts which convey a more complete picture of proceedings and debates.

Toombs' congressional career is recorded in *The Congressional Globe: Containing the Debates and Proceedings of . . . Congress*, 46 vols., (Washington, 1834–73). "Journal of the Committee of Thirteen," *Senate Reports*, No. 288, 36th Congress, 2nd Session is a valuable document for the secession crisis in which Toombs played a major role.

The Confederate civil career of the Georgian can be followed in several sources. James D. Richardson, editor, *A Compilation of Messages and Papers of the Confederacy Including the Diplomatic Correspondence, 1861–1865*, 2 vols. (Nashville, 1906) contains much of his correspondence as Secretary of State. Also useful here is the *Official Records of the Union and Confederate Navies in the War of the Rebellion*, 30 vols. (Washington, 1895–1929). James M. Matthews, editor, *The Statutes at Large of the Provisional Government of the Confederate States of America . . .* (Richmond, 1864) describes the early organization of the Confederate State Department. "Journal of the Congress of the Confederate States of America, 1861–1865," *Senate Documents*, No. 234, 58th Congress, 2nd Session, 7 vols., records Toombs' brief tenure in the Confederate Congress. Georgia's secession movement is documented in Allen D. Candler, editor, *The Confederate Records of the State of Georgia*, 6 vols. (Atlanta, 1910).

The great storehouse of information on the Civil War is *The War of the Rebellion: A Compilation of the Official Records of the Union and Confederate Armies*, 130 vols. (Washington, 1880–1901). Of value in studying Toombs' military career are Lillian Henderson, compiler, *Roster of the Confederate Soldiers of Georgia, 1861–1865*, 4 vols. (Hapeville, Ga., 1955–60); the *Southern Historical Society Papers*, 38 vols. (Richmond, 1876–1910); and Robert U. Johnson and Clarence C. Buel, editors, *Battles and Leaders of the Civil War*, 4 vols. (New York, 1956).

The indispensable source for Toombs' work in the Georgia constitutional convention of 1877 is Samuel W. Small, reporter, *Georgia*

Constitutional Convention, 1877. A Stenographic report of the proceedings of the Constitutional convention held in Atlanta, Georgia, 1877 . . . (Atlanta, 1877).

The most valuable single collection of letters for a study of Robert Toombs is Ulrich B. Phillips, editor, *The Correspondence of Robert Toombs, Alexander H. Stephens, and Howell Cobb* in *Annual Report of the American Historical Association for the year 1911*, II (Washington, 1913). Useful is Marion Alexander Boggs, editor, *The Alexander Letters, 1787–1900* (Savannah, 1910), the correspondence of a neighbor family from Washington, Georgia. "The Correspondence of Thomas Reade Rootes Cobb, 1860–1862," *Publications of the Southern History Association*, XI (May, 1907) is particularly helpful in the information it gives on Toombs during the Montgomery convention and the early years of the war. Other printed correspondence of value includes R. P. Brooks, editor, "Howell Cobb Papers," *Georgia Historical Quarterly*, V–VI; George C. Osborn, editor, "Sherman's March Through Georgia: Letters from Charles Ewing to His Father Thomas Ewing," *Georgia Historical Quarterly*, XLII (September, 1958); Dunbar Rowland, editor, *Jefferson Davis Constitutionalist, His Letters, Papers and Speeches*, 10 vols. (Jackson, 1923); and Douglas Southall Freeman, editor, *Lee's Dispatches* (New York, 1915).

Newspapers are extremely important for nineteenth century biographical studies. Indispensable for Toombs and his era are the Augusta *Chronicle and Sentinel*, a supporter, then opponent of the general; the Democratic Milledgeville *Federal Union;* and the progressive Atlanta *Constitution*. Frequently the papers of this era reprint articles from other journals, giving the reader a wide sweep of news and opinions from several sources. Other newspapers useful to a study of Toombs are the Athens *Southern Banner* and the *Southern Watchman;* the Atlanta *Daily Intelligencer* and the *Southern Confederacy;* the Columbus *Daily Sun;* the *Daily Richmond Examiner* and the Richmond *Dispatch;* the Milledgeville *Southern Recorder;* the New York *Times* and the *Tribune;* the

Rome *Tri-Weekly Courier;* the Sandersville *Central Georgian;* the Savannah *Morning News;* the Washington, D. C. *Daily National Intelligencer;* and the Washington, Georgia *Gazette* and the *News.*

The following articles have information profitable for this study: Henry W. Cleveland, "Robert Toombs," *The Southern Bivouac* (January, 1886), 449–59; Tom S. Gray, Jr., "Bob Toombs," *Georgia Alumni Record* (May–June, 1928), 193–98; Willard Range, "Hannibal I. Kimball," *Georgia Historical Quarterly*, XXIX (June, 1945), 47–70; William P. Brandon, "Calling the Georgia Constitutional Convention of 1877," *Georgia Historical Quarterly*, XVII (September, 1933), 189–203; *ibid.,* "The Galphin Claim," *Georgia Historical Quarterly*, XV (June, 1931), 113–41; E. Merton Coulter, "The Toombs Oak," *Georgia Historical Quarterly*, XLVI (March, 1962), 34–40; Peter S. McGuire, "The Railroads of Georgia," *Georgia Historical Quarterly*, XVI (September, 1932), 179–214; Judson Clements Ward, Jr., "The New Departure Democrats of Georgia: an Interpretation," *Georgia Historical Quarterly*, XLI (September, 1957), 227–236; and Ralph Wooster, "The Georgia Secession Convention," *Georgia Historical Quarterly*, XL (March, 1956), 21–55.

DIARIES, AUTOBIOGRAPHIES, AND MEMOIRS

There are many personal journals which touch on various facets of Toombs' life. One of the most important is Eliza Frances Andrews, *The War-Time Journal of a Georgia Girl, 1864–65,* (New York, 1908), which affords important observations on Washington, Georgia, just before and during Union troop occupation. T. C. DeLeon, *Belles Beaux and Brains of the 60's* (New York, 1907) and *Four Years in Rebel Capitals* . . . (Mobile, 1892) abound in colorful comment on life in wartime Montgomery and Richmond. Another observer and sometime gossip, J. B. Jones, affords valuable comment on embattled Richmond in *A Rebel War Clerk's Diary at the Confederate States Capital,* 2 vols. (New York, 1935). Very important also on many phases of Toombs' life is Myrta A. Avary, editor, *Recollections of Alexander H. Stephens, His Diary Kept When a Prisoner at Fort Warren, Boston Harbour, 1865* . . . (New York, 1910). Toombs appears several times in Mary B. Chesnut's charming *A Diary From Dixie* (Boston, 1949), edited by Ben Ames Williams.

Shedding some light on the Creek uprising of the 1830's are James F. Sunderman, editor, *Journey Into Wilderness, An Army Surgeon's Account of Life in Camp and Field During the Creek and Seminole Wars, 1836–1838* (Gainesville, Ga., 1953) and *Memoirs of Lieutenant-General Scott, LL.D. Written by Himself* (New York, 1864).

A study of Toombs in Washington, D. C., is aided by Thurlow Weed Barnes, *Memoir of Thurlow Weed* (Boston, 1884); Mrs. Virginia (Clement C. Clay) Clay-Clopton, *A Belle of the Fifties* . . . (New York, 1904); Percival G. Melbourne, editor, Christian F. Eckloff, *Memoirs of a Senate Page, 1855–1859* (New York, 1909); Benjamin Perley Poore, *Perley's Reminiscences of Sixty Years in the National Metropolis* . . . , 2 vols. (Philadelphia, 1886); Carl Schurz, *The Reminiscences of Carl Schurz*, 3 vols. (New York, 1907–08); and Henry Watterson, *Marse Henry: An Autobiography*, 2 vols. (New York, 1919).

Insights into the Confederate years are afforded by Wirt A. Cate, editor, *Two Soldiers: The Campaign Diaries of Thomas J. Key and Robert J. Campbell* (Chapel Hill, 1938); Jefferson Davis, *The Rise and Fall of the Confederate Government*, 2 vols. (New York, 1881); *Diary of Gideon Welles, Secretary of the Navy Under Lincoln and Johnson*, 3 vols. (Boston, 1911); Henry Kyd Douglas, *I Rode With Stonewall* (Chapel Hill, 1940); Joseph T. Durkin, editor, *John Dooley Confederate Soldier: His War Journal* (Georgetown, 1945); Richard B. Harwell, editor, Richard Taylor, *Destruction and Reconstruction: Personal Experiences of the Late War* (New York, 1955); E. R. Jones, *Four Years in the Army of the Potomac* (London, n.d.); A. L. Long, *Memoirs of Robert E. Lee* (New York, 1887); James Longstreet, *From Manassas to Appomattox* (Philadelphia, 1896); *Memoirs of General William T. Sherman. By Himself* (Bloomington, 1957); [Mrs. Sarah Putnam], A Richmond Lady, *Richmond During the War* (New York, 1867); John H. Reagan, *Memoirs, With Special Reference to Secession and the Civil War* (New York and Washington, 1906); G. Moxley Sorrel, *Recollections of a Confederate Staff Officer* (New York, 1905); Alexander H. Stephens, *A Constitutional View of the Late War Between the States* . . . , 2 vols. (Philadelphia, 1868–70); and Robert Stiles, *Four Years Under Marse Robert* (New York, 1910).

Useful for a contemporary lawyer's comments on Toombs before the bar is Richard M. Johnston, *Autobiography of Col. Richard Malcolm Johnston* (Washington, 1900). Briefly used are Lucian Lamar Knight, *Reminiscences of Famous Georgians* (Atlanta, 1907) and James Z. Rabun, editor, "Alexander H. Stephens's Diary, 1834–1837," *Georgia Historical Quarterly*, XXXVI (March, 1952), 71–96.

BIOGRAPHIES

Two early biographies of Toombs have been most useful in the preparation of this volume: Ulrich B. Phillips, *The Life of Robert Toombs* (New York, 1913) and Pleasant A. Stovall, *Robert Toombs: Statesman, Speaker, Soldier, Sage: His Career in Congress and on the Hustings—His Work in the Courts—His Record with the Army—His Life at Home* (New York, 1892). Phillips' work is largely a political study emphasizing Toombs' antebellum public career. Stovall, a friend of the senator's, writes sympathetically but affords valuable insights into Toombs' character in his highly personalized account.

Important on Toombs' public career are J. F. H. Claiborne, *Life and Correspondence of John A. Quitman*, 2 vols. (New York, 1860); Mary Ann (Mrs. C. C.) Coleman, *Life of John J. Crittenden, with Selections from his Correspondence and Speeches*, 2 vols. (Philadelphia, 1871); Joseph T. Durkin, *Stephen R. Mallory: Confederate Navy Chief* (Chapel Hill, 1954); Brainerd Dyer, *Zachary Taylor* (Baton Rouge, 1946); Herbert Fielder, *A Sketch of the Life and Times and Speeches of Joseph E. Brown* (Springfield, Mass., 1883); Percy S. Flippen, *Herschel V. Johnson of Georgia: State Rights Unionist* (Richmond, 1931); Holman Hamilton, *Zachary Taylor: Soldier in the White House* (Indianapolis and New York, 1951); Albert D. Kirwan, *John J. Crittenden: The Struggle for the Union* (Lexington, Ky., 1962); and Philip S. Klein, *President James Buchanan: A Biography* (University Park, Pennsylvania, 1962).

Quotations in Vincent H. Cassidy and Amos E. Simpson, *Henry Watkins Allen of Louisiana* (Baton Rouge, 1964) give a delightful look at the festivities surrounding the marriage of Toombs' daughter Louisa. Varina Howell Davis, *Jefferson Davis, Ex-President of the Confederate States of America, A Memoir by His Wife*, 2 vols. (New York, 1890) contains revealing comments on both Toombs and Alexander H. Stephens and the relationship between Toombs and the Confederate president. Richard Malcolm Johnston and William Hand Browne, *Life of Alexander H. Stephens* (Philadelphia, 1878) is a valuable study which contains several quoted observations on Toombs by Stephens. Useful also is James D. Waddell, editor, *Biographical Sketch of Linton Stephens, . . . Containing a Selection of His Letters, Speeches, State Papers, Etc.* (Atlanta, 1877). Douglas Southall Freeman, *R. E. Lee: A Biography*, 4 vols. (New York, 1934–35) is indispensable for the Civil War career of Toombs. An interesting, if unflattering, comment on Toombs by General Edmund Kirby Smith is found in Joseph Howard Parks, *General Edmund Kirby Smith, C.S.A.* (Baton Rouge, 1954).

MONOGRAPHS, GENERAL AND MISCELLANEOUS WORKS

The best general history of Georgia is E. Merton Coulter, *Georgia: A Short History* (Chapel Hill, 1947). Also beneficial on the history of the state are I. W. Avery, *The History of the State of Georgia from 1850 to 1881* (New York, 1881); T. Conn Bryan, *Confederate Georgia* (Athens, 1953); Amanda Johnson, *Georgia As Colony and State* (Atlanta, 1938); Horace Montgomery, *Cracker Parties* (Baton Rouge, 1950); Ulrich B. Phillips, *Georgia and State Rights . . .* (Washington, 1902); Richard H. Shryock, *Georgia and the Union in 1850* (Durham, 1926); and Ethel K. Ware, *A Constitutional History of Georgia* (New York, 1947).

Useful works on the University of Georgia are E. Merton Coulter, *College Life in the Old South* (New York, 1928); Robert Preston Brooks, *The University of Georgia Under Sixteen Administrations 1785–1955* (Athens, 1956); and Thomas Walter Reed, "History of the University of Georgia," (typescript), University of Georgia Library. Augustus L. Hull, *Annals of Athens, Georgia, 1801–1901* (Athens, 1906) has been used briefly in this study.

Standard histories frequently consulted have been Avery Craven, *The Coming of the Civil War* (New York, 1942); George Fort Milton, *The Eve of Conflict: Stephen A. Douglas and the Needless War* (Boston, 1934); Allan Nevins, *Ordeal of the Union*, 2 vols. (New York, 1947) and *The Emergence of Lincoln*, 2 vols. (New York, 1950); Alice Nichols, *Bleeding Kansas* (New York, 1954); Roy F. Nichols, *The Disruption of American Democracy* (New York, 1948); David M. Potter, *Lincoln and His Party in the Seces-*

sion Crisis (New Haven, 1942); James G. Randall, *The Civil War and Reconstruction* (Boston, 1937); Henry H. Simms, *A Decade of Sectional Controversy, 1851–1861* (Chapel Hill, 1942); C. Vann Woodward, *Origins of the New South, 1877–1913* (Baton Rouge, 1951); and E. Merton Coulter, *The Confederate States of America, 1861-1865* (Baton Rouge, 1950).

The ablest work on Southern diplomacy is Frank Lawrence Owsley, *King Cotton Diplomacy: Foreign Relations of the Confederate States of America* (Chicago, 1959). This can be supplemented by James M. Callahan, *The Diplomatic History of the Southern Confederacy* (Springfield, Mass., 1957); William M. Robinson, *The Confederate Privateers* (New Haven, 1928); Samuel B. Thompson, *Confederate Purchasing Operations Abroad* (Chapel Hill, 1935); and Thomas A. Bailey, *A Diplomatic History of the American People* (New York, 1950).

An excellent study which was of considerable help in this biography is Arthur C. Cole, *The Whig Party in the South* (Gloucester, Mass., 1962). Equally fine is George R. Poage, *Henry Clay and the Whig Party* (Chapel Hill, 1936). Four works which are useful in specialized areas are Holman Hamilton, *Prologue to Conflict: The Crisis and Compromise of 1850* (Lexington, Ky., 1964); Charles Robert Lee, Jr., *The Confederate Constitutions* (Chapel Hill, 1963); Rembert W. Patrick, *Jefferson Davis and his Cabinet* (Baton Rouge, 1944); and Louise B. Hill, *Joseph E. Brown and the Confederacy* (Chapel Hill, 1939).

Two of the finest military histories ever written are Douglas Southall Freeman, *Lee's Lieutenants: A Study in Command*, 3 vols. (New York, 1942–44) and Kenneth P. Williams, *Lincoln Finds a General*, 5 vols. (New York, 1949–59). They have been particularly helpful to this study of Toombs.

An excellent study of post-war Georgia is Judson Clements Ward, Jr., "Georgia Under the Bourbon Democrats, 1872–1890" (Ph.D. dissertation, University of North Carolina, 1947). Other valuable unpublished studies are Robert T. Segrest, "History of Banking in Georgia Before 1865" (M.A. thesis, University of Georgia, 1933); Hugh O'Neal Richardson, "A History of Toombs' Brigade, 1861–1863" (M.A. thesis, Emory University, 1962); and Harold E. Davis, "The Civil War Career of Robert Toombs" (M.A. thesis, University of Georgia, 1950).

Miscellaneous sources include *A Lecture Delivered in the Tre-*

mont Temple, Boston, Massachusetts, on the 24th January, 1856 by R. Toombs (pamphlet, Emory University); Fred C. Cole, *Union Worthies, Number Sixteen. Robert Augustus Toombs, Class of 1828* (Schenectady, n.d.); Charles C. Jones, Jr., *Brigadier General Robert Toombs. An Address Delivered Before the Confederate Survivors Association in Augusta, Georgia, At Its Eighth Annual Meeting, On Memorial Day, April 26th, 1886* (Augusta, 1886); Nelle Womack Hines, editor, *A Treasure Album of Milledgeville and Baldwin County, Georgia* (Milledgeville, 1936); and *Sesqui-Centennial of Milledgeville and Baldwin County, Georgia, 1803–1953* (souvenir program, Georgia Department of Archives and History).

Index

271

Robert Toombs (*continued*):
retary of state, 165n; description of
duties as secretary of state, 166;
work with Confederate commissioners to Washington, 167–68; opposes firing on Fort Sumter, 168–
69; opinion on King Cotton diplomacy, 170; routine secretarial work,
170–71; accompanies Davis to Richmond, 171–72; Julia Toombs comes
to Richmond, 172; criticizes Confederate officials, 172–74; pledges
one-hundred bales of cotton for
Confederacy, 173; dissatisfied with
defensive posture of Confederacy,
173; resigns state post, 174; family
opposes entrance into military, 175;
criticizes Confederate military effort, 177–78, 181, 183–84, 188, 194–
95, 208; described by Mrs. Chesnut
at Richmond fair grounds, 177; organization of his brigade, 178, 178n;
as member of Confederate Provisional Congress, 179–81; appraisal
of as brigade commander, 179–80;
loses to Ben Hill in Confederate
Senate election, 180; lavish entertainment by the Toombses, 180;
"Address to the People of Georgia," 180–81; description of during
troop movement, 182; leads troops
in battle at Dam No. 1, p. 182; T. R.
R. Cobb hears of his threatened
resignation, 184n; Lee comments on
fortifications of, 185; involved in
controversy over cotton planting,
185–87; in battle of Garnett's Farm,
188–90; in battle of Golding's Farm,
190–91; in battle of Malvern Hill,
192–93; challenges Daniel H. Hill
to duel, 193–94; rebuked by Stonewall Jackson, 195; placed under
Longstreet's command, 195; his
brigade occupies Malvern Hill, 196;
visits T. R. R. Cobb, 196; put under
a r r e s t by Longstreet, 196–98;
reaches second Manassas at close of
hostilities, 198; his brigade occupies
Hagerstown, 199; in battle of Antietam, 200–203; resigns from army,
203; appraisal of military career,
204; illness of, 205, 205n; opposes
Davis and Richmond war policy,
205–206, 208–209, 210, 216–17; declines to run in 1863 Georgia gubernatorial contest, 206; speaks for
reelection of Brown, 206–207; letter
on fiscal policy, 207; commissioned
colonel in State Guard, 208; runs
unsuccessfully for Confederate Senate, 209, 209n; clashes with railroad
agent, 209–10; makes incendiary
speech to troops near Savannah,
210; charges brought against by
railroad, 210; regiment disbands,
210; enters state military service
again, 211; in battle of Atlanta,
212–13; description of during siege
of Atlanta, 212; condemns citizens
of Atlanta, 213; cautions Stephens
against "peace conspiracy," 214;
with Georgia m i l i t i a opposing
Sherman's march to the sea, 214–
16; comment on by General
Richard Taylor, 215; goes home on
sick leave, 216; spends last days of
war in Washington, Georgia, 217;
attitude toward Davis during cabinet flight through Washington,
217–18; description of in Washington, 218; turns part of Confederate
treasury over to Federal authorities,
218n; flees from Federal authorities,
219–21; goes to Cuba, 221; condemns President Johnson's Reconstruction policy, 221–22; exile in
Europe, 222–25; description of in
Paris, 223; letter to Stephens criti-
cizing events at home, 223–24; death
of daughter Sallie, 224; softens in
attitude toward Johnson, 224–25;
returns to U.S. and to Georgia, 225;
remains "unreconstructed," 225; es-
timate of wealth in 1860 and at end
of war, 226; post-war management
of land holdings, 227; post-war legal practice, 227, 227n; inflexibility
of post-war political attitude, 227,
231, 235–36; denounces Radical Reconstruction at Bush Arbor meeting, 228; speaks in Augusta and
Cedartown, 229–30; denounces Negro suffrage, 230, 242, 244; speaks
against New Departure, 231; con-